WOVEN STRETCH AND TEXTURED FABRICS

Woven Stretch and

Interscience Publishers

Textured Fabrics

Berkeley L. Hathorne

CHEMICAL ENGINEER AND CONSULTANT

SEDGEFIELD LABORATORIES, INC.

GREENSBORO, NORTH CAROLINA

A DIVISION OF JOHN WILEY & SONS, NEW YORK · LONDON · SYDNEY

Library of Congress Catalog Card Number: 64–20068
Printed in the United States of America

To my loving wife
whose inspiration and help made this book possible.

Preface

This book was written to give a comprehensive view of the woven stretch and textured fabric industry. The "stretch fabric explosion," with its daily increase in production capacity, has created a need for knowledge of stretch and textured yarns and fabrics, their characteristics, methods of manufacture, probable growth rates and directions, and various other information.

In this book are covered the different yarns, texturing techniques, yarn properties, fabric design, and weaving, dyeing and finishing methods of the woven stretch and textured fabric industry.

Stretch cotton has been emphasized because the low cost of cotton (and rayon) indicates that the use of continuous high-speed false twisting and resin treating of cellulosic fibers will bring about increased production of this material in the immediate future.

In areas where stretch and recovery properties constitute the primary objective, elastic fibers, core, plied, and spun with "hard" fibers, are due for rapid production expansion. However, these fibers are so new and in such short supply that their future cannot be accurately predicted at this time.

The post-treated false-twisted thermoplastic yarns, used in materials in which aesthetic properties, softness, drape, surface interest, and easy stretch are of importance, as well as the various thermoplastic yarns used in the manufacture of stretch and textured yarns, such as nylon 6 and 66, polyester, and polypropylene, are all discussed in detail.

All patents of current texturing processes are given in the book, including the claims and illustrations that are considered most revealing by the United States Patent Office.

I hope that I have succeeded in my attempt to give complete coverage of the subject ranging from the basic yarns and fibers through texturing, fabric design, fabric manufacturing, dyeing and finishing, to marketing.

I am most appreciative of the assistance given me by the various licensors of texturing processes, manufacturers of texturing machines, synthetic yarn producers, throwsters, designers, weavers, and dyers and finishers, most of whom expressed a desire to remain anonymous.

BERKELEY L. HATHORNE

April 1964

Contents

I

Development and Future
of Woven Stretch Fabrics

Stretch and textured woven fabrics, developed from permanently crimped thermoplastic yarns, have grown so fast, and in so many directions, that considerable confusion exists in many segments of the designing, manufacturing, and marketing branches of the textile and garment industries utilizing these yarns. This book has been written to clarify the facts relating to the use of crimped thermoplastic yarns, thermoplastic yarns textured by other processes, and other means of producing stretch and textured woven fabrics. It will benefit technicians and others working in these fields who are not thoroughly familiar with all phases of the new and rapidly expanding developments.

Crimped fibers are not new; wool fibers have a pronounced crimp, and natural cotton fibers have numerous convolutions and crimps. Certain other natural fibers are crimped to a greater or lesser degree. To enhance their spinning properties manufacturers of viscose process rayon, and other cellulose and cellulose-based fibers crimped these fibers mechanically. Later fibers were given latent crimping power by combining, in one fiber, two components that possessed different latent shrinking properties, forming crimps when wet out, whether in yarn or fabric form.

With the arrival of the yarns now called "synthetic" as differentiated from the earlier cellulose, cellulose derivatives, and regenerated natural fibers, the possibility of producing permanent or durable crimps and durable latent crimping power occurred to inventors working in the synthetic yarn fields. Invention of means of producing durable crimps followed. They have made possible the development and growth of the stretch and textured fabric industry. The increas-

1

ing aesthetic appeal and utility of properly designed and manufactured stretch and textured fabrics and garments indicate that the industry is destined for many years of continued growth and expansion.

At this point it appears advisable to list trademarks and certain descriptive and technical terms and tradenames that will be used freely in the pages to follow. Each word will be defined as it is used in the stretch and textured yarn, fabric, and allied industries. Wherever possible these are taken verbatum from, or are minor modifications of definitions given under oath in court in the case of Scragg & Sons vs. Leesona Corporation. The case was tried in 1961 and 1962 in Ottawa, Canada, and utilized the sworn testimony of experts in the field including: Chester J. Dudzik, Timothy Nesbitt-Dufort, Donald Finlayson, Dr. George Preston Hoff, Ernest Philip, Rushton Scragg, Warren A. Seem, and John Bamber Speakman. Following these definitions are several quotations from the American Society of Testing Materials.

Technical Terms and Tradenames

ACRILAN®. A trademark owned by Chemstrand Company, New York, New York.

ACRILAN® YARNS are acrylic yarns manufactured and sold by the Chemstrand Company.

AGILON®. A trademark owned by the Deering Milliken Research Corporation, Spartanburg, South Carolina.

AGILON® YARNS are made by the procedure whose generic name is "edge crimping." The trademark is available to licensees of the Deering Milliken Research Corporation.

A.R.C.T. MACHINES. Machines manufactured by Ateliers Roannais de Construction Textile Roanne, Loire, France, sold in North America by Whitin Machine Works of Whitinsville, Massachusetts, their use licensed by Deering Milliken Research Corporation of Spartanburg, South Carolina, for the purpose of producing torque and no-torque, stretch and stabilized, false-twist-crimped thermoplastic yarns.

ARNEL®. A trademark owned by Celanese Fibers Company, Charlotte, North Carolina.

BACK WINDING. A process of winding yarn from any form of put-up to a bobbin or other device suitable for use in further processing of the yarn.

BAN-LON®. A trademark owned by Joseph Bancroft & Sons Company, Wilmington, Delaware.

BAN-LON® GARMENTS and FABRICS are made primarily of Textralized® yarns, according to specifications and quality standards prescribed and controlled by Joseph Bancroft & Sons Company, Wilmington, Delaware.

BATCH-HEAT SETTING. Twist setting a multiple of units of crimped thermoplastic yarns in a container, such as an autoclave; capable of being controlled with respect to temperature and pressure, the autoclave being exhausted of air and filled with steam, or water vapor.

BELFAST®. A trademark owned by Deering Milliken Research Corporation, Spartanburg, South Carolina.

BELFAST® CLOTH is cotton cloth cross-linked under license from Deering Milliken Research Corporation in accordance with procedures originated by Deering Milliken Research Corporation. Belfast® cloth recovers from a wrinkled condition when wet out in water and drip-dried.

BULKED. Yarns which have had their voluminosity increased by any process whatsoever.

CELLULOSE ACETATE YARN. A yarn spun from cellulose diacetate; two acetate groups per cellulose group.

CELLULOSE TRIACETATE YARN. A yarn spun from cellulose triacetate; three acetate groups per cellulose group.

CONTRACTILE FORCE. The force that must be applied to prevent yarn contracting.

CREPE TWIST. A high degree of twist, of the order of 60 turns per inch in 100-denier yarn and 70 turns per inch in 70-denier yarn.

CREPE SETTING. A form of twist setting.

CRIMPED YARN. A yarn deformed by inserting a considerable number of crimps per inch; heat set to make the crimp durable; subsequently untwisted in the case of torque-crimp yarns.

CRIMPING EDGE. A unit of an edge-crimping machine over which hot thermoplastic yarns are drawn under tension to produce a type of durable crimp.

DACRON®. A trademark owned by E. I. du Pont de Nemours and Company, Wilmington, Delaware.

DACRON® YARNS are thermoplastic yarns manufactured by E. I. du Pont de Nemours and Company, Wilmington, Delaware.

DOUBLING. A process that combines yarns on a single spool bobbin, cone, or other type of unit.

DOWNTWISTER. A device or machine that rapidly revolves a vertically placed bobbin and slowly winds the yarn twisted by these revolutions on this same bobbin, the supply package being above the delivery package. Generally speaking, downtwister spindles revolve slower than uptwister spindles, so they are usually used when a low number of turns are required.

DUCTILITY. The ability to be drawn out and extended in length without elastic recovery. A yarn is ductile to the extent to which it does not recover.

DURABLE. Long lasting with respect to the anticipated useful life of the yarn or fabric.

EDGE CRIMPING. A means of crimping thermoplastic yarns by drawing heated and stretched thermoplastic yarns over a crimping edge and cooling. Edge-crimping machines are used to make Agilon® yarns.

ELASTICITY. The ability of yarn to return to its original length after being extended in length. A yarn is elastic to the extent to which it recovers.

EVERGLAZE®. A trademark owned by Joseph Bancroft & Sons Company, Wilmington, Delaware.

EVERGLAZE® FABRICS are cotton fabrics finished with a durable glaze or luster and fine soft hand by licensees of Joseph Bancroft & Sons Company, Wilmington, Delaware, in accordance with the teachings of the company.

FALSE TWIST. Running yarn is prevented from rotating at two points along its length and caused to rotate between these points by a suitable false-twisting device.

FALSE-TWIST YARN. Thermoplastic yarn properly processed through a false-twist machine.

FLUFLON®. A trademark owned by the Permatwist Company, Coatesville, Pennsylvania, and the Leesona Corporation, Providence, Rhode Island.

FLUFLON® YARNS are thermoplastic yarns durably torque-crimped on reconverted uptwisters equipped with units that uniformly tension and uniformly heat set thermoplastic yarns while processed through this type of false-twist machine.

HEAT SET. A thermoplastic textile material is heat set when a deformation is imposed upon it at a temperature high enough so that the internal molecular structure of the yarn may adapt itself to these new conditions and then the temperature is dropped, allowing it to cool. It will retain or attempt to retain the new dimension until such time as more severe conditions are applied.

HELANCA®. A trademark owned by the Heberlein Patent Corporation, used to merchandise torque-crimp thermoplastic yarns and fabrics meeting Heberlein's specifications and produced by its licensees. Originally the yarns were processed by the step-by-step process. Later the trademark was applied to false-twist thermoplastic yarns and fabrics made from these yarns meeting the rigid specifications established by the corporation.

LATENT CRIMPING POWER. Crimping power imparted to thermoplastic yarns which does not manifest itself until activated by heat or tension or by other means.

LATENT TORQUE-CRIMP ENERGY. Useful or available energy, temporarily quiescent as a result of processing, releasable at will by relaxing under controlled conditions, utilizing release of strain, heat, moisture, or motion, singly or in combination, depending on material to be relaxed and equipment available.

LYCRA®. A trademark owned by E. I. du Pont de Nemours and Company, Wilmington, Delaware.

LYCRA® YARNS are fine denier elastic filament yarns spun from segmented polyurethane by E. I. du Pont de Nemours and Company, Wilmington, Delaware.

MILLIUM®. A trademark owned by Deering Milliken Research Corporation, Spartanburg, South Carolina.

MILLIUM® FABRICS are fabrics coated with a flexible metallic coating material that reflects heat. Coating and methods of application developed and licensed by Deering Milliken Research Corporation, Spartanburg, South Carolina.

MODULUS. The stiffness of a material or its resistance to longitudinal expansion.

NYLON 6 YARN. A yarn spun from polycaprolactam.

NYLON 66 YARN. A yarn spun from polyhexamethyleneadipamide.

ORLON®. A trademark owned by E. I. du Pont de Nemours and Company, Wilmington, Delaware.

ORLON® YARNS are acrylic yarns manufactured and sold by E. I. du Pont de Nemours and Company, Wilmington, Delaware.

OVERFEED. A device that feeds yarn continuously to a winding mechanism, the linear speed of the yarn through the feeding device being greater than the linear speed of the yarn taken up by the winding mechanism. The yarn may run directly to the winding mechanism or may be processed through an intermediate unit as it runs from feed to take-up.

POLYESTER YARN. A yarn spun from polyester resin such as polyethylene terephthalate.

PURPOSE OF TWIST SETTING. The purpose of twist setting and crepe setting is to make the torsional forces temporarily dormant so that yarn will not snarl or otherwise misbehave while being processed through subsequent yarn or weaving or knitting operations.

REAL TWIST. Real twist results from holding a yarn at one end and twisting at the other end.

SAABA®. A trademark owned by Leesona Corporation, Providence, Rhode Island.

SAABA® YARNS are thermoplastic yarns torque-crimped, reheat set in a partially relaxed state to control the crimp. Saaba® yarns are exceedingly soft, cover well, and are very uniform with respect to crimp. Each turn of torque crimp imparted to each filament during the initial twist process becomes an individual crimp in finished Saaba®.

SANFORIZED®. A trademark owned by Cluett Peabody and Company, Waterford, New York.

SANFORIZED® FABRICS are preshrunk during finishing to eliminate shrinkage during subsequent wearing, washing and drying.

SAYELLE®. A trademark owned by E. I. du Pont de Nemours and Company, Inc., Wilmington, Delaware.

SAYELLE® YARNS are spun yarns manufactured by spinners from Sayelle® tow supplied by E. I. du Pont de Nemours and Company. Sayelle® filaments are double or dual component filaments consisting of two joined filaments of acrylic material each having a different shrinkage factor. When permitted or caused to relax the shrinkage differential causes crimping.

SPANDEX. A generic term approved by the Federal Trade Commission that describes manufactured fibers in which the fiber forming substance is a long chain synthetic polymer comprised of at least 85 per cent of a segmented polyurethane.

STRETCH YARN. Yarns made from modified thermoplastic fibers, usually in the form of continuous filaments which are capable of a pronounced degree of stretch and rapid recovery. This property is conferred on yarn (having a multiple of filaments) which has been subjected to an appropriate combination of twisting, heat setting, and untwisting treatments.

STUFFER BOX. A unit of the stuffer box machine for crimping yarn, into which thermoplastic yarn is impelled at a high rate of speed, the force being sufficient to crumple the yarn and push the crumpled yarn up to a lightweight tube through which it is drawn from the stuffer box. The stuffer box is heated to cause the deformation of the crumpled filaments to be more durable.

SUPERLOFT®. A trademark owned by the Leesona Corporation, Providence, Rhode Island.

SUPERLOFT® YARNS are thermoplastic yarns durably torque-crimped on false-twist machines designated as 550, 551, 552, and 553.

TASLAN®. A trademark owned by E. I. du Pont de Nemours and Company, Inc., Wilmington, Delaware.

TASLAN® YARNS are crimped by air bulking. The yarns are fed into a venturi where they are air bulked by a stream of compressed air released into the venturi.

TEXTRALIZED®. A trademark owned by Joseph Bancroft & Sons Company, Wilmington, Delaware.

TEXTRALIZED® YARNS are thermoplastic yarns crumpled by being impelled against a mass of previously crumpled yarn; heat set in this position by being passed through a heated stuffer box tube.

THROWSTER. One who is primarily concerned with the processing of continuous filament yarns, preparing them for further processing into knitted and woven fabrics, carpets, etc.

TORQUE CRIMP. The crimp formed by twisting thermoplastic yarns to a high degree of twist, for example, but not limiting to, 60 to 80 turns per inch in a 70-denier nylon yarn, then heat setting and untwisting. When relaxed, each filament assumes, or attempts to assume, the helical shape in which it was heat set. This produces texture, softness, and stretch properties in fabrics, depending on their design and processing.

TORQUE FORCE. Same as torsional force.

TORSIONAL FORCE. Torsional force is the force which causes or tends to cause the yarn to twist on its axis after having been twisted.

TWIST SETTING. A process carried out in a yarn processing plant to render the torsional forces resulting from the twisting temporarily dormant.

TYCORA®. A trademark owned by Textured Yarn Company, Inc., Philadelphia, Pennsylvania.

TYCORA® indicates a source of manufacture rather than a method. Tycora® covers a variety of processes: nylon, polyester, and acrylic fibers textured in different ways for specific end uses.

UNDERFEED. A device that feeds yarn continuously to a winding mechanism, the linear speed of the yarn through the feeding device being less than the linear speed of yarn taken up by the winding mechanism. The yarn may be processed through an intermediate unit as it runs from feed to take-up.

UPTWISTER. A device or machine that winds yarn up to a slowly revolving horizontally positioned bobbin from a rapidly rotating vertically positioned bobbin.

VENTURI. A unit on an air-bulking machine into which yarns are led meeting there compressed air, that, expanding in the venturi, air bulks the filaments.

VOLUMINOSITY. Volume occupied by a given weight.

YARN SET. A thermoplastic yarn is yarn set when a deformation is imposed upon it at a temperature high enough so that the internal molecular structure of the yarn may adapt itself to these new conditions and then the temperature is dropped, allowing it to cool. It will retain or attempt to retain the new dimension until such time as more severe conditions are applied.

550 MACHINE. A machine manufactured and sold by the Leesona Corporation for the purpose of false-twisting thermoplastic yarns. This was the first machine sold commercially by the Leesona Corporation for this purpose. It was followed by the 551, 552, and 553 Hi-Speed Machines.

551, 552, AND 553 MACHINES. Machines manufactured and sold by the Leesona Corporation for producing torque-crimped thermoplastic yarns at high speeds. The most recently designed machine, the 553, runs at speeds even higher than the Hi-Speed 551 and 552 machines.

511 MACHINE. A downtwister equipped with two sets of tension control rolls and an aluminum heater block similar to that used on the 550, 551, and 552 machines for reprocessing false-twist yarn, partially reheat setting while relaxed to the desired predetermined extent.

As stated earlier, whenever possible the foregoing definitions embody the sworn statement of the experts listed. They were edited when necessary by the author. We quote below from the publication of the American Society for Testing Materials, Definitions of

Textile Terms (D123-58), Appendix 1, Part B—Related Terminology on Textile Materials.

BULK YARN, N.   A class term for various yarns that have been prepared in such a way as to have greater covering power, or apparent volume, than that of conventional yarns of equivalent yarn number and of the same basic material with normal twist.

There are three categories of bulk yarns (bulky, textured, and stretch), as follows:

1. Bulky Yarn, n.   A generic term for yarns formed from inherently bulky fibers such as man-made fibers that are hollow along part or all of their length, or for yarns formed from fibers that cannot be closely packed because of their cross-sectional shapes, fiber alignment, stiffness, resilience, or natural crimp, or both.

2. Textured Yarn, n.   A generic term for filament or spun yarns that have been given notably greater apparent volume than conventional yarn of similar fiber (filament) count and denier. The yarns have a relatively low stretch. They are sufficiently stable to withstand normal yarn and fabric processing, including wet finishing and dyeing treatments, and conditions of use by the ultimate consumer. The apparent increased volume is achieevd through physical, chemical, or heat treatments, or a combination of these. (In the United Kingdom, it has been proposed to designate such yarn as "bulked" yarn.)

There are three types of textured bulk yarns (loopy, high bulk, and crimped) as follows:

a. Loopy Yarn, n.   Yarns essentially free from stretch that are characterized by a relatively large number of randomly spaced and randomly sized loops along the fibers or filaments. (These yarns are produced by an air jet acting on yarn fed through the jet at a greater speed than the final yarn take-up speed.)

b. High Bulk Yarn, n.   Yarns essentially free from stretch in which a fraction of the fibers (in any cross section) have been forced to assume a relatively high random crimp by shrinkage of the remaining fibers which, in general, have very low crimp. (This effect is produced by heating or steaming a yarn containing a proportion of thermally unstable fibers so that the latter shrink, producing a permanent crimp in the other fibers.)

c. Crimp Yarn, n.   (1) Thermoplastic textured yarns having relatively low elastic stretch (usually under 20 per cent) and frequently characterized by high saw-tooth type crimp, or curl. (These yarns are produced by a variety of mechanical methods, the use of stuffer boxes, heated gears, knife edges, a knife-set-ravel technique, or false twisting. (2) Non-thermoplastic textured yarns with irregular crimp and relatively high elastic stretch but low power of contraction. (A tight crimp in these yarns is produced by release of internal strains following immersion of the fabric in water, or by chemical treatments.)

3. Stretch Yarn, n. A generic term for thermoplastic filament or spun yarns having a high degree of potential elastic stretch and rapid recovery, and characterized by a high degree of yarn curl. (These yarns have been produced by an appropriate combination of deforming, heat setting, and developing treatments to attain elastic properties.)

There are two types of stretch yarn (torque and non-torque):

a. Torque Yarn, n. Stretch yarns that, when permitted to hang freely, rotate in the direction of the unrelieved torque resulting from previous deformation.

Note 1. Torque yarns include those whose deformation has been produced by a suitable combination of twisting, setting, untwisting or plying resulting in potential stretch and torque.

b. Non-Torque Yarn, n. Stretch yarns that have no tendency to rotate when permitted to hang freely.

Note 2. Non-Torque yarns include: (1) those whose deformation is wave-like, crinkled, crimped, or curled produced by a suitable combination of mechanical deformation followed by a setting treatment resulting in potential stretch without torque, and (2) plied yarns whose single yarn torque properties have been balanced by plying.

Note 3. Stretch yarns should be distinguished from elastic yarns based on rubber or other elastomers. The stretch of elastic yarns either as monofilaments or covered core yarns is a basic polymer property not associated with yarn curl.

Stretch nylon yarns, containing durable latent torque crimp, were developed, promoted, and marketed by the Heberlein Patent Corporation of Wattwil, Switzerland, shortly after World War II. Their method, involving a multiple number of steps, back winding, twisting, batch heat setting, back twisting, doubling, and winding produced yarns that were rapidly utilized in knitted stretch fabrics. Finished garments made from these yarns were very well promoted and merchandised under the tradename of Helanca®.

The Heberlein Patent Corporation guided the development in all phases; manufacture of yarn, manufacture of garments, dyeing and finishing, and promotion. Through judicious licensing arrangements they were able to exert a considerable amount of control over the quantity of yarn produced and the quality of the garments sold. By merchandising and promoting, by utilizing a single word to describe the product, they were able to identify the product as new, different, and of very high quality.

Spindles designed for the twisting of continuous filament yarns that had been idle for years were reactivated, and put to work producing Helanca®. Soon most of the spindles originally installed to produce rayon crepe were fully occupied. This expansion, rapid as it was, lagged well behind the demand even though the growth had to be limited to fabrics so designed that the variations inherent in the process, discussed in detail further on, would not cause, pronounced visible variations in the finished garments.

Meanwhile Warren A. Seem and Nicholas A. Stoddard, working as a team of inventors, discovered that the false-twist principle combined with control of heat, tension, and cooling within specified limits could be utilized to produce uniform durably crimped thermoplastic yarns in a continuous multistep process. This could be done rapidly, economically, and, most important, uniformly.

Practically the entire thermoplastic yarn twisting industry in the United States applied for, and obtained, a license to use the new process on a patent applied for basis. Paying royalties started at sixty ($0.60) per pound at the outset, twenty-five ($0.25) per pound later, then a flat paid up royalty on a per spindle basis; this was followed by six ($0.06) per pound for new machines operating at high speeds.

The wise pricing policy contributed greatly to the development of the industry. Royalties were reduced as rapidly as required to broaden the operating base and increase fields and sales. The very rapid development and expansion of markets for durably crimped thermoplastic yarns in the United States was a direct result of this policy. The European market for torque-crimp nylon produced in the United States, a multi-million pound market, is a further tribute to the wise and fair licensing policy of Seem and Stoddard.

The demand for stretch yarns, created by the very excellent promotional activities of the Heberlein Patent Corporation around their trademark Helanca® became so substantial that the knitting industry eagerly purchased the entire production of all false-twist spindles as rapidly as they were installed, and at the same time utilized surprisingly large poundages of "conventional" multi-step Helanca®.

At this time, while spindles and yarns were in very short supply, Messrs. Seem and Stoddard, together with their associates and the

Leesona Corporation, purchaser of their patent applications, elected to reinvest substantial percentages of their royalties in exploring the possibility of utilizing torque-crimp thermoplastic yarns in the weaving industry. They decided to produce woven stretch fabrics and soft, silky, textured fabrics, the latter by heat setting in such a manner that the crimps produced bulk, covering power, softness, and drape, rather than stretch. They retained the author, B. L. Hathorne, and instructed him to work with their licensees, weavers and dyers and finishers, in developing new and novel fabrics, and with yarn producers, converters, and cutters, to arouse industry interest in the new fabrics. This work, which extended over a four-year period and involved the expenditure of hundreds of thousands of dollars, resulted in the development of hundreds of samples of textured and stretch fabrics, and in the perfection of techniques of quilling, weaving, and dyeing and finishing that are in general use today.

A European firm, Moulinage et Retarderie de Chavanoz of Paris, France, that started later than Seem and Stoddard, eventually developed machines for producing false yarns varying in detail but not in principle from the concept of Seem and Stoddard. Early "Chavanoz" patent applications are limited in scope when compared to those of Seem and Stoddard, especially with respect to methods and the details of apparatus required to carry out the methods. As a result European and United States development proceeded along parallel lines, eventually resulting in parallel developments in both areas.

The Joseph Bancroft & Sons Company of Wilmington, Delaware, acquired from Alexander Smith Company Incorporated, now Mohasco Industries, Inc., Amsterdam, New York, an exclusive license covering the production of crimped yarn by forcing the yarn into a stuffer box under controlled conditions. This process produces crimped thermoplastic yarns that have some stretch, though not nearly as much as the torque-crimp yarns, and yarns that are very bulky, very soft, and full in hand.

Thermoplastic yarns processed through stuffer box machines by licensees of Joseph Bancroft & Sons Company that adhere to the rigid specifications set up and policed by the company may be, and usually are, sold as Textralized® yarns. Textralized® is a trademark owned by Joseph Bancroft & Sons Company that is made available to their licensees and controlled as stated above. Fabrics and garments manufactured from Textralized® yarns meeting the specifications set up and policed by this company may be sold as Ban-Lon®. Ban-Lon® is a registered trademark owned by Joseph Bancroft & Sons

Company that is made available to licensees manufacturing fabric and garments from Textralized® yarn in accordance with the company's specifications. In the weaving field Textralized® yarns have been utilized primarily for their texture, covering power, and softness, rather than for stretch properties. To date the production of woven fabrics from Textralized® yarns has been somewhat limited because of variations in crimping, etc., that adversely affect the uniformity of the finished fabrics, although the same variations do not produce objectionable visible variations in knitted garments. Many feel that these variations are due to differences in the heat transfer of hot metal to crumpled thermoplastic yarns vs. the heat transfer of heated air to these yarns and that it would be possible to so vary the machine as to eliminate the variations that have retarded its progress in weaving to date.

The Deering Milliken Research Corporation owns the patented process of producing crimped yarns by processing previously heated thermoplastic yarns over a crimping edge, then cooling and relaxing them. Considerable progress has been made in the knitting industry with these edge-crimped yarns. As in the case of Textralized® yarns weaving has been limited. Edge-crimped yarns may be sold as Agilon® yarns by licensees of the Deering Milliken Research Corporation adhering to the specifications of this corporation. Agilon® is a registered trademark owned by Deering Milliken Research Corporation that is made available to licensees meeting their requirements.

Air-bulked yarns have been used to make many excellent and unusual woven fabrics, some are woven in multi-millions of yards annually. As with Textralized® and edge-crimped yarns unavoidable variations caused by the equipment utilized to date have limited the development of this particular means of producing textured thermoplastic yarns.

Air-bulked yarns are produced by leading yarns into a stream of air in a venturi tube, where the yarns become air bulked. The yarns are increased in bulk and size to the extent permitted by the per cent of overfeed utilized. The air-bulking process is not limited to thermoplastic yarns or to continuous filament yarns. All yarns twisted properly for the process can be air-bulked.

Air-bulked yarns manufactured by licensees of E. I. du Pont de Nemours and Company, Inc., in accordance with their specifications, may be sold as Taslan® yarns. Taslan® is a registered trademark owned by du Pont, that is made available to licensees adhering to the rigid specifications of the company.

Recently new types of textured thermoplastic yarns have been made available to knitters, weavers, and tufters. These are producer-textured yarns. Current activity in this field may make much that is written here on this subject appear out of date before this book is published.

Heavy denier thermoplastic yarns, carpet yarns, are being textured by variations of the gear crimping and stuffer box crimping processes, the improvements incorporated into the process by its producers eliminating the variations inherent in the original hot stuffer box yarns.

Use of special trilobal cross-sectional yarns, good control of processing, good promotion, and establishment of prices below those charged by throwsters enabled producers to develop quickly a multi-million pound market for producer-textured carpet yarns.

Dual component yarns, which crimp when relaxed, have already won an established place in the textured yarn family.

Certain producers are preparing to invade the fine denier textured yarn field. It is anticipated that these yarns will be very well promoted and will open new markets to textured thermoplastic yarns, increasing their use to several times the poundage now used.

Spandex yarns, continuous filament, spun, and spun combined with fibers relatively inert insofar as stretch and recovery are concerned, have been woven into fabrics and have produced unusually excellent stretch fabrics. Depending upon construction and wet processing these fabrics can be substantially superior in stretch and recovery to the older torque-crimp fabrics. Weavers anticipate that smart merchandising of these new yarns by the producers will tremendously expand existing markets for woven stretch fabrics and will in addition open many new markets, all of which will provide an umbrella to cover increased and expanding activity in the torque-crimp field. Also anticipated is a combination of torque-crimp textured yarns and Spandex yarns to produce new and novel effects and superior hand and drape over the effects that are anticipated from Spandex itself.

The so-called "cotton" stretch fabrics are made by combining torque-crimped thermoplastic yarns and cotton in such a manner that the final fabric resembles cotton in appearance and feel, yet produces the stretch and recovery of torque crimp. The growth in the popularity of these fabrics induced a reactivation of earlier work in producing cotton stretch by slack mercerizing and by resin treating twisted cotton and subsequently untwisting it to a predetermined extent. At this writing there has been little practical application of the slack mercerizing process, other than in bandages, because of the poor recovery of so-called stretch fabrics produced in this manner. Considerable work is continuing in this field and will undoubtedly eventuate into development of processes that would combine slack mercerizing effects with other methods of producing stretch in the same fabric, each augmenting the other.

Excellent woven fabrics have been produced in experimental quantities by and for the Southern Regional Research Laboratory (Division of U.S.D.A.) by using durable resins to impart durable memory to crimped cotton yarns. Basically the S.R.R.L. work has followed the teachings of Heberlein reproducing durable crimp in thermoplastic yarns; it varies from Heberlein in that cross-linking and thermosetting resins are present in the fibers when they are batch heat set following initial twisting, and preceding the back twisting operation.

This process, a multistep process, is necessarily very expensive, and subject to the lack of uniformity problems that beset the original Heberlein process.

The concept of imparting durable memory to processed resin-treated cotton yarns is disclosed in U.S. Patent 3,025,659 issued to Messrs. Seem and Stoddard who pioneered in this field and who are the inventors of the process of producing durably crimped thermoplastic yarns by the false-twist process. Their concept makes the production of durably crimped cotton yarns practical, economical, and sufficiently uniform to warrant their use in woven fabrics. The Seem-Stoddard concept produces durably crimped cotton and other durably crimped cellulostic yarns by continuous twisting, curing, cooling, and untwisting cotton and other cellulostic yarns treated with resins, cellulose reactive or non-cellulose reactive, or a combination of cellulose reactive and non-cellulose reactive, a portion of which can be durably set by heat. The resins are applied continuously during processing or prior to processing, the twisting, setting and untwisting is accomplished by passing the yarn through a heating unit and a false-twist spindle. Current activities in this field indicate that it will be very important in the future and may become the principal source of stretch fabrics. Cotton, resin, and false twisting are all very economically priced.

The major portion of woven stretch fabrics have been produced by utilizing the stretch and recovery properties of thermoplastic yarns twisted, heat set, and untwisted. These for the most part have been torque-crimp yarns made by the false-twist principle although, particularly in Europe, considerable use has also been made of the older "conventional" Helanca® process.

There was a long lag between the development of good woven stretch and textured fabrics, based on proper utilization of torque-crimp yarns in the United States, and substantial sales of these fabrics because of a price ceiling of $1.00 per yard, which was imposed by cutters. Finally J. P. Stevens & Company, Inc., boldly marketed a polyester fabric based on torque-crimp yarn at a price well above the so-called ceiling. The new fabric was an instant success, both aesthetically and profit-wise, and was followed by a host of imitators and by variations produced by Stevens and their competitors. This blasted once and for all the arbitrary ceiling that had previously retarded the development and growth of woven stretch and textured fabrics, and has led to the utilization of this increasingly large new family of fabrics.

In Europe the development took a different tack than in the States. Europeans wove the best possible fabrics that could be made at the time from torque-crimp yarns, priced these at and above $8.00 per yard, and achieved an immediate success in Europe. This was followed by the adoption of these fabrics to a greater or lesser extent by many countries throughout the temperate zones of the world. These early European fabrics, following the production of fabrics in the United States, were warp stretch fabrics, as opposed to the United States development of filling stretch fabrics, and were much heavier on the average than the different types of United States fabrics.

In the States, earlier developments involved primarily the production of filling stretch fabrics, although lightweight warp-textured fabrics were also made available fairly early. At present the bulk of the development in the United States continues to be stretch filled and the bulk of the European developments are stretch warp.

The success of woven stretch and textured fabrics, based primarily on torque-crimp thermoplastic yarns, has stimulated continuing work on many other approaches to the development of woven stretch and textured fabrics. Two such developments, mentioned previously, appear to be on the verge of a major breakthrough. These are: utilization of resin to impart a durable "memory" of crimp to resin-treated cellulastic yarns and fibers, twisted, heat set, and untwisted; and utilization of yarns consisting of or containing durable elastomers such as polyurethane.

A third development, new only with respect to its existence becoming generally known (patent applied for in 1956), was disclosed by representatives of E. I. du Pont de Nemours and Company, Inc., in December 1961. Shortly after the issuance of U.S. Patent 3,009,309 assigned to du Pont, representatives of the company informed segments of the nylon-consuming industries and related industries that du Pont had produced a major breakthrough in producing stretch and textured nylon and polyester yarns by "molecular rearrangement at the spinnerette," and that du Pont would market these yarns in an orderly fashion during the ensuing two years. This unexpected announcement has been a major cause of the increasing interest in woven stretch fabrics. At present opinions of those who will use these yarns appears to be rather evenly divided between belief that the process depends on utilizing the disclosures of U.S. Patent 3,009,309, which describes false twisting at speeds above one million turns per minute, using a stream of air as source of power, and belief that the "molecular rearrangement at the spinnerette" involves texturing and drawing at the same time, continuously drawing to a crimped condition rather than in a straight line.

Hundreds of workers are actively designing woven stretch fabrics and seeking to improve the elastic and aesthetic properties given them by known methods; other workers are seeking diligently to devise new and improved methods and techniques of producing woven stretch fabrics. The known methods of producing woven stretch fabrics utilize the following.

1. Thermoplastic yarns containing latent torque crimp energy.

2. Thermoplastic yarns containing latent crimping energy imparted by gear or stuffer box.

3. Thermoplastic yarns containing latent "producer crimp" energy.

4. Thermoplastic yarns containing latent crimping energy imparted by scraping heated yarns over a crimping edge.

5. Multifilament elastomer yarns and fibers resistant to degradation.

6. Dual component yarns that crimp when relaxed under controlled conditions.

7. Chemical treatment of fabrics, as in the slack mercerizing of especially designed loosely woven cotton fabrics, and chemical treatment of loosely woven woolen and worsted fabrics.

8. Fabrics as in (7) augmented by stretch imparted by other means.

9. Cellulose fibers and yarns, cotton and rayon, twisted, cross-linked and resin-treated, and untwisted.

Textile mills and related organizations are spending literally millions of dollars per year on the development and improvement of woven stretch fabrics for one reason only; they recognize that this new family of fabrics is destined to increase rapidly in popularity and volume, and that the first firms to market each improvement will benefit more in increased volume and profit than those that adopt a "me too" policy.

Depending on the yarns employed, design of fabric, methods of imparting stretch, manufacturing efficiency, and efficacy of relaxing and dyeing and finishing methods employed, stretch fabrics as a group possess unique properties that will win for them an ever increasing volume of the woven fabric market.   For example, woven stretch fabrics:

1. Improve the appearance of garments, when new or freshly pressed, and especially after being worn for a considerable period of time.   This is because strain is spread over a wider area, stretch compensates for strain, and recovery properties cause the garment to return quickly to its unstrained condition as strain is relaxed.

2. Improved comfort of garments.   Stretch characteristics permit the body to move with minimum restraint from stretch garments, thereby increasing comfort.   This freedom from restraint is so pronounced that women wearing stretch fabrics for the first time often remark that they feel almost naked.

3. Improve fullness or thickness of fabric causing a pleasing illusion of lightness or featheriness of hand.

4. Improve drape of garment.

5. Improve crease retention of fabrics that are pressed with a crease.

6. Improve wash and wear characteristics of fabrics that are utilized in wash and wear garments.

7. Increased utility.   The garments maintain their "new" well-groomed look for a longer time and applied strain is spread over a greater number of threads thereby increasing snag resistance and tear strength.

It was stated above that millions of dollars are being spent on research on woven stretch fabrics.   One firm conclusion must be drawn from the increase in beauty, drape, comfort, and utility which was created by adding stretch to woven fabrics; that the development, manufacture, and sale of these fabrics will increase rapidly and steadily for the next several years.

2

Methods of Producing Durably Crimped Thermoplastic Yarns and Details of Durable Torque-Crimp Processes

Thermoplastic yarns are textured or crimped by five major methods, four of which involve energy exchange that produces latent crimping power in the yarns, releasable under controlled conditions. When these four conditions, energy input, fabric design, yarn and fabric manufacture, and energy release, are correctly controlled the resultant fabric is a stretch or textured fabric, depending on result required and controls utilized.

The fifth method, air entangling of fibers, produces textured yarns only, although a variation of this method, disclosed in U.S. Patent 3,009,309, assigned to E. I. du Pont de Nemours and Company, Inc., can be used to produce stretch yarns as well.

The methods used to produce durably crimped yarns may be roughly grouped as follows:

METHOD	POPULAR OR TRADENAME OF PROCESS
Torque crimp (twisting, setting, and untwisting)	False twist (Fluflon®, Superloft®, Whitin-A.R.C.T.) and conventional Helanca® multistep process
Stuffer box and gear crimp	Textralized® and related processes
Heated yarn drawn over a crimping edge	Agilon®
Entangle with stream of air	Taslan®
"Molecular Rearrangement at the Spinnerette"	Producer crimped yarn

A study of the methods used to produce crimped thermoplastic yarns makes it very evident that much more latent energy can be inserted in thermoplastic yarn by torque-crimp processes than by any other process currently known, or likely to be devised, for processing single component thermoplastic yarns.   In all fields of science it is accepted that for every action there is an equal and opposite re-action.   It defies the imagination to conceive of any method or means of subjecting a thermoplastic yarn to more abuse (stretching, twist-ing, and heating) so as to obtain a greater reaction which might be used functionally in creating useful effects in yarn and/or fabric. Visualize a rubber band wrapped tightly about your finger and imagine the additional stress if the rubber band were also highly twisted while being tightly wound.   The tendency of the rubber band to untwist plus the tendency to return to its relaxed length would create an unbearable pressure.   This is essentially what hap-pens in the production of multistep Helanca® yarn.

MULTISTEP HELANCA®

The yarn is very highly twisted as it is wound under tension upon a metal-headed bobbin.   The stresses are so great that skill is re-quired to prevent the metal heads from exploding or becoming loose from the barrel or the crushing of the metal or solid maple wood barrels.   This truly violent force must be tamed to be utilized func-tionally in textiles.   This is accomplished by subjecting the wound spools of highly twisted yarn to steam under pressure for at least several hours.   The temperature of the steam plus the moisture (to a lesser extent) plasticizes the thermoplastic material and conse-quently all of the stresses come to rest through a shifting or re-orien-tation of the molecules of the yarn in its then plastic condition.   This is but the first step in the production of torque-crimp yarn by the conventional Helanca® method.   The second functional step is carried out after the yarn is cooled to stabilize the molecules to their new position and is rewound onto a spinner bobbin.   Again the yarn is highly twisted but this time in the opposite direction.   The violent force is still present, but in this instance the many filaments of the multifilament yarn are substantially parallel instead of being tightly twisted together.   Basically this is the finished product with its strong tendency to contract and untwist untamed.   These forces are use-fully tamed or utilized in numerous ways, for example:

a. One right-twist yarn is plied with one left-twist yarn so that the opposing forces balance each other.   Only the plied yarn *per se* is dormant, as each of the two yarns and each of their many individual filaments remain "alive" with torsional forces. The balance of the opposed forces prevent bias in knitted or woven fabrics, but the forces (torsion) that continue to fight each other to bring about the balance give life to a fabric in the form of hand, resilience, stretch, and recovery from stretch, crease resistance, dimensional stability, and drape.

b. A single yarn may be used as a crepe yarn is used to create fabric effects but in either (*a*) or (*b*) the parallel relationship of the filaments is unnatural; strong torsional forces and crimps tend to separate them and when the yarn or fabric is not held taut the filaments will separate causing the yarn or fabric to shorten as the yarn attains greater bulk. However, in yarn or fabric form, the degree of bulking and shortening may be controlled by subjecting the yarn or fabric to the required heat while under a required stress.

FALSE-TWIST METHOD

The differences between the multistep Helanca® process and the false-twist process are given in detail later in this chapter. At this point it is merely being pointed out that the false-twist process inserts the same strong torsional forces in a continuous one-step process as the multistep process does in a series of steps. In the torque-crimp process every fraction of an inch of each fiber is subjected to a strong torque force during twisting. Thus the entire length of each filament attempts to wind up or crimp in a helical direction when the yarn, or fabric made from the yarn, is relaxed. This produces a uniformly irregular crimp condition in each filament, as per the shadowgraphs in Figs. 1 and 2. Depending on the type, denier and filament count of the yarn, the heat, twist, etc., used during crimping, the conditions of relaxing, wet or dry, hot or room temperature, torque-crimp thermoplastic yarn will shrink, to a varying degree, up to 85 per cent of its length when relaxed as a single yarn, without restraint. When the yarn is restrained, as in a fabric, the latent energy may be expended uselessly if design and relaxing conditions are improperly employed; when design and relaxing conditions are favorable, the energy can produce texture in the yarn and fabric, interesting surface effects, or stretch and recovery properties as intended.

Yarns crimped by the stuffer box and gear crimp methods can retain energy only where it is applied and this is at the intermittent positions throughout the yarn where the filaments are bent while passed through the stuffer box, gear or other device. A glance at

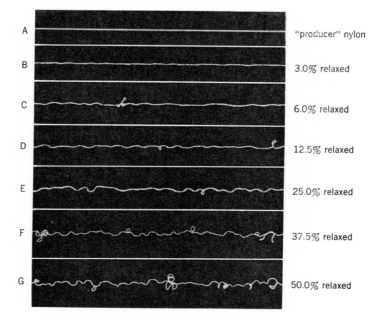

Fig. 1. Shadowgraphs of seven single filaments of 70-denier, 32-filament, semi-dull, type-6 nylon taken from a single pirn. Filament A is from yarn taken directly from the pirn. Filaments B, C, D, E, F, and G are from yarns false-twisted 80 tpi on the 553 machine then permitted to relax as indicated.

the individual filament shown in Fig. 3 clearly illustrates that the latent energy in the stuffer box or gear-crimped yarn can be only a fraction of the energy in yarn crimped by the torque-crimp process. When multifilament thermoplastic yarns are tightly twisted, heat-set, and untwisted, energy is set into every minute length of each filament, and the entire length of each filament tries to return to its twisted heat-set condition when permitted or caused to relax. When multifilament thermoplastic yarns are stuffer box or gear-crimped and heat set in this condition, energy is set in the fiber only where the fibers are bent, thus the total amount of latent energy that can be set into the yarn, releasable during relaxing, is only a fraction of the amount of energy that can be built into torque-crimp thermoplastic yarn.

The process involving drawing a hot yarn over an edge, thereby producing edge-crimped or Agilon® yarns can impart more crimping power than is possible in the stuffer box or gear-crimped yarn because the filament is crimped continuously. However, the crimp

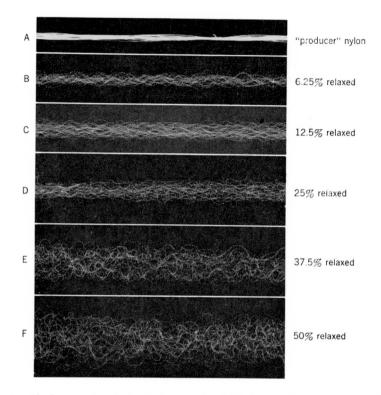

Fig. 2. Shadowgraphs of six single strands of 70-denier, 32-filament, semi-dull, type-6 nylon taken from a single pirn. Yarn A is yarn taken directly from the pirn. Yarns B, C, D, E, and F are from yarns false-twisted 80 tpi on the 553 machine then permitted to relax as indicated.

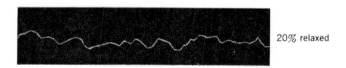

Fig. 3. A shadowgraph of a single filament of Textralized® nylon. The filament was taken from a strand of 70-denier, 32-filament, semi-dull, type-6 nylon, Textralized® and relaxed 20%.

form is usually such that not as much force of retraction is present in edge-crimped yarns as is present in torque-crimped yarns of the same material.

The air-bulking method of crimping thermoplastic yarns, Taslan®, as used commercially to date, produces a textured yarn but does not impart usable latent energy to the fibers.   U.S. Patent 3,009,309, assigned to E. I. du Pont de Nemours and Company, Inc., discloses a means of using a stream of air to insert false twist in a yarn.   This is a totally different concept of the use of air to modify a yarn and should not be confused with the process of leading yarn into a venturi where it is bulked by escaping compressed air thereby producing Taslan®.

Unlike other methods of texturizing or crimping thermoplastic yarns, the air-bulking process does not use heat to plasticize and cooling to stabilize, so as to set the filaments bulked by air under pressure. Taslan® yarns do not contain latent energy able to form crimps when the yarns are relaxed.

The popular understanding of the methods utilized at this time to produce "molecular rearrangement at the spinnerette" and "producer textured yarns" vary from the belief that the yarns result from combining two dissimilar polymers in a single filament, through crimping while drawing, by stuffer box, gear-crimping and torque-crimp procedures, in effect drawing into crimp positions rather than in straight lines, air bulking, and additional undisclosed processes.   It is probable that grounds exist for all the various popular beliefs, that "producer textured yarns" continue to be in a state of flux, work progressing rapidly along many directions, and that when commercially available in fine deniers, "producer textured yarns" will vary in latent energy from the energy content of Textralized® and related yarns to the energy content of false-twist yarns.

From the foregoing it is evident that the torque-crimp process of texturing thermoplastic yarns imparts substantially more latent energy or force of retraction to the yarn than any other known commercial process.   The value of this latent force cannot be overemphasized.   This energy, present in every minute portion of each individual filament enables fabrics to stretch and recover from the normal strains of wearing throughout the life of the fabric.   It produces the millions of minute spaces between crimped filaments that absorb perspiration and allow it to evaporate slowly as from hydrophilic fabrics.   This latent crimping and shrinking power is used by designers to produce stretch and recovery properties, when required, a soft full hand when desired, and an endless multitude of interesting surface effects most of which have not yet been merchandized.

The need for the maximum possible amount of latent crimping energy in the yarn is matched only by the need for uniformity throughout the entire length of individual units of yarn and from unit to unit.

Fabrics, knitted and woven, vary in type, pattern, methods of manufacture, etc., to such an extent that any generalized statement regarding the magnitude of the need for uniformity in either group is bound to be considered erroneous by many, and can be successfully challenged with positive evidence in specific instances. Nevertheless depending on the type of nonuniformity, certain textured yarns, commercially successful in the knitting industry, have been notably unsuccessful in weaving because of variations in the yarn, readily visible in woven fabric, yet very difficult to discern in knitted fabrics. The reason for this is the nature of the textured yarns, the type of nonuniformity, and the nature of knitted fabrics.

The mechanics by which knitted fabrics cover or substantially reduce the extent to which variations in textured yarns are visible in finished fabrics due to the effect of the relaxing process and the use of constructions in knitting that permit the textured yarns to crimp more in certain knitted fabrics than in woven fabrics, can be dramatically illustrated by a specific woven fabric, 30-denier nylon batiste warp, normally filled with a fine-count polyester cotton, 65–35 blend.

To illustrate the manner in which crimped thermoplastic yarns hide fabric variations otherwise visible, fill one cut with low or producer twist 70-denier nylon and another with 70-denier nylon textured by the false-twist process. Dye and finish each cut separately, using the best known commercial techniques for each.

The usual warp streaks found in this type of fabric filled with continuous filament nylon will be clearly visible in the cut filled with plain nylon and will be completely invisible in the cut filled with torque-crimp textured nylon, provided that the warp is properly prepared from good nylon. A reprocessing of the textured fabric, consisting solely of reframing and reheat-setting to the widest possible width, thus eliminating the effect of texturing of the filling, will permit the warp streaks, normal to the construction, to become visible. In this example the latent crimping power of torque-crimp yarn *used in the filling* successfully hides or covers streaks normally visible in the *warp*. This happens because the release of the latent crimping power in the filling distorts the warp in various directions, thus effectively breaking up the parallel light reflections that cause the luster streaks. These luster streaks, because of variations in strain unavoidably applied to the nylon during its manufacture, again become visible when the warp threads are again drawn into a parallel position by reframing and reheat setting.

As stated previously, thermoplastic yarns can be durably crimped by five distinctly different methods, torque crimp, stuffer box and gear crimp, edge-crimped, air-bulked, and yarn-crimped during spinning or drawing.

Torque crimp, utilizing every portion of every filament to carry and retain memory or latent crimp energy, produces the most stretch and recovery of any yarns produced by throwsters and will be covered in detail first.

Latent torque-crimp energy can be put into a thermoplastic yarn in two ways: by the conventional multistep Helanca® process, and by the various continuous false-twist processes.

By utilizing the slow, expensive multistep process, operating under the very best conditions, it is often possible to build into a thermoplastic yarn a very small increment of torque-crimp energy over and above the best that can be done by the various false-twist machines. It is believed that this is due to three factors, namely: moisture and heat are used in the multistep process, as compared to dry heat alone in the false-twist process; a much longer heat treatment is used, more than one hour in the multistep process, compared with less than one second of time by the false-twist method; and the yarn is cooled thoroughly before untwisting in the multistep process. It is generally believed that if the false-twist process were sufficiently reduced in speed, and temperatures approaching the melting point were utilized, more nearly equal results would be obtainable. However, since false-twist yarns generally have more than adequate torque, the practice has been to favor the economy of high-speed operation. The A.R.C.T. machine, having a longer dwell time in the heated zone, is said to give a higher crimp modulus than other high-speed machines. Note that although torque-crimp yarn made from nylon, by the multistep process, may have some increment of torque-crimp energy over and above the best false-twist yarn, this may not apply in every instance with all thermoplastic yarns. On the contrary, acceptable torque-crimp yarn of polyester and certain other thermoplastic yarns cannot be produced by conventional means with the multistep process; the deficiency is that the crimp is not durable and pulls out too easily. The false-twist process can deal with this problem because any required tension may be applied to the heated yarn being twisted so as to preclude ductility in the finished yarn. However, in the multistep process there are definite limitations to the tension that may be applied, and in this process the tension is applied to the unheated yarn which in some instances becomes ductile after twisting and heating.

Most multistep process, torque-crimp yarn produced in this country has been produced on spindles designed primarily for rayon crepe. This, and use of a batch process for heat-setting bobbins of yarn under pressure in an autoclave, has resulted in variations in stretch and recovery and especially rate and depth of dyeing that have been very troublesome.

In the following pages of this chapter we will discuss in detail the conventional Helanca® process (the step-by-step or discontinuous process) and will continue with the false-twist process and the various machines used to produce false-twist yarns.

Conventional Helanca® or Step-by-Step or Discontinuous Process of Producing Torque-Crimp Thermoplastic Yarns

The process was patented by the Heberlein Patent Corporation of Wattwil, Switzerland, the original process patent for the twist, heat set, de-twist method was granted in 1935, additional patents relating to thermoplastic yarns were issued after World War II (see Chapter 17) and was licensed throughout the world. It produced new and novel stretch fabrics and was immediately successful in the knitting field, particularly the men's half-hose field producing half-hose known as stretch socks. A carefully guided licensing, control, and promotional program contributed very substantially to the rapid profitable growth of the market for Helanca® knitted half-hose and garments. Within two years of the issuance of the patents most of the spindles originally built to produce rayon crepe were fully occupied producing Helanca®. This happy and profitable situation continued for two years after the introduction of false-twist machines in 1955, because of the growth of the market, which is still continuing at an ever-accelerating pace.

By 1957 the production of false-twist machines had grown to such proportions that the inevitable price drop made production of conventional Helanca® unprofitable except for certainly highly specialized end uses; some of these continued into 1963 and show indications of continuing for years.

Step-by-Step or Discontinuous Process

The step-by-step or discontinuous process consists of five primary steps, these are usually followed by two secondary steps as follows:

REDRAW

Thermoplastic yarn is wound on a redraw machine from the producer delivery package to a bobbin suitable for use on an uptwister.

UPTWIST

Bobbins from the redraw machine are moved to the uptwister and are uptwisted at maximum possible speed, as high as 16,000 rpm in some instances, inserting twist of the order of magnitude of crepe twist, usually in the neighborhood of 75 turns per inch in 70-denier nylon, the twist being proportionally higher and lower for other deniers.

All efforts are made to use tensions as uniform as possible from bobbin to bobbin, from top to bottom, and from inside to outside of individual bobbins. Unfortunately the nature of the equipment is such that variations from bobbin to bobbin, from top to bottom of individual bobbins, and from outside to inside of individual bobbins, cannot be entirely eliminated. Tension increases as the yarn approaches the top of the bobbin and as the yarn approaches the barrel or core of the bobbin. These variations cannot help but manifest themselves as variations in finished fabrics, the degree of visible variation modified by the construction of the fabric, and the type of dyestuffs and techniques used in wet processing.

YARN SET OR HEAT SET

The bobbins of twisted thermoplastic yarn are placed on racks and then in an autoclave where they are treated at elevated temperature for substantial time periods with steam under pressure. Various manufacturers have their own techniques, varying pressure, vacuum when used prior to or intermittently with the introduction of steam, and time. All seek to obtain a complete and full yarn set or heat set, that is, all seek to give the yarn the maximum possible "memory" of the highly twisted condition. In general, temperatures range from 240°F to 270°F, and the pressure between 25 and 50 pounds above atmospheric pressure; the treatment usually consists of two or more steam applications, each preceded by a vacuum exhaustion of the autoclave to promote maximum possible penetration to the barrel of the bobbin.

This batch heat-setting process is, for many reasons, the worst offender in the step-by-step process with respect to causing variations in the crimp, crimp retention, and dye index of the finished yarn.

Moisture and heat, in the order of magnitude used in yarn setting, tends to cause thermoplastic yarns to shrink. If they cannot shrink, the contractile force must cause the yarn to become stretched. In this manner elongation is reduced and modulus increased.

When twisted thermoplastic yarns wound on bobbins are heat set, the yarn next to the barrel of the bobbin is unable to shrink. Successive layers are able to shrink more and more due to the drawing in of the innermost layers of yarn, resulting in a gradual variation in dye affinity from the yarn next to the barrel to the yarn on the outside of the bobbin. This primary cause of variation in the step-by-step process has been minimized somewhat by wrapping the bobbin with collapsible corrugated cardboard (U.S. Patent 2,394,639, W. A. Seem). Even with the use of corrugated cardboard, which does minimize the inside to outside variation, this still constitutes a major cause of visible variations in finished merchandise from step-by-step thermoplastic torque-crimp yarns.

Another cause of variation in this process is the outside and inside variation due to the effect of heat. Obviously the outside layers are effected by the heat first and most, causing serious variations in finishing merchandise. Also yarn adjacent to the flanges or heads of headed take-up packages receives different heat treatment.

REDRAW

After heat treatment to plasticize the twisted yarn under severe stress, the yarn is permitted to cool, to stabilize, or yarn-set the yarn, and is then redrawn to a twister bobbin.

REVERSE TWIST

The heat-set yarn redrawn to the twister bobbin is again placed on an uptwister and again twisted, this time in such a direction that the twist is removed from the yarn; attempts are made to so adjust the machines that the finished untwisted yarn will contain zero twist yarn, when zero twist is desired, or a definite number of turns when this condition is required preliminary to plying. As the yarn untwists, it lengthens or loses its contraction due to prior twisting and, therefore, it is necessary that a lesser number of turns per inch be taken out than is put in to accomplish a zero twist result in the yarn on the take-up bobbin.

Differences in tension and turns of twist from bobbin to bobbin during the first time twisting, differences in shrinkage and heat effect during yarn setting, and differences in tension and turns of twist from bobbin to bobbin during uptwisting, none completely avoidable, all contribute to the differences observed in the finished single yarn. Particularly in the case of completely untwisted yarn, what might appear to be relatively minor variations in twist per inch cause very serious visible variations in many types of fabric.

DOUBLE

Most, though not all, of the step-by-step or discontinuous-type stretch yarns have been doubled, one end S and one end Z, the doubling being of a very low order of magnitude usually 3 to 5 turns. There are instances where much greater doubling twist is required, to avoid picking and in some cases to provide increased available torque energy in the finished yarn.

The doubling operation, simple as it is, can become very costly when the yarns doubled vary from the outside to the inside of the bobbins. In this situation it is necessary to waste the tailings (expensive) or tie knots in the single-end magnifying dye differences by causing yarn from the outside of one bobbin to be plied with yarn from the inside of another bobbin after the practice has been carried out continuously for a sufficient length of time.

CONE

For shipping purposes it is usually desirable to cone the yarn by running it over an oil trough and applying 2 to 5 per cent of oil to facilitate further processing. The coning operation is the least sensitive of those used, although even in coning, variations in cone density can cause visible variations in finished merchandise.

———————————

Following its quick success in the men's half-hose field, Helanca® was knitted and woven on various machines and introduced into many types of garments ranging from ladies' sheer panties to men's heavy duty ski pants. Two of the most successful items were leotards and ski pants.

Leotards which were properly designed, quality controlled, and well promoted were very successful and would have continued to have been sold in far greater quantities than at present, particularly as a staple in the children's field, had it been possible to control the type of machines on which the fabrics were made. Fabrics which were similar in appearance but much cheaper in price, knitted on multi-end simple circular knit machines, were offered to and quickly purchased by the public who expected this merchandise to have the utility of the initially produced and quality controlled tricot knit and double-knit Helanca® leotards. Unfortunately the cheap circular knit fabrics, particularly in children's wear, snagged readily, broke into holes, and proved to be very expensive in terms of actual wear per dollar expended. Better constructed, run-proof leotards continue to be used in substantial quantities in the colder regions. Control of quality at the outset would have maintained sales at and above their initial high level.

Fortunately this did not happen in ski pants. European manufacturers used good yarns, good constructions, and packed in a sufficient number of ends to assure that the fabric had enough latent torque-crimp memory to enable it to pass through the dyeing and finishing operations without undue loss of elasticity. The utility of these garments and their fine appearance, even after long and hard usage, contributed greatly to the growth of stretch yarns in various fields.

Eventually, as would be anticipated, cheaper versions, which used fewer ends per inch and which were undesirable in other ways, caused trouble in this and related fields. Fortunately this did not happen until after a sufficient number of high-quality garments had been produced, sold, and used. Poor quality warp stretch merchandise delayed stretch growth somewhat but did not in any way hurt the continuing growth of high-quality stretch merchandise. In 1955 the Heberlein Patent Corporation recognized the inevitable and permitted their trademark Helanca® to be applied to garments made from false-twist yarns, but maintained a very strict testing and policing program for the protection of their trademark and their trademark licensees.

The Heberlein Patent Corporation should be, and is, hereby highly commended for its most excellent promotional, merchandising, and quality control program that has contributed much to the success of fabrics made with torque-crimp thermoplastic yarns.

As stated previously, thermoplastic yarns are still being processed by the conventional Helanca®, or step-by-step process, particularly when true twist is desired in addition to ply twist, in order to reduce picking and increase torque. It is probable that this method will

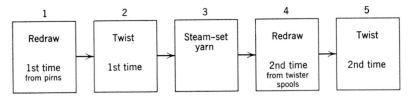

Fig. 4. Minimum steps in producing stretch yarn by conventional process.

continue to be used for years, in relatively small quantities when compared to current production of false twist, yet substantial in special fields where true twist in addition to false twist is considered necessary by some operators. Further growth of the process is unlikely because of the unavoidable variations inherent in the process, as explained previously, and the cost differential. The step-by-step process requires more than five times the floor space needed by the early Fluflon® and Superloft® machines, in excess of twenty times the floor space required by the new high-speed 553 machines, more elapsed time from start to finish of the processing, more labor, and more power. Top twisting speeds for the conventional or step-by-step process are 16,000 rpm, where two twistings are necessary, com-

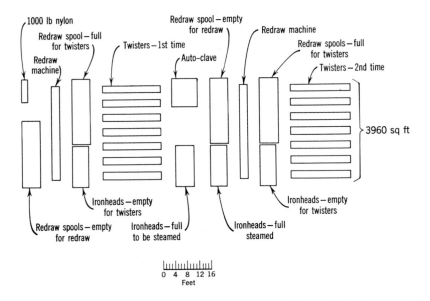

Fig. 5. Floor space requirements to produce 1000 pounds stretch nylon per week
CONVENTIONAL PROCESS.

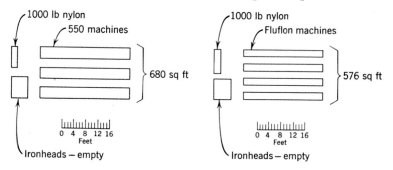

Fig. 6.   Floor space requirements to produce 1000 pounds stretch nylon per week on 550 machines.

Fig. 7.   Floor space requirements to produce 1000 pounds stretch nylon per week on Fluflon® machines.

pared with 360,000 rpm for false twist on the most recent machines, where only one twisting operation is required because the yarns are twisted, heated, cooled, and untwisted in a single operation.

Figure 4 shows, diagrammatically, the five basic steps of the conventional or multistep process of producing stretch yarn from low twist or zero twist thermoplastic yarns. Figures 5, 6, and 7 show the relative floor space and machine requirements of the conventional process and the early false-twist processes. Floor space requirements for the 553, the newest machine, are too small to warrant a drawing. Less than one-third of one 553 machine is required to produce 1000 pounds per week.

The False-Twist Process

Commercial production from one full-scale Fluflon® machine started in early 1953. A limited exclusive license prevented further licensing until late 1954 when The Permatwist Company of Coatesville, Pennsylvania, licensed nine manufacturers to produce false-twist thermoplastic yarns on converted uptwisters utilizing very low priced but very excellently designed parts added to conventional uptwisters. Thus it was made possible for manufacturers to enter this new field without risking undue amounts of capital based on annual pounds of anticipated production. These initial licensees were all sworn to secrecy, and the licenses were based on patents applied for rather than issued patents.

In December 1954, The Permatwist Company sold their inventions, covered by patents applied for, to the Universal Winding Company, which subsequently became the Leesona Corporation, one of the largest if not the largest firm producing twisting machines for continuous filament yarns utilized in throwing and weaving mills. The Universal Winding Company (later The Leesona Corporation) then proceeded to sell the equipment designed and developed by the Permatwist Company and their own version of a machine which was developed to accomplish a similar result. More about this later. At this point we believe we should describe the initially developed and now patented false-twist process for imparting latent torque-crimp memory to thermoplastic yarns.

This false-twist process is described so clearly and concisely in the claims of their U.S. Patent 2,803,109 issued August 20, 1957, that we present Claim 1 in its entirety as the simplest way of introducing readers unfamiliar with this process to the invention. For the benefit of those totally unfamiliar with the process we have divided this claim into sections, numbering each important correlated phase. (The claim as printed by the patent office does not show this breakdown into numbered steps, as it is intended for teaching those familiar with the art, rather than for the edification of others interested in all phases of this new family of yarns and fabrics.)

CLAIM 1 U.S. PATENT 2,803,109

1. A method of producing evenly and permanently crimped, (1)
wavy or fluffed multifilament thermoplastic yarn having improved and uniform physical characteristics which comprises, continually drawing the yarn from a source of supply,

continually twisting the yarn drawn from said supply, (2)

continually passing the yarn at a selected linear speed (3)

under uniform tension (4)

through a restricted thermally isolated and uniformly heated zone (5)

to uniformly heat the yarn (6)

to a prescribed temperature (7)

to reorient the molecules of the yarn (8)

to the twisted formation of the yarn (9)

and yarn-set the same, (10)

controlling the supply of heat energy to said zone (11)

to thereby maintain said heated zone uniformly (12)

at the temperature required to uniformly heat said yarn (13)

to said prescribed temperature, (14)

continually cooling the yarn   (15)

to stabilize the same after passage under tension through said   (16)
heated zone,

continually twisting the yarn after cooling the same,   (17)

and finally continually collecting the processed yarn,   (18)

the tension upon the heated yarn being co-related to said pre-   (19)
scribed temperature of the heated yarn

to maintain the yarn under tension adequate to preclude sub-   (20)
stantially any ductility in the cooled yarn.

To facilitate understanding of the false-twist process we have prepared two line drawings, Figs. 8 and 9. Figure 8 shows twist stop,
yarn, and twist trapper only. Figure 9 shows the path the yarn
travels on a converted uptwister equipped with the necessary parts
to effect conversion of an uptwister to a Fluflon® machine. Below
we discuss each unit of the machine, explaining the constitution and
action where explanation appears necessary.

a. A Pirn Holder. This consists of a pin, and a base fastened to
a creel built above the machine. When tubes replace pirns as a supply source for the yarn, pads are placed under the tubes to reduce
under wind problems. Two of these units are available for each spindle to permit tailing from package to package to increase through-put
by eliminating the need for rethreading.

b. Supply Package. This is customarily a pirn or a tube of thermoplastic yarn with low or zero twist.

c. A Yarn Guide. A rod over which the yarn runs, placed so that
yarn can be drawn from pirn or tube with a minimum of plucks.

d. A Tensioning Device. This device applies a very light tension
to the yarn, which is necessary to assure proper operation of spring-
loaded gate tension (*f*), and to prevent yarn from continuing to ravel
from the supply package when a spindle position is not in operation.

e. Yarn Guides. These guides are fastened to and are part of the
gate tension, their function is to guide the yarn properly into the
tension device.

f. A Spring-Loaded Gate Tension Twist Stopper. This is a very
important part of the equipment. Its function is fourfold:

1. Its functions as a twist stopper preventing the twist from passing back through the gate. The smooth nature of untwisted thermo-

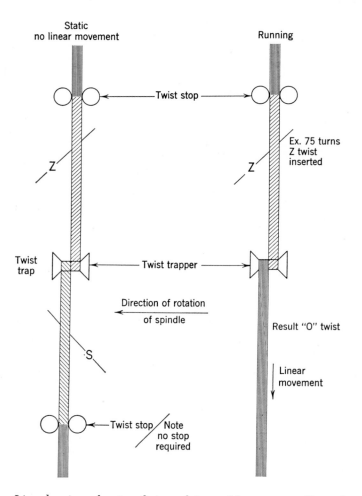

Fig. 8. Line drawings showing that revolving a false-twist spindle with a stationary yarn wrapped around the twist trapper inserts S twist on one side of the spindle and Z twist on the other side, whereas revolving a false-twist spindle with a *running* yarn wrapped around the twist trapper inserts twist on the input side of the spindle and simultaneously takes it out on the output side.

When means of heating and cooling are utilized, between twist stop and twist trapper, on the input side, the running yarn is twisted, heat-set, cooled, and untwisted, in the distance between twist stop and the output side of the twist trapper.

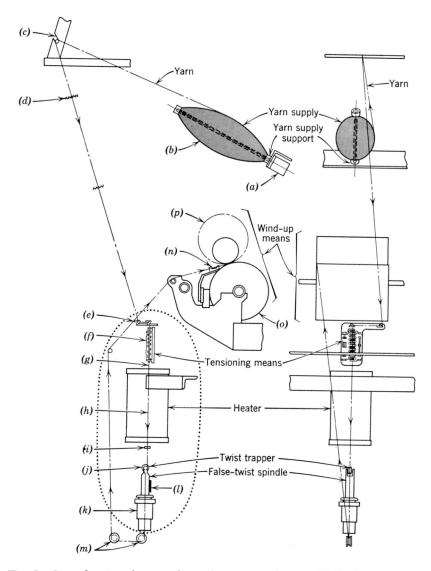

Fig. 9. Line drawing showing the path yarn travels on a Fluflon® machine, a converted uptwister.

plastic yarns permit yarn to be drawn through the spring-loaded gate tension as needed. The relatively rough file-like nature of the twisted yarn in the lower portion of the twist stop prevents any reverse slippage.

2. It maintains the required tension; this varies from denier to denier and from type of yarn to type of yarn but is very uniform. Once set for a given yarn it maintains the tension uniformly until yarn or tension device is changed.

3. The spring loading compensates for plucks and/or intermittent incoming tension variations.

4. The low inertia of the spring-loaded gates causes this tensioning means to become an additive tension device, i.e., it functions to add to the tension of the incoming yarn rather than to multiply incoming tension variations, which would occur if the gate were set in a fixed position.

g. *A Restricting Device.* A ceramic unit with a small hole in the center, the purpose of which is to center the twisted yarn in the heated tube, and reduce loss of heated air from the heating unit due to a chimney effect.

h. *The Heater.* This consists of a small metal tube extending through the heater, the outside of which is heated by a resistance wire coiled so that the tube remains uniformly heated throughout the greater part of its length. This tube and resistance wire are small in diameter and are surrounded by a large quantity of insulating material, protected in turn by metal covering to maintain its uniformity intact. Electrical energy is supplied to this heater through devices which accurately correct variations in incoming voltage and reduce the high incoming voltage to low voltage for personal safety. It is important to note that these devices are controlled by thermal sensing means in such a way that regardless of changes in room temperature the heating devices are heated and controlled to any temperature required and to an accuracy of plus or minus 1 per cent. It and the heater design permit a uniformly high temperature to be maintained with a minimum amount of electrical energy, effecting a double saving because heat dissipated into the room by heaters (and all the heat used is dissipated into the room) must be removed by the air-conditioning system, doubling the energy cost. Low initial heat cost assures low heat removal cost.

i. A Yarn Guide. The purpose of this yarn guide is to keep the yarn in the desired position, substantially in the center of the tube; however, it is of such a size and so located that the yarn can balloon slightly to increase the cooling action that takes place between the bottom of heater unit (*h*) and the beginning of twisting and untwisting unit (*k*).

j. Rotating Wheel Twister Trapper. This wheel is very small in diameter at the center and functions to prevent twist inserted by the spindle, of which the wheel is a part, from passing beyond this point. In practice it is found desirable to wrap the yarn two turns around this wheel to assure complete twist trapping. Depending upon the denier of the yarn used, this wheel may be metallic or nylon. For certain special results a pin may replace the wheel.

k. The Complete Spindle. This consists of the twist trapper (*j*), a hole directly under (*j*) extending straight through the spindle, ball bearings that make the rapid twisting possible, a housing for the bearings, and a cover preventing dirt from the belt from falling into the bearings.

l. A Belt. This is the belt that revolves the spindle.

m. Ball-Bearing Guide Wheels for the Yarn.

n. A Yarn Guide. A moving guide assures a uniform build-up of yarn on ironhead.

o. Cork Roll. A roll mounted on a shaft that extends the length of the machine, and supplies the power to pull the yarn through the machine at the desired rate.

p. An Ironhead Bobbin. This bobbin rides on cork roll (*o*), pulls the yarn through the machine, holds the finished single-end torque-crimped yarn. Operators replace full bobbins with empty bobbins without stopping the machine or rethreading the yarn. Many initial, and most recently installed units utilize headless packages instead of ironhead bobbins.

It is interesting to note that although (*a*) to (*e*) and (*m*) to (*p*) are necessary to hold the low twist or zero twist yarn and the finished crimped yarn, and to move the yarn through the machine, the work is all done withi nthe space indicated by the ellipse in Fig. 9. Spindle (*k*) activated by belt (*l*) twists the yarn above twist trapper (*j*) and removes the twist as the yarn leaves twist trapper (*j*). The twist must run back to the first effective restricting point, this is the spring-loaded gate tension twist stopper (f). As the yarn progresses through the machine it is twisted at point (f). (by the spindle, the twist runs back), plasticized in heater (h), air-cooled to yarn set between (h) and (j), and is untwisted as it leaves twist trapper (j).

A study of Fig. 9 and the descriptive matter pertaining to it makes it clear that the really pertinent units in the Fluflon® machine are:

1. Combined Tensioning Device and Twist Stopper.
2. Heating Device, Followed by Cooling Area.
3. Combined Spindle and Twist Trapper.

Although a study of patents and literature indicates that it is possible to effectively false-twist and yarn-set thermoplastic yarns by many means, the machines currently producing the millions of pounds of torque-crimp yarns produced annually in the United States all embody variations of the three units listed above and, in fact, any and all false-twisting necessarily requires some tensioning means to hold the yarn so that it might be twisted, some means to heat the yarns, and some means to trap the twist so that twist will be inserted into the revolving yarn.

Well over 90 per cent of all false-twist yarns produced in the United States have been produced on five machines: Fluflon®, 550, 550 converted to Hi Speed (551), 552, and 553. These are all sold by the Leesona Corporation who owns the patents. As the 552 varies from the 551 only in that the 552s are newly built and the 551s are converted 550s, the number of truly different units is reduced to four. The remaining yarns, less than 10 per cent of production, were processed on a number of other machines.

Two of these machines, the Joe Smith spindle operated on Leesona-built 550 machines and the Whitin A.R.C.T. machines built by Ateliers Roannais de Constructions Textiles, Roanne, France, and sold in North America by Whitin Machine Works, have received enough publicity to warrant their being covered herein.

Deering Milliken Research Corporation licenses the use of the A.R.C.T. equipment in North America on behalf of Moulinage et Retarderie de Chauanoz, Chauavez, France, a French throwster who holds a number of patents; the numbers and official patent office Gazette published data on this will be presented in Chapter 17.

The Joe Smith spindle is a unit designed to fit on Leesona's 550 machine replacing the original spindle, increasing the speed of throughput by several hundred per cent.

Fig. 10. A Fluflon® machine, actually a converted uptwister.

Fluflon® Machine

Although this machine, shown in Fig. 10, has already been described in detail to make comparisons with the really pertinent units of the other machines easier, we shall review some of its parts.

Combined Tension Device and Twist Stopper. The Fluflon® tension device and twist stopper consists of a spring-loaded gate tension so designed that any desired amount of tensioning from a few grams to more than 100 grams can be obtained and accurately retained by setting the spring load as shown. It is necessary to determine the required tension on specific yarns by test. The device very effectively stops the twist yet permits untwisted yarn to be drawn through it as required.

Heating Device Followed by Cooling Area. The Fluflon® heating device consists of a small-diameter metallic tube extending through the heater and constricted at the top by a ceramic button which centers the yarn in the heater and reduces to a minimum the heat losses caused by the chimney effect. The tube is wrapped with resistance wire, surrounded by insulating material, and protected by a metallic outer covering. Its heat loss is very low because the hot area is very small. Uniformity of temperature from unit to unit is very great because the units are individually finely adjustable and are controlled in groups by a voltage control unit to maintain the desired voltage and resultant temperature regardless of normal variations inherent in commercial alternating current and room temperature changes. Cooling is effected in a short distance, controlled ballooning of the yarn contributing materially to its rapid cooling. The yarn-set is completed by the cooling.

Combined Spindle and Twist Trapper. Fluflon® spindles are ball-bearing spindles; one of the "secrets" of their extraordinary long operating life is that the bearings are incased in rubber for protection. Most of the spindles installed prior to and during 1955 have operated around the clock, seven days a week, continuously since their installation and are still operating in spite of the fact that they were represented to be operable at 20,000 rpm and have been operating during most of this time at speeds as high as 42,000 rpm.

In most instances the twist trapper in the top of the hollow tube that goes through the spindle is a metallic wheel although nylon wheels have been used in some spindles and, occasionally, pins have replaced the wheels.

550 Machine

The 550 machine, shown as a line drawing in Fig. 11, and as a picture in Fig. 12, varies radically from the Fluflon® machine in appearance, even though each of its pertinent units operates quite similarly to the Fluflon® machine.

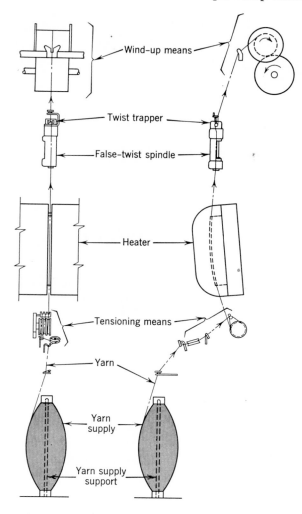

Fig. 11.   A line drawing showing the path yarn travels on a 550 machine.

Combined Tension Device and Twist Stopper. This is in the form of a power driven roll which restricts the flow of the yarn from the supply package so that it might be shrunk or stretched as provided in the "Fluflon® U.S. Patent 2,803,109." By maintaining a low tension relative to the contractile force of the heated yarn, the yarn will be permitted to shrink in the processing, while by subjecting it to a relatively high tension, a corresponding amount of stretching or elongation will take place during the heating.

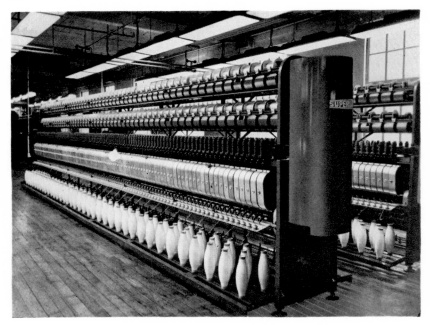

Fig. 12. A photograph of a 550 machine.

Two or more wraps of the yarn about the roll effectively stop the twist from running back to the supply package. Plucks and/or intermittent tension variations of the incoming yarn are compensated for as the yarn passes around the roll and the roll serves as an additive tension device same as the Fluflon® gate-tension device.

The tension controlling roll of the 550 machine, as with the Fluflon® tensioning device, is preceded with a lighter tensioning device, in this instance a conventional disk tension. It is well known that the relation of tension on the input and output sides of a revolving roll determines the traction or slippage of a yarn wound about such a roll and consequently the disk tension is also utilized for this function, especially when processing heavier denier sizes of yarn.

Heating Device Followed by Cooling Area. The 550 heating device is a very slightly curved electrically heated aluminum plate that can be operated as a contact heater, and is capable of being converted into a radiant heater by cutting grooves as necessary to permit the yarn to be radiantly heated in the grooves. By permitting the yarn to contact the rear of a deeply cut groove, the heater may serve as a combination contact and radiant heater. The plate is very well insu-

lated for conserving heat and to reduce the load on the air-conditioning system that must remove all heat put into the unit. Thermom-
eters and thermostats are placed at strategic points, the temperature
is adjusted when necessary by individual rheostats, each controlling the
heat of one plate, each plate in turn serving a number of yarns. As
with Fluflon® the cooling is effected by causing the yarn to balloon
as it leaves the spindle after heating.

At this point it might be well to mention that the yarn direction
in the 550 is directly opposite to the direction used in Fluflon®. In
the Fluflon® machine the yarn runs down and in the 550 machine
the yarn runs up.

Combined Spindle and Twist Trapper. The spindle, as the Fluflon®
spindle, is ball bearing, and is capable of running at speeds greater
than those employed in uptwisting, it having been found practical
to run as high as 50,000 rpm although the initial recommendation
was for 30,000 rpm. The twist trapper is a nylon unit resembling a
very small spool in appearance, and is supported from one side only
to facilitate easy and rapid threading of the unit. Twist trapping is
made quite complete by two wraps around the trapper.

551 and 552 Machines

These machines are treated together because they are so similar,
the 551 being a converted 550, and the 552s having been newly built
to supply the increasing demand for 551s that exceeded the available
installed 550s.

Combined Tension Device and Twist Stopper. These are identical
with the tension device and twist stoppers used on the 550 machine.
We state this in the plural because after several years of operation
an improved tension device and twist stopper was made available to
owners of 550 machines.

Heating Device Followed by Cooling Area. This is identical with
the heating device and cooling area employed in the 550 machine.

Combined Spindle and Twist Trapper. The spindle is totally different from the spindle used on the 550 machine, it consists of a
very small tube attached to the upper end of which is a spindle head
which holds an Alsamag twist-trapping pin. The spindle is rotated
by a very rapidly moving narrow belt that holds the spindle against
tungsten carbide units recessed in brass blocks made by compressing
brass powder; the porosity of these blocks makes possible the con-

stant lubrication of the tungsten-carbide bearings through the oil porous brass blocks. These spindles, engineered for high speed, constituted a tremendous forward step in the art of false-twisting thermoplastic yarns as they increased the speeds at which the machines may operate by more than four times the original speed.

553 Machine

Theoretically the 551 and 552 machines should be able to run at much higher speeds than are currently used, since the bearings in the spindle and the pin-type twist trapper are capable of being operated at higher speeds. However, the balance of the machine was not engineered for these higher speeds and the length of the heater constituted a constricting factor as all thermoplastic yarns have a minimum dwell time in the heated area; this varies with the yarn, the tension, the temperature, and the heat employed in processing. The 553 machine, shown as a line drawing in Fig. 13 and as a photograph in Fig. 14, provides the longer heater found necessary and the engineering required to assure years of trouble-free production.

Combined Tension Device and Twist Stopper. As in the 550, 551, and 552 machines this is a rotating power driven tension control means. Because of the vastly increased yarn speed it is designed for more positive control, but otherwise it functions essentially the same as that of the 550 machine previously described. It is preceded by a light disk tension to control the yarn prior to entering the tension. It is positively connected to a similar device on the output side of the spindle, the second device controls the forward movement of the yarn to the take-up package so that the package may be wound with the desired density. Stated more simply, the 553 controls the tension of the yarn in the processing zone and independently controls the tension of the yarn being wound onto a large headless package (4 pounds or more).

Heating Device Followed By Cooling Area. This is similar to the heating device employed in the 550, 551, and 552 machines; in the case of the 553 machine the vertical direction is increased from 9 to 27½ inches. This permits higher speeds to be employed by providing a longer heating area. The yarn can run faster yet remain long enough in the hot zone to make possible a full set. To facilitate threading a manually operated threading device draws the yarn to the bottom of the spindle to enable skilled operators to thread the machine easily.

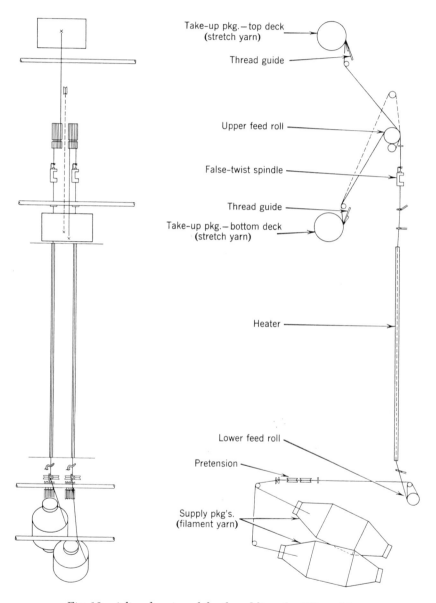

Take-up pkg.—top deck
(stretch yarn)

Thread guide

Upper feed roll

False-twist spindle

Thread guide

Take-up pkg.—bottom deck
(stretch yarn)

Heater

Lower feed roll

Pretension

Supply pkg's.
(filament yarn)

Fig. 13.   A line drawing of the thread line of a 553 machine.

Fig. 14.   A photograph of a 553 machine.

Combined Spindle and Twist Trapper.   This is identical with the spindle and twist trapper used in the 551 and 552 machines.

Speeds Attainable.   The machine is engineered for, and is capable of operating at very high speeds, 360,000 rpm being an acceptable operating speed for 70 denier at this time.

Value of Take-up Overfeed Arrangement.   Certain yarns such as polyester and polypropylene are very substantially benefited by being overfed to the take-up bobbin rather than being tightly wound on the bobbin. Also to produce very large headless take-up packages, flexibility in tension control, independent of processing tension, is essential.

Joe Smith Spindle

The Joe Smith spindle is a clever device built to increase the production of 550 machines, utilizing the same principle as that employed in converting 550s and 551s, and differing from the 551 concept only in that each spindle has its own step-up device, which is a small diameter unit contacting the belt, a larger diameter wheel attached to it drives the spindle. Although it is limited in distribution it is still running on certain machines.

Whitin A.R.C.T.-F.T. 1 and F.T. 3 Machines

False-twist machines manufactured by Ateliers Roannais de Constructions Textiles Roanne, Loine, France, are sold in the United States by Whitin Machine Works, Whitinsville, Massachusetts, and are licensed in the North American continent by Deering Milliken Research Corporation, Spartanburg, South Carolina. The F.T. 1 machine is shown as a line drawing in Fig. 15 and as a photograph in Fig. 16. The F.T. 3 machine has a 48-inch heater providing a longer dwell time in the hot zone, and a faster through-put.

The A.R.C.T.-F.T. 1 and F.T. 3 machines are quite similar in concept to the 553 machine in that they have similar means of controlling the processing-zone tension and wind-up tension, and the take-up package is headless. The heaters, both electrically controlled, vary in shape and size. The 553 heater is a plate, the A.R.C.T. heaters are curved tubes. The 553 heater is $27\frac{1}{2}$ inches long, the A.R.C.T. heaters are 22 inches long in the F.T. 1 machine, $47\frac{1}{4}$ inches in the F.T. 3 machine.

The A.R.C.T.-F.T. 1 machine is designed to operate at 80,000 rpm and it is claimed that, operated at this speed, it produces a better set than when it, or competitive machines, are operated at higher speeds, thus reducing dwell time in the heated zone.

The A.R.C.T.-F.T. 3 machine, utilizing a longer heater ($47\frac{1}{4}$ inches vs. 22 inches) and equipped with high speed, is designed to operate at higher speeds, from 100,000 to 300,000 rpm.

Both A.R.C.T.-F.T. 1 and A.R.C.T.-F.T. 3 machines heat the yarn by a combination of contact and radiant heat. This means of heating is undoubtedly more efficient than contact heat only.

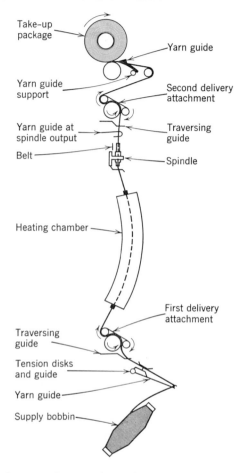

Fig. 15. A line drawing showing the path yarn travels in an A.R.C.T.–F.T. 1 machine.

Litigation involving alleged patent infringement is pending. The industry is hopeful that at least some clarification of the situation may occur during 1964.

Detailed Item-by-Item Discussion of False-Twist Manufacture. The false-twist process of twisting, yarn setting, and untwisting thermoplastic yarns makes possible the manufacture of an endless variety of durably crimped yarns, most of which have yet to be commercially exploited. Durably crimped yarns can be produced varying from rough bouclés to yarns softer and smoother than the most delicate silks, yarns with large prominent crimps to crimps so delicate they are hard to discern, yarns that have texture only, the stretch properties having been eliminated by processing, yarns that will shrink and that can be stretched and relaxed thousands of times, all so durably crimped that the crimps remain throughout the useful life of garments made therefrom; yarns varying in respect to other properties are too numerous to enumerate in full detail herein.

In the following pages we discuss in some detail a number of the factors that can be utilized to produce the numberless variations in texture, cover, softness, stretch, etc., possible within the confines of the process of durably torque-crimping thermoplastic yarns.

Tensions. Tensions are measured, usually, between the spindle and the take-up bobbin or overfeeding device and every effort is made to maintain uniform tension from spindle to spindle and within the confines of individual spindles.

It is known that there is a definite relationship between the tension as measured between the spindle and the take-up and the tension in the hot zone, and it is known that this relationship varies with spindle thread-up and temperature.

The exact tension in the hot zone is unknown. Accurate means of

Fig. 16. A photograph of an A.R.C.T.–F.T. 1 machine installation.

determining this tension do not exist, and in any event an exact measure of the longitudinal tension would not constitute a measure of the tangential tension caused by the twist. As the turns per inch are increased, the tangential tension due to twist is increased, this becomes a very substantial though unmeasured force as the twist approaches the saturation point. It is known and recognized that the magnitude of the tangential tension due to twist is greater than the measured longitudinal tension in the hot zone, and that the effect of this tension in deforming the filaments as desired is increased by the high temperatures employed that soften the filaments and make them easier to deform.

Another force, contractile force, complicates the situation still further. The contractile force is the force exerted by the yarn as it tends to shrink when subjected to heat. This force increases as the temperature is increased up to a point which is called, by some workers in the field, the second-order transition; after this the force diminishes, although the extent to which the yarn will shrink, if free of tension, increases.

Tangential tension, contractile force, softening due to heat, and contraction in length due to twist, cause tension in the hot zone even when the yarn is overfed during false-twisting. Overfeeding reduces tension but does not eliminate it, otherwise the apparatus could not function. Unless both the tension and heat employed deform the individual filaments into helical crimps, the entire operation is a useless waste of time and money. Actually, great care is exerted to so balance heat and tension that the required deformation takes place, and the yarn is set in the new position as it cools.

Tensions measured between the output side of the spindle and the take-up or overfeed roll vary from 5 to 40 grams for 70-denier nylon, and proportionally for other deniers, although because of machine limitations in the older-type machines, tensions employed with very heavy denier yarns have been lower than would be anticipated or desirable, necessitating higher temperatures to achieve full set.

Heat. Temperatures are measured very accurately, in most commercial machines temperatures are maintained from position to position, and within positions, with an accuracy of plus or minus 1 per cent. The exact temperature that the yarn attains is unknown. Near estimates are made by gradually raising the temperature of the heater while processing the yarn, noting the temperature of the heater when the yarn itself melts. As the melting point of the yarn is known it can be reasonably assumed that the temperature of the yarn is the temperature of its melting point at the time it melts. By noting the recorded temperature of the heater when the yarn melts, and the known melting point of the yarn, a relationship can be determined and correlated to the slightly lower temperatures used during false-twisting. Thus we know the approximate, but not the exact, temperature that the yarn attains.

There is a distinct difference between temperature and energy absorption by the yarn. Fluflon® yarns, radiant-heated, are always whiter than Superloft® yarns. Superloft® yarns, contacting the surface of the hot aluminum plate, are always slightly discolored when the heating plate is run at the maximum temperature necessary to set the yarn. It appears that the outside filaments of yarn running over contact heaters absorb more energy as heat than filaments near the center of the yarn, resulting in a slightly better set and a slight yellowing of the yarn.

As per the teachings of U.S. Patent 2,803,109, the correlation between temperature and tension is exceedingly critical, a change in either necessitates a change in the other to make possible the processing of the yarn in such a way that ductility in the finished yarn is substantially precluded. As a practical matter the helical crimps must be sufficiently permanent to withstand the stress and temperatures of subsequent yarn operations, fabrication, dyeing and finishing, and end use. Higher temperatures and higher tensions increase both the degree and the rate of the deforming of the filaments during false-twisting. The optimum for each in any specific yarn is currently determined by trial and error based on experience, in most instances higher temperatures permit the use of lower tensions and vice versa. It is to be anticipated that increased use will be made of the mechanical aids now available to replace trial and error methods with a minimum amount of actual trials, followed by production of usable curves, graphs, and charts from data fed to the "thinking machines," and that these curves will further improve utilization of equipment and result in production of yarns more exactly meeting requirements. A start in this direction has been made by licensors.

In most instances thermoplastic yarns are deformed as desired and durably torque-crimped at temperatures only slightly ($20°–30°$) below their actual melting point. It should not be assumed that such temperatures are always utilized as, by controlling other conditions, it has been found possible to set the yarn durably at temperatures ranging all the way down to room temperature. This, however, requires yarn drawn to a lesser extent than normal or, when desired, torque-crimping and drawing in a single operation, in effect drawing the yarn in twisted position rather than drawing the filaments parallel.

Dwell Time in Heated Zone. It is necessary that thermoplastic yarns remain under tension in the heated zone for a sufficient length of time to permit the filaments to become yarn-set in the helical position as desired. This time varies with temperature, tension, filament denier, yarn denier, and the chemical constitution of the thermoplastic yarn. In some instances the minimum desirable dwell time is as long as 2 seconds, although the time actually employed is closer to 1 second, to increase through-put to the maximum. Longer dwell time assures better set. Slightly less than the absolute maximum is usually sufficient for commercial purposes.

Twist. Many detailed studies have been made to determine the effect of turns of twist on the properties of various false-twist yarns. As might be anticipated the available data are fragmentary and inconclusive, and the conclusions drawn by various workers from the available data are contradictory.

There are various reasons for the contradictory opinions currently held. One is twist slippage. During twisting the number of turns of twist inserted in the yarn are often less than the number of turns determined by calculation because of twist slippage at the twist trap in the spindle. This does not mean to say that these yarns are not good yarns, they are. Nevertheless the twist to which they are subjected is often less than the twist determined by calculating the spindle speed and linear travel of the yarn.

Another reason for the contradictory opinions lies in the relatively small amount of work that has been done in the texturing, as opposed to the stretch field, and the differences in types of warps used in many of the preliminary trials. In a very light warp filled with relatively heavy filling yarn relatively low twist during false-twisting produces large, coarse pebble effects and tremendous shrinkage in width. This, however, creates an accordion-like effect with typical crepon-type ripples running warpwise. This apparent extra shrink is due to most of the creping or shrinking power being concentrated at the bends of the fabric, the intervening portions remain relatively flat. As the turns of twist are increased the number of pebbles or bends increase, the size of the pebbles decrease resulting in more uniform appearing fabrics; each individual bend has less force than when a lesser number of larger bends are present. The total distortion of the warp is greater, and the shrinkage of the fabric is reduced. Thus more latent torque-crimp power in lightweight warp fabric produces less shrink-age but more desirable surface interest effects.   When the same yarns are woven in heavier warps utilizing more floats in the construction the reverse situation appears to occur; the higher twisted yarns pro-duce more shrink and more permanent shrink and recovery effects, all or most of the latent torque crimp produces shrinking rather than distorted surface effects.

It is believed by many that 70-denier nylon shrinks to the maximum extent in woven fabrics when twisted 75 to 80 turns per inch, the opti-mum twist with other deniers varying proportionally.

When extra softness and extra fine pebble effects are required, higher twists are employed.   When the maximum in coarse, relatively harsh crepon-like effects are desired, lower twists are utilized.

Denier, Filament Count, Filament Diameter.   The effect of denier, filament count, and filament diameter on the properties of torque-crimped yarns are so interrelated that they must be considered to-gether.   Shrinking power, or creping power, or latent torque-crimp energy varies with denier, a situation that is readily understandable when considered in relation to the radius of the crimps.   As the radius increases, latent retained energy per denier decreases.

Retained energy or latent torque power increases directly with the diameter of individual filaments.   The coarser the filament the greater the energy that is required to distort, and the greater the retained energy after distortion and setting.   The other side of the coin is that as filament diameters increase harshness increases, this often requires the use of finer denier filaments than would be desired to produce the required hand in specific fabrics.

Spin Finish.   It has been thoroughly demonstrated that the type of spin finish applied by the yarn producer affects the rate at which thermoplastic yarns can be deformed during false twisting, thus af-fecting the rate of through-put.   No explanation has been offered by yarn producers as to why spin finish affects the rate of deformation as it does.   A possible explanation is that the many filaments of a multifilament yarn must slip or slide over each other if they are to be highly twisted and spin finish could, if desired, be varied to permit free movement or very little movement of the filaments, one against the others.   Thus if the filaments do not slide into the intended posi-tion, each one around the others, they are not deformed as expected or required.   A further partial explanation is that spin finish has a direct effect on the amount of friction developed at the twist stopper and trapper.

Chemical and Physical Constitution of Yarns. The physical as well as the chemical constitution of yarns affects the tension, temperature, and twists that must be employed during false twisting, the necessary dwell time in the heated zone, and the degree of permanency of crimp.

The bulk of the nylon that has been false-twisted in the United States is type-66 nylon, as a result of which it is generally believed that type-66 nylon accepts torque crimp faster and more durably than does type-6 nylon, the primary reason being that throwsters have learned how to properly process type 66.

In Europe type 6 predominates and throwsters there have learned how to process it properly to give the optimum in speed of through-put and latent torque-crimp memory. Type-6 nylon properly torque-crimped is the full equivalent of torque-crimped type-66 nylon with respect to stretch and recovery, texture, covering power, etc.

As made in the United States type-6 nylon varies from producer to producer with respect to its elongation at the breaking point, in some instances this is very similar to the elongation of type-66 nylon at the break. Actually the greater the elongation at the break the easier it is to produce durable torque-crimp memory in type-6 nylon; although the greater the elongation before processing the finer will be the denier of the yarn after processing, as it is necessary to strain the yarn sufficiently during torque-crimping to preclude substantially any ductility in the finished torque-crimped yarn (if, after crimping, the yarn is ductile, it is clear that the crimps could not be permanent). As with type-66 nylon, most U.S. throwsters must learn the best technique of producing the optimum results through temperature-tension correlation. As with type-66 nylon the temperature must be adequate to make the yarn plastic and sufficient tangential stress (longitudinal tension plus torsion caused by twisting) must be employed to permanently deform the filaments to their twisted position before cooling.

With polyester yarns there is a further consideration in that the yarn must be drawn out sufficiently in processing to prevent it from being easily drawn out in the finished yarn. When some such yarns are woven into fabrics, properly relaxed with the use of the proper quantity of the right carriers and fabric set, the yarn subsequently retains its torque-crimp memory approximately as well as nylon. For this reason the lesser torque-crimp memory of polyester in torque-crimp yarn form does not constitute a handicap for polyester yarns. Fabrics woven from torque-crimped polyester yarns are believed to have better hand, better cover, and better crease resistance than similar fabrics made from nylon yarns.

Given sufficient incentive, and adequate research funds, it is probable that the torque-crimp process combined with thermal processing can be utilized to make possible the production of fabric from nylon, the full equivalent of the best that can be produced from polyester, even in the most difficult property, crease resistance.

Polypropylene retains torque-crimp memory fully as well as nylon. The nature of polypropylene is such that polypropylene yarns require more time in the heated zone than either nylon or polyester, necessitating the use of longer heaters or slower through-put during processing. Offsetting this to a very pronounced extent is the hiding or covering power of polypropylene, and its low specific gravity, both properties create a very pleasing illusion of lightness of hand.

Stretch and Recovery. The stretch and recovery of fabrics woven from torque-crimped thermoplastic yarns is a function of many factors in addition to the yarn itself and the conditions employed during the torque-crimping operation. To obtain the maximum in stretch and recovery, throwsters tension and heat the yarn in such a manner that the tensile strength at the break is reduced by 35 to 50 per cent of the tensile strength of the yarn as received by the producer. They use the minimum permissible number of filaments for the denier required, the permissible minimum being governed by the required hand in the finished fabric. See Post and Ply Twist.

Cover or Hiding Power. This is a function of the delustering agent used in the yarn, the chemical nature of the yarn, the number of filaments, and the number of turns of false twist imparted to the yarn during the crimping process.

There is a very substantial difference between nylon, polyester, and polypropylene with respect to the cover or hiding power, nylon being the lowest, polyester intermediate, and polypropylene outstandingly better in hiding power than either polyester or nylon, other conditions being equal.

The effect of the delustering agents is too well-known to require any discussion herein.

The hiding or covering power is directly proportional to the number of turns of torque crimp employed, the hiding power increases, as would be anticipated, as twist increases.

Crimp Size. Crimp size is varied by the number of turns of false twist inserted and by the manner in which the yarn or fabric is subsequently heat-treated prior to relaxing during boil off. The higher the twist the smaller the crimp sizing, provided relaxing is so controlled that each turn of twist becomes a crimp. When this control is not exercised the tendency to crimp runs along individual filaments causing excessive crimping at some points and minimum crimping at others, this difference is due to the location of the filament in the yarn at the time of crimping. Obviously some filaments must be near the center of the yarn and others near the surface; the location of individual filaments changes throughout the length of the yarn, causing or permitting the tendency to crimp to be irregular unless certain known controls are exercised.

Post treatment in yarn form, discussed in a separate chapter, is undoubtedly the best means of assuring uniform crimping and assuring that every turn of twist inserted in each filament becomes a crimp in the finished fabric. When this operation is not used, for reasons of economy, it is possible to approximate this condition by partially heat treating the fabric prior to relaxing; this operation when properly carried out produces a result part way between torque crimp alone and the torque crimp followed by post treatment in yarn form.

To obtain different textures and surface-appearance effects it is desirable to modify crimp size although little use of this valuable variable factor has been made to date, presumably because the bulk of the torque-crimp yarns woven have gone into stretch fabrics. It is anticipated that this situation will change and that much greater use will be made of the tremendous differences in appearance, hand, and drape that can be produced by proper control of crimp size.

Post and Ply Twist. Ply twist is utilized for a number of reasons. It reduces or precludes picking and piling in fabrics so designed that more than half of the torque-crimp yarn is caused to be on one side of the fabric. Its use enhances the stretch and recovery by permitting more crimps to be utilized in a yarn of given denier. For example, a 140-denier nylon yarn can be twisted 65 turns, whereas a 70-denier yarn can be twisted 75 or more turns producing a total twist of 150 more turns in a two-ply 70 denier. It is not surprising that 150 turns of twist produce more stretch and recovery than 65 turns.

In certain fabrics a balance twist is desired, this is obtained by plying an S and a Z a very low number of ply turns, the result being a yarn almost completely balanced.

Post twist is employed when single ends of torque-crimped yarn are used in the warp, and when the need for additional stretch and recovery indicates that a few turns of twist against the torque will increase the composite torque in the finished yarn to a point making its use economically feasible.

3

Post-Treated Torque Crimp

False-twist thermoplastic yarns can be post-treated in yarn form to produce a number of different effects, these are: control of crimp, control of stretch, increased softness of hand, increased bulk, stabilization, control of or elimination of torque.

Five of the above-listed six controllable variables are controlled by processing torque-crimp yarns through a heated zone during which time they are relaxed or stretched to a predetermined extent. Stretching, desirable for certain specific results, is limited in its possibilities. Relaxing offers a much wider range of possibilities; it is feasible to relax up to and above 30 per cent, when desired, on existing installed equipment.

The extent and distribution of latent crimping power in individual filaments of false-twist yarns vary throughout the length of each filament. Post-treating controls the amount and release of latent crimping power as explained in detail in the following paragraphs.

The crimping power in individual filaments of torque-crimped thermoplastic yarns varies throughout the length of the filaments, depending on the location of each filament within the group of filaments comprising the yarn at the time of heat-setting. The size of each crimp depends on the distance of individual filaments from the center of the yarn at the time of crimping. In 70-denier 32-filament nylon this can vary from zero to four times the diameter of the individual filaments as shown in Fig. 17. At all times one filament, not the same filament, must be at or almost at the center of the yarn, and several must be at or very near the perimeter of the yarn. The remainder of the filaments occupy intermediate positions as in Fig. 17. The effect of this on the size and distribution of crimps is shown in Fig. 18, in which filament D shows the maximum variation possible,

60

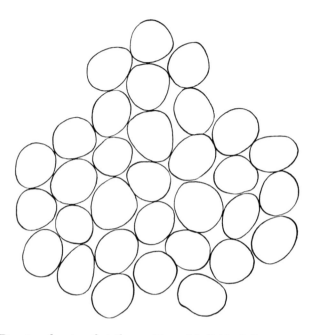

Fig. 17. Drawing showing that the position of individual filaments in 70-denier, 32-filament nylon, tensioned and twisted, varies from center to outside by as much as four diameters.

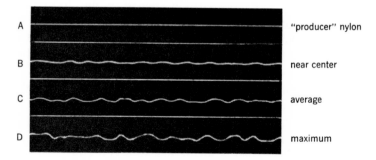

Fig. 18. Shadowgraphs of four filaments of 70-denier, 32-filament, semi-dull, type-6 nylon. Filament A is from a strand of "producer" nylon. Filaments B, C, and D are from a single strand of false-twisted nylon. They show the crimping differences due to location of the filament in the highly twisted strand in the hot zone.

filament *C* represents an average filament, and *B* represents a filament near the center of the yarn at the time of twisting.

It is obvious that whereas each filament has a similar amount of total latent torque-crimp energy over a long length of yarn, the crimping power can and does vary throughout individual filaments to the extent shown in Fig. 18. When the latent torque-crimp energy is released, for instance, when a skein of torque-crimped thermoplastic yarn is immersed in a beaker of water, stirred gently, and the temperature of the water is slowly raised to the boiling point, the variation in degree of available torque energy at various points throughout each filament causes crimps to develop in some locations prior to others. This permits the energy to move toward the point of least resistance, magnifying the effect of the variation in energy in specific locations, causing the formation of double, triple, and quadruple kinks, and producing the effect shown in Fig. 1, filament "G."

Inventors Seem and Stoddard devised a means of controlling the release of torque-crimp energy in thermoplastic yarns and the amount of torque-crimp energy left in the yarn, and assuring release of energy at the location of each crimp heat-set into the original torque-crimped yarn. This invention enables texturers to control better the effects produced by torque-crimp thermoplastic yarns during relaxing, boil-off, and finishing operations. The result is more uniform fabrics, softer fabrics when desired, control of the extent to which the fabrics can shrink, and other benefits to be described in detail in the following pages.

The invention consists of partially reheat-setting torque-crimped thermoplastic yarns under controlled conditions with respect to temperature, time, and degree of relaxing or stretching during the partial heat-setting. The yarn is free to shrink to the permitted degree when controlled overfeed is used.

The first machine built for post-treating torque-crimp thermoplastic yarns was basically a 10B downtwister with a second set of capstan rolls, necessary yarn guides, and a temperature-controlled, heatable aluminum block inserted between creel and bobbin. This machine, designated as a 511 machine by its builders, the Universal Winding Company, now the Leesona Corporation of Providence, Rhode Island, enables yarns to be fully tensioned, heat treated, stretched, or shrunk as desired within the limitations possible in each yarn, plied if desired, twisted and wound on a bobbin, all in one continuous operation.

Figure 19, a line drawing, shows the path the yarn travels on a 511 machine and the principal working parts. Figure 20 is a photograph of the machine. Below we discuss the individual units, explaining the constitution and action of each.

a. A Creel. This consists of a number of pins so placed in relation to the working parts that yarn can be drawn from a number of bobbins to each spindle of the machine.

b. Supply Packages. These are usually ironheads or headless packages from a false-twisting machine.

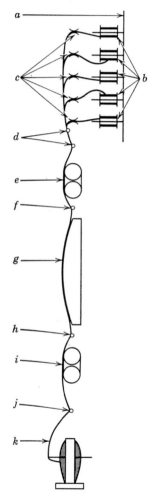

c. A Tensioning Device. This device applies a light tension to the yarn, which is necessary to assure proper operation of the rolling tensioning and yarn-feeding device that follows.

d, f, h, and j. Yarn Guides.

e. A Pair of Capstan Rolls. The yarn is guided around these rollers five or six times, frictional contact increasing with each turn; the contact with the surface provides the pull necessary to draw the yarn from bobbins (*b*) and the tension required prior to heat processing.

g. The Heater. In a heated aluminum block, the temperature can be accurately controlled as desired. The heat causes the yarn to be partially reheat-set, relaxed, or stretched to the degree desired by the difference in the surface speeds of rollers (*e*) and (*i*).

i. A Pair of Capstan Rolls. As in the case of capstan rolls (*e*) the yarn is guided around the rolls five or six times to assure full frictional engagement. The surface speed of the second set of capstan rolls can be adjusted as desired in relation to the first set of rolls, assuring uniform constant overfeed or underfeed and related yarn tension between the two sets of rolls.

Fig. 19. Line drawing of the thread line on a 511 machine.

Fig. 20. A photograph of a 511 machine, experimental size, manufactured and sold by the Leesona Corporation, Providence, R.I.

k. Twisting and Take-up Device. This is actually the ring, traveler, and bobbin of a 10B downtwister.

As the yarn travels from (*b*) to (*k*) it is lightly tensioned at (*c*), more firmly tensioned at (*e*) and drawn by (*e*) from the bobbins, reheat-set by heater (*g*). The degree of relaxing or stretching, more usually relaxing, is controlled by the ratio of surface speeds of rollers (*i*) to rollers (*e*). The yarn continues to the twisting and take-up device (k) that inserts the desired turns of twist and takes the yarn up on a bobbin.

The heart of the machine consists of the two sets of rolling tension devices that control the degree of relaxing or, occasionally, stretching; and of the heated aluminum plate that resets the yarn relaxed or stretched to the predetermined per cent.

The first yarns from the first 511 machine, available early in 1957, were used to produce stretch-filled fabrics, some finished with stretch properties, some finished with surface interest effects, utilizing torque-crimp to produce softness, fullness, drape, and pebble.

One of these early fabrics, woven 55 inches in the reed, with 90 picks of 70-denier polyester torque-crimp yarn in a 135-sley, 30-denier, 3-turn nylon warp, illustrates some of the advantages of post-treating torque-crimp yarns. When filled with Fluflon® and boiled-off slack, this construction shrank to 11 inches during relaxing and boil-off. When filled with post-treated yarns the width after boil-off increased in direct proportion to the increase in temperature during post-treating and in inverse proportion to the per cent of overfeed used.

Although it is commercially impractical to finish fabrics that are narrower after slack drying than the minimum width obtainable on the frame used during finishing, sample quantities of the very narrow fabric were finished by hand guiding them into a very slow moving frame. The narrow fabric was relatively wiry in hand, crepon-like in appearance, and much less opaque than all of the fabrics woven from post-treated yarns. The fabrics filled with post-treated yarns were all wide enough to be processed commercially, "full" in hand, opaque, as desired, in appearance, stretchy or stabilized, as desired, with respect to stretch. Because of the bulk of the filling these fabrics produced an illusion of being lighter in weight than an equal-weight fabric finished from straight torque-crimp yarns.

As an added dividend the warp streaks, actually luster streaks, visible in 135-end, 30-denier nylon warps filled with unprocessed continuous filament yarns, disappeared completely when the fabrics were filled with post-treated torque-crimp yarns, and were much less visible in the fabrics filled with straight torque-crimp yarn.

This warp streak disappearance is due to the very slight and pleasing warp distortion caused by the uniformly irregular surface of the post-treated torque-crimp filling, augmented by the slow shrinking that takes place during relaxing. When these fabrics are deliberately pulled as wide as possible during the final framing, the streaks reappear.

These and similar fabrics woven from various post-treated yarns in various constructions were so pleasing in appearance, soft and full in hand, drapy, and indicated such a tremendous range of fabrics possible by utilizing the controls of temperature and the per cent of relaxing available on the post-treating machine that great interest was aroused in the mills participating in this work. This interest led to requests for reasonably substantial quantities of post-treated yarns for further semi-commercial runs.

Unfortunately parallel work with post-treated yarns in the knitting field had led to the development of extra soft, extra full, very uniform dyeing knitted garments, and knitters had bought up the entire available production from the few machines already constructed.

These knitted garments, excellent in every way, were produced in limited quantities for a time, never controlled, merchandised, or promoted; they fell by the wayside owing to a sudden increase in demand for torque-crimp yarns not post-treated. This demand temporarily increased the price of straight torque-crimp yarns to such a point that throwsters could obtain as much return from the single-processed yarn as they asked for post-treated yarns; and their customers for single-treated yarns all demanded the maximum possible quantities of single-processed yarns. Throwsters abruptly ceased production of post-treated yarns and their manufacture in even moderate quantities has never been resumed. It is unlikely that there will be any activity in this most excellent field for textured thermoplastic yarns until some organization undertakes to produce, control, merchandise, and promote specific yarns and carry the control and promotion through to finished garments.

Actually the throwster work in this field was centered solely on the production of yarns that could produce garments similar in appearance and hand to Ban-Lon® yet free from the dye variations that have curtailed the development of items made from Textralized® yarns in certain fields. The superior hand and dye index of post-treated torque-crimp yarns could not successfully combat Joseph Bancroft & Sons Company's excellent quality and quantity control and merchandising and promotional program.

Meanwhile widespread sampling continued in the weaving field utilizing post-treating in fabric form rather than in yarn form, this being accomplished in three entirely different ways: by embossing, by calendering, and by processing through heat-setting units at temperatures well below that of heat setting.

Torque-crimp yarns can be post-treated in this manner, in fabric form, with results that constitute definite improvement over similar fabrics wet-processed without preliminary heat treatments. The restraining influence of the warp yarns and warp size prevent the torque-crimp yarn from relaxing as completely and as uniformly as when processed in single-end yarn form.

Torque-crimp yarns were post-treated in fabric form at the outset solely because post-treated yarns were commercially unavailable. Later, in the absence of promotional programs, futile attempts were made to produce fabrics to sell to cutters below the then existing arbitrary $1.00 per yard ceiling. Regrettably the objective, good fabrics filled with post-treated torque-crimp yarns to sell below $1.00 per yard, could have been easily attained at normal converter mark-ups. Understandably, converters were unwilling to gamble on new unproven fabrics in the absence of free promotion, except at mark-ups that precluded any sale whatsoever.

A very large number of fabrics, soft in hand, showing good surface interest effects and good drape, were produced by post-treating the yarn in fabric form, and were then shown to cutters. New, different, superior in many ways to fabrics then being made in quantity, these fabrics were offered at high prices without benefit of promotion, and their rejection was a foregone conclusion because converters are interested in purchasing only fabrics that cutters want. Cutters in turn purchase fabric specifically requested by buyers, and buyers seek fabrics promoted by yarn producers. Any synthetic fabrics offered cutters at prices exceeding the $1.00 per yard ceiling, without promotion, cannot be expected to sell in appreciable quantities.

At first glance there appears to be certain exceptions in that some torque-crimp fabrics, post-treated in fabric form and priced above $1.00 per yard, did become very successful. A close examination of the circumstances reveals that these fabrics had the benefit of control of production, merchandising, and promotional programs under specific tradenames chosen by the weaver.

As stated above, until garments made from good fabrics woven from post-treated thermoplastic yarns are promoted to garment buyers there will be no really substantial usage of these items despite their outstanding excellence in quality and desirable properties.

RADIANT HEAT FOR POST-TREATING

The 511 machine was designed primarily for the processing of fine denier yarns and has proven to be well adapted for doing the work for which it was intended. When heavier denier yarns are employed, and when yarns other than nylon are torque-crimped, and overfeeds are utilized to a pronounced extent during torque-crimping, the 511 contact heater has been found to be less satisfactory than the newer version, a radiant heater. This consists of a tube that heats the yarn through radiant heat and contact with the heated air within the tube. This radiant heater has been found especially beneficial for processing heavier denier yarns, and yarns overfed to take-up packages from false-twist spindles. Use of radiant heat provides more control and improves the bulk and uniformity of the finished yarn.

CONTINUOUS PROCESS, FALSE TWIST, AND POST-TREATMENT

Whitin Machine Works, Whitinsville, Massachusetts, offers a continuous process machine manufactured by Ateliers Roannais de Constructions Textiles Roanne, Loire, France, designated as Whitin A.R.C.T. type F.T.-F. machine, that processes thermoplastic yarns from supply package to finished yarn, singles or plied (without twist), producing torque-crimp post-treated yarns in a single pass. The yarn is continuously tensioned, twisted, heated, cooled, untwisted, retensioned, relaxed, reheat-treated, retensioned, and wound up on a package suitable for further processing or shipment.

The basic elements of the machine, shown diagrammatically in Fig. 21, and photographically in Figs. 22 and 23, comprise three yarn delivery attachments, a false-twist spindle and two heat zones. The first stage of the two-stage continuous process produces false-twist stretch yarn. The second stage post-treats the yarn to modify stretch and bulk by overfeeding or underfeeding through a second heat zone. The machine consists of two units, one containing creel and take-up packages, the other the spindle, heater, and yarn delivery attachments. Yarn passes from creel to processing unit under a false floor and from processing unit to take-up packages over the operator's head (see Figs. 21 and 22).

The influence of the yarn delivery attachments, the twist, and the temperatures of the heating treatment can be varied to produce an infinite variety of yarn characteristics tailored to the requirements of the fabric for which the yarns are intended. Stretch can be varied from a high degree of stretch with good recovery to stabilized yarns with very little stretch and recovery. Bulk can be varied from very low to very high, as desired. Torque can be reduced and controlled.

Until late 1962 through-put was limited by a relatively (for 1962) slow spindle speed, the top speed being 80,000 rpm. In late 1962 Whitin offered the machine equipped with magnetic support-type spindles, by virtue of an exclusive arrangement concluded with Heber-

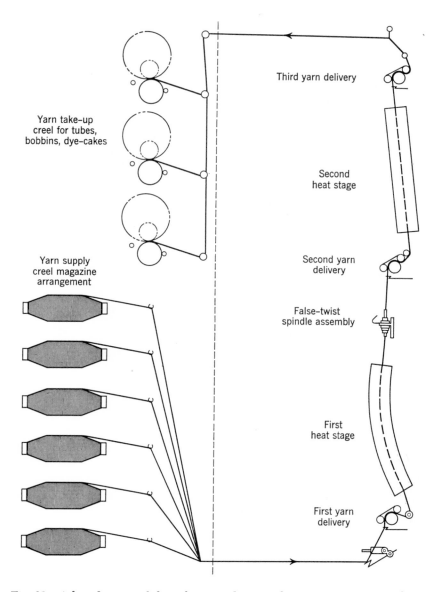

Fig. 21. A line drawing of the Whitin Machine Works A.R.C.T.–F.T.F. machine.

Fig. 22.   A photograph of the Whitin Machine Works A.R.C.T.–F.T.F. machine. Note that creel and take up are in one unit, tension controls, first and second time heaters and spindles in a second unit.   Yarn passes creel under false floor to second unit, is processed, and returns overhead to take up unit.

Fig. 23. Close-up photograph of second, or production unit, of Whitin Machine Works A.R.C.T.–F.T.F. machine.

lein, Watwill, Switzerland.   The Heberlein magnetic spindle is claimed to be operatable up to 500,000 rpm.

Pending patent litigation involving alleged patent infringement is complicating the situation.   It is to be hoped that 1964 will see some clarification in respect to the validity of the patents allegedly being violated.

CONTINUOUS PROCESS, FALSE TWIST, POST TREATMENT, NO TORQUE

Whitin Machine Works, Whitinsville, Massachusetts, offers a combined false-twist post-treatment no-torque machine manufactured by Ateliers Roannais de Constructions Textiles Roanne, Loire, France, that processes thermoplastic yarns from supply package over two heaters and two spindles, producing torque-crimp post-treated no-torque yarns in a single pass.   This machine designated as Whitin A.R.C.T. type F.T.U. machine is similar in over-all appearance and operation to the A.R.C.T. type F.T.F. Machine, differing primarily in respect to the presence of a second spindle.   The second spindle false-twists the yarn in a direction opposite to the direction of the first spindle, inserting only the amount of torque required to balance, or almost balance, torque due to first-time twisting producing a finished yarn, stretch, or bulk with essentially no torque.

By properly controlling heats, tensions, overfeed, spindle speeds, etc., it is possible to produce a great variety of yarns, stretch and bulk, with minimum or essentially no torque.

As with the A.R.C.T.-F.T.F. machine, pending patent litigation involving alleged patent infringement was complicating the situation at the end of 1963.

Item-by-Item Discussion of Post Treating

The reheat setting, or partial resetting of torque-crimped thermoplastic yarns under controlled conditions makes it possible to produce a wide variety of modified torque-crimped yarns having properties that make them of special value in many instances.   Post-heat-treating of torque-crimp yarn can produce exceedingly soft silk-like yarns in which every turn of twist inserted in each filament during the torque-crimping process becomes a crimp in the finished reheat-set yarn.   Its use enables texturers to eliminate shrinkage in the yarns and fabrics made therefrom, or to reduce shrinkage and stretch to a predetermined extent.   It makes possible the control of width after boil-off, control of surface characteristics of knitted and woven fabrics, and control of bulk, softness, resilience, and other desirable characteristics. The elimination of shrinkage is especially valuable in certain woven fabrics, where texture, softness, and drape are the primary perquisite, and in carpet yarns, rug yarns, and pile-type upholstery fabrics, where loft or height of pile is important.

In the following pages we will discuss in detail a number of the more important factors and their effect on yarns processed through reheat-setting equipment.

TENSION

Surprisingly, when certain torque-crimp yarns are reheat-set under high tension, such as is characteristic of underfeeding, the finished yarn has good crimp and good texture up to tensions that elongate the yarn as much as 8 to 10 per cent. These yarns do not have the cover of yarns relaxed while reheat-set, but do have good cover. Fabrics made from them vary in hand and appearance from yarns heat-set while relaxed, assuring this type of yarn a place in the family of textured thermoplastic yarns, although necessarily a specialized place.

PER CENT OF RELAXING

Most yarns are relaxed from in the neighborhood of 6 to 35–40 per cent, the appearance and properties of the yarns relaxed to varying degrees being just about what would be anticipated with respect to appearance, covering power, bulk, etc. The per cent of overfeed used depends on the results desired in the finished fabric, balanced against economics. Obviously a fabric woven from a yarn relaxed 30 per cent will vary substantially from one relaxed 6 to 7 per cent. The 30 per cent relaxed yarn will produce a fabric with some stretch and recovery properties, a very high degree of covering power, and a full hand. On the dollar and cents side it requires the use of more yarn per yard and must be finished narrower to obtain the full effect or benefit of the higher per cent of relaxing. The yarn reheat-set at 6 to 7 per cent will produce more yards of cloth, must be finished wider but has less cover, softness, less fullness of hand and drape.

TEMPERATURE

Temperatures employed are usually a full 100°F and more below the temperature employed during the torque-crimping operation.

The degree of reset varies directly with the temperature, and for this reason various temperatures are used, the actual temperature depending on the results desired. For example, when the maximum of softness, together with stretch, is desired in a finished woven fabric, lower temperatures and a higher per cent of overfeed are employed than when texture and drape only are the objectives.

DWELL TIME IN HEATED ZONE

As in the case of the initial false-twisting operation, this is critical and definitely controls the speed at which yarns can be post-heat-set. Because the requirements of reheat-setting are less than the requirements of the initial setting, it is usually possible to reheat-set at a faster rate than the initial set, although it is not necessary that the yarns be processed in the minimum possible time. Actually, a longer dwell time is desirable. Dwell times utilized vary from 1 to 2 seconds.

PLY TWIST

Many, but not all, of the yarns reheat-set are so treated during a plying operation; this is to effect economy of operation. The true economy is not always as great as it appears to be owing to the need of time in the heated zone, which often reduces the through-put of the machine.

DENIER, FILAMENT COUNT, AND DIAMETER

As the denier of the yarn and the diameter of individual filaments increase, the dwell time in the hot zone during reheat-setting must increase. When very coarse yarns are processed it is better to use a radiant type heater rather than a heated plate. This is especially true when heavy denier yarns are overfed to the take-up package during false twisting. Otherwise variations in heat from filaments contacting the plate to filaments an appreciable distance away will cause visible variations in the finished yarn.

CHEMICAL AND PHYSICAL CONSTITUTION OF YARNS

The tensions, temperatures, dwell times, and even ply twists employed are necessarily varied as the physical and chemical constituents of the yarn varies. Type 6 must be processed at much lower temperatures than type 66. Polyester yarns benefit by a longer dwell time in the heated zone. It is necessary to reheat-set polyester more completely than nylon because the carrier used during dyeing awakens polyester beyond the effect achieved with nylon, and this tends to overcome the beneficial effect of reheat-setting if temperatures or dwell times are too low. Polyesters are benefited by overfeeding during torque-crimping and by reheat-setting with radiant heat.

Polypropylene requires the longest dwell time in the heated zone, both during the original torque-crimping and during reheat-setting. When possible, polypropylene torque-crimped yarns should be reheat-set with radiant heat.

STRETCH AND RECOVERY

Per cent of overfeed used, temperature, and dwell time in the hot zone all affect the stretch and recovery properties of reheat-set yarn. When maximum stretch and recovery are required the yarns should not be reheat-set. In certain woven fabric constructions, reheat-setting prevents the fabric from shrinking in too much during boil-off and very beneficially modifies the surface of the fabric, producing a more uniform and finer type of pebble in crepe-type fabrics, and at the same time reduces the rate and extent of recovery. Many light-weight fabrics do not require the immediate strong snap-back properties of ski fabrics, and such fabrics are very substantially improved in appearance and hand by reheat-setting after torque-crimping.

COVER OR HIDING POWER

The covering power of reheat-set torque-crimped yarns is increased to a very pronounced degree over the covering power of the torque-crimped yarns from which they are made, because in the reheat-set yarn every turn of twist inserted in every filament becomes a helical torque crimp. Often the covering power is doubled by reheat-setting.

SOFTNESS, HAND, AND DRAPE

Fine denier, fine filament, reheat-set yarns are softer, fuller, much more silk-like in hand than the torque-crimp yarns from which they are made. Heavy denier, coarse filament yarns are also less wiry, softer and fuller in a different manner. Fullness in a torque-crimp carpet yarn produces a firm, yet resilient, hand, which is very desirable in carpets.

HEIGHT OF PILE

Carpet yarns and pile-type upholstery yarns require rather thorough reheat-setting to prevent the pile from "squatting," slowly in the greige and rapidly during dyeing and finishing operations. It may safely be said that torque-crimp yarns have little value in pile fabrics until they are well reheat-set to provide the necessary stability. When yarns other than nylon yarns are torque-crimped radiant heat is mandatory during reprocessing, and nylon yarns also are improved by radiant heat reprocessing.

Anticipated Growth of Post-Treated Torque-Crimp Thermoplastic Yarns. Post treatment of torque-crimp yarns, performed in a one- or two-step process, can control the subsequent release of latent force, uniformity, size, and number of crimps, softness and fullness of hand, bulk of the yarn, degree of stretch or stabilization of fabric made from the yarn, and many other important factors.

Torque-crimp thermoplastic yarns, post-treated, constitute a tremendous "sleeper" in knitted and woven fabric fields.

Unfortunately timing, lack of vision, absence of new yarn development departments, and merchandising and promotional programs by throwsters, coupled with the fabric manufacturers' dependence on the synthetic yarn producers' development and promotional programs, have permitted this sleeper to continue to sleep.

Now that high-speed production reduces machine cost per pound to a very reasonable figure it is to be anticipated that some throwster, fabric manufacturer, or, more likely, synthetic yarn producer, will awaken the sleeper, and open and create new and profitable markets for torque-crimp post-treated yarns.

Photomicrographs of Post-Treated Yarns

Figures 24 and 25, photomicrographs of 70-denier, 32-filament, type-6 nylon, false-twisted 80 turns per inch and post-treated to uniformly distribute the torsional forces in the yarn, graphically show the increase in uniformity of crimp induced by post-treating. Compare Figs. 24 and 25 with Figs. 1 and 2. The yarns used are from the same cone; the difference is due to post-treating only. The greater number of smaller crimps in post-treated yarns increases bulk, covering power, softness, and uniformity.

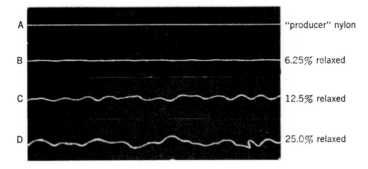

Fig. 24. Shadowgraphs of four single filaments of 70-denier, 32-filament semi-dull, type-6 nylon taken from a single pirn. Filament A is from yarn taken directly from the pirn. Filaments B, C, and D are from yarns false twisted 80 tpi on the 553 machine, relaxed to the extent indicated, and post-treated.

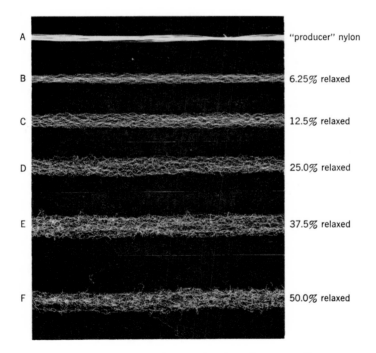

Fig. 25. Shadowgraphs of six single strands of 70-denier, 32-filament, semi-dull, type-6 nylon taken from a single pirn. Yarn A is yarn taken directly from the pirn. Yarns B, C, D, E, and F are from yarns false twisted 80 tpi on the 553 machine, relaxed to the extent indicated, and post-treated.

4

Stuffer Box Crimping —
Textralized® Yarn

The stuffer box process of crimping yarns was invented and patented by Alexander Smith Incorporated, now Mohasco Industries, Inc., of Amsterdam, New York, manufacturers of carpets. The first patent, U.S. Patent 2,575,837, was issued September 20, 1951, and reissued May 4, 1954, under U.S. Patent 23,824. All large manufacturers of carpets were then seeking additional fibers suitable for manufacture into carpets, to augment the static and dwindling supply of carpet wools, which was already insufficient to meet the growing demand for carpets because of increased population and increased prosperity. Alexander Smith Incorporated developed their crimping process primarily for wool in order to be able to utilize South American carpet wool instead of Chinese and Indian wool, which had been cut off due to political changes in that part of the world. The research on crimping expanded into the crimping of thermoplastic yarns and rayon.

On June 4, 1953, Alexander Smith Incorporated granted Joseph Bancroft & Sons Company, of Wilmington, Delaware, an exclusive license, including rights to sublicense, for all of their stuffer box rights. Bancroft also obtained the services of Lee W. Rainard and Ewart H. Shattuck, the inventors of record, who continue to mastermind and guide the development and growth of the process and its application.

Joseph Bancroft & Sons Company, experienced in the development and licensing of inventions in and to the textile industry (Everglaze® is their development), supplied sufficient funds and personnel to enable the process to be developed properly and, later, funds and personnel to guide the industry in the use of the invention and the merchandising of the yarn and fabrics made from the yarn.

Licenses and trademark agreements, covering a constantly increas-

78

ing number of patents and trademarks, were issued as required by industry demand. This demand had been created by a most excellent promotional, merchandising, and quality control program planned and executed by Joseph Bancroft & Sons Company. The first license was issued in September 29, 1953, to Hess Goldsmith & Company, now operating under the name of Atwater Throwing Company. Currently fifty-six license agreements have been issued (world-wide), and essentially all installed machines are running 24 hours a day, 7 days a week throughout the year. The garments or fabrics made from Textralized® yarns have been trademarked Ban-Lon®, a word that through judicious planning, yarn development, garment development, quality control, and excellent promotional and merchandising programs has created in the public mind a most excellent image, designating high-quality, durable, soft, lightweight, form-fitting garments, high styled at very attractive popular prices.

The Stuffer Box Process of Durably Crimping Thermoplastic Yarns

Thermoplastic yarns are continuously:

1. Drawn into the stuffer box by two rollers operating at linear speeds varying from 100 to 2000 ypm depending on the machine, the yarn processed, the denier used, and the results desired. Seventy-denier, type-66 nylon is usually processed below 400 ypm when optimum results are desired.

2. Propelled at a high rate of speed as described in (1), against a mass of crimped yarn in the stuffer box tube.

3. Crimped in a uniformly random manner when the yarn is forced against the mass of yarn in the stuffer box tube.

4. Slowly pushed upward by the impelling force of the yarn. The impelling force of the yarn is much greater than would be anticipated by those not familiar with the process, the force of a single strand of 70/32 type-6 nylon being sufficient to push several hundred yards of previously stuffed yarn constantly upwards, against its own weight and against the weight of the tube that maintains the yarn in the stuffed position and serves as an exit tube for the yarn.

5. Heated well above the second-order transition while slowly pushed upward through the heated tube.

6. Removed from the tube through a smaller tube partially within the heated tube that serves as a weight to help pack the yarn in the stuffer box tube and as an egress for the crimped and heated yarn.

7. Led to a cone and wound on same.

The Stuffer Box Machine for Durably Crimped Thermoplastic Yarns

Line drawing, Fig. 26, shows the most important working parts of the crimping unit for Textralized® yarn. Yarn is drawn from the supply package (*a*) by rollers (*b*) through nip (*c*) pushed or impelled at a high rate of speed into a heated tube (*e*), striking against the mass of yarn at (*d*), slowly, during 40 to 60 seconds, pushed through heated tube (*e*) to the smaller egress tube (*h*), through

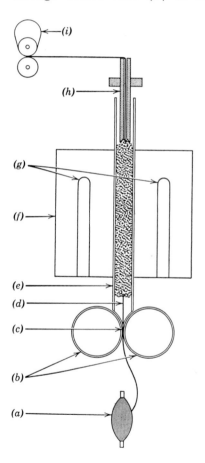

which it is drawn to the finished yarn package. Heated tube (*e*) is maintained at a uniform temperature by cast aluminum block (*f*) heated by electric heating units (*g*). Crimps are formed at (*d*). Crimps are not formed by the rollers pushing the yarn against the mass of crimped yarn, but rather by the yarn striking the mass of crimped yarn at a high rate of speed.

Figure 27 shows the relative position of the nip of the rollers, the yarn, and the mass of crimped yarn ready to be heat-treated. The actual distance from the nip to the mass of crimped yarn varies surprisingly from as little as one-eighth of an inch to as much as 1 inch, depending on yarn, denier, filament count, speed of operation, etc. As the diameter of individual filaments of 70-denier, 32-filament nylon is less than one-thousandth of an inch (actually 0.00066 inch), the length of each filament between nip and yarn mass is several hundred times the diameter of individual filaments. Each filament is free to act individually.

The amount of twist in one-eighth of an inch to 1 inch of producer-

Fig. 26.   Line drawing of thread line and working units of stuffer box machine used to produce Textralized® yarn for manufacture of Ban-Lon® garments.

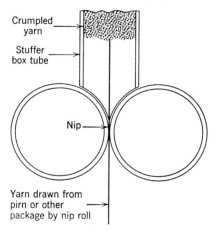

Crumpled yarn

Stuffer box tube

Nip

Yarn drawn from pirn or other package by nip roll

Fig. 27. Feeder yarn, nip roll, lower end of stuffer box tube, and crumpled yarn in Textralizing unit.

twist thermoplastic yarn is not sufficient to prevent each filament from acting individually. The pressure at the nip tends to flatten the yarn, spreading the filaments, providing extra space for the free movement of each filament when it strikes the relatively soft surface of the mass of previously crimped yarn. The crimps are formed as the filaments hit the mass of yarn. For this reason the crimps are not all V-shaped, as originally thought and planned. Many are N-shaped, or partially looped as in the written letter N, and individual crimps vary in size and direction; this produces a round, full yarn rather than the flat, ribbon-like effect that would be produced if the crimps were formed by gears or other positive mechanical means. The crimps are actually formed by a sort of crumpling action, as each section of filament thrust at high speed by the nip rolls strikes the irregular surface of the previously partially crimped yarn in the stuffer box tube. (If the crimps were formed in a flat, ribbon-like arrangement, a little twist, in the order of 1 to 3 turns, would disarrange the ribbon-like structure and produce a round, full yarn.)

Over-all Machine. Machines for Textralized® yarn are essentially coners, individually equipped with variable drives to enable speeds to be controlled as required for different yarns, and equipped at each position with a unit known as a crimping head, this being the compact unit that does the crimping.

The Yarn Supply Package. This can be any type of package as delivered by the producer, usually a pirn or tube.

The Crimping Head. This is a compact unit placed between the yarn supply package and the finished yarn package, and is the unit that does the actual crimping.

The Nip Rolls. Yarn is drawn at a very high rate of speed from the yarn supply package by two metal nip rolls that continuously impel the yarn upward into a metal tube known as the stuffer box tube. The rollers tend to flatten the yarn in a ribbon-like form, each filament being free to act as it will.

The Stuffer Box Tube. The lower end of this tube is so designed that the bottom end of the cutaway portion can be inserted rather close to the nip of the rotating rollers; this is to prevent yarn from being pushed out of the tube. When the machine is started yarn accumulates in the tube, quickly filling it almost to the bottom, and thereafter the impelled yarn continuously holds the mass of previously crimped yarn above the rotating nip rolls, against the weighted tube; the remainder of forces resulting in crumpled yarn slowly being pushed upwards through the stuffer box tube.

The Heated Aluminum Block. The tube is inserted in a cast aluminum block several times the diameter of the tube, the block covering approximately three-quarters of the length of the tube and supplying a steady source of constant heat to the tube.

The Chromolox Heater. Two electric heating devices are inserted in holes or wells in the block, these heaters maintaining the block at a uniform temperature. When 70-denier, 34-filament, type-66 nylon is crimped the heaters are set, usually, to maintain the temperature of the aluminum block at 380° to 390°F. When "excessive" speeds are used temperatures range as high as 410°F. Type-6 nylon is processed at lower temperatures, usually at about 320°F.

The Egress Tube. A small tube partially inserted in the top of the heated tube serving as a weight to maintain the desired pressure on the yarn as it passes through the stuffer box and serving as a means of continuously withdrawing the crimped heated yarn from the tube. Tubes weighing approximately 1½ ounces are used when 70-denier nylon is processed.

The Coning Head. This is a regular cone-wind-up unit of a coning machine, and functions to draw the yarn from the crimping unit and wind it into a usable form for shipment or further processing.

Quantity Through-put. Through-put varies with denier and machine setting. The average through-put for one crimping unit is calculated at approximately 1900 pounds per spindle year, basis 70-denier nylon, when the machine is operated at recommended speeds. In many instances speeds actually used exceed the recommended speeds by as much as 80 per cent.

Operation of Machine for Textralized® Yarn

Thermoplastic yarns are drawn from a supply package by a pair of nip rolls, thrown or impelled against a mass of previously crimped yarn at the bottom of the heated stuffer box at linear speeds of 100 to 2000 yards per minute, crumpled or crimped, and slowly pushed up through the tube to the weighted egress tube through which the hot crimped yarn is drawn to the take-up package, a cone. Seventy-denier nylon usually is impelled at speeds just below to substantially above 300 ypm.

The dwell time in the hot zone for 70-denier nylon is 40 to 90 seconds depending upon the objective of the crimper, whether he seeks to produce the best possible yarn, or the highest possible through-put. Temperatures employed for 70-denier, type-66 nylon range very close to 400°F, between 370° to 410°F in most instances. Temperature is only part of the story. Part of the mass of crimped nylon contacts the walls of the hot stuffer box while passing through the heated zone, whereas the bulk of the yarn must receive its heat by contact with the hot air in the tube, and by radiant heat extending inwardly from the walls of the tube.

The radiant heat cannot reach all of the yarn uniformly; the yarn nearest the walls receives the most radiant heat. The specific heat of heated air is only a small fraction of the specific heat of metal at the same temperature, and the metal constituting the tube is continuously supplied with energy as heat from the aluminum block surrounding it.

As a result of the above, crimped thermoplastic yarns passed through a hot stuffer box tube vary somewhat when finished, particularly with respect to dye index. When plied yarns are utilized and the most level dyeing dispersed-type dyestuffs are used, the finished garment may be very uniform in appearance despite differences in dye index of parts of the yarns.

When stuffer box crimped thermoplastic yarns are woven single-end and dyed with fast colors, many of which are much less level dyeing on nylon heated to varying degrees, the result is a fabric having a skittery or noticeable uneven dyed effect that has delayed the entrance of stuffer box crimped yarns into the weaving field.

Obviously there are ways of overcoming this problem, some means having been developed by Joseph Bancroft & Sons Company, and made available to licensees. The market for stuffer box crimped yarns in fabrics utilizing plies of these yarns has developed so rapidly and steadily that licensees have not yet made the necessary investment in capital equipment to produce the degree of uniformity required in woven fabrics.

The hot crimped yarn is drawn continuously from the hot stuffer box through the small weighted tube to the cone. This necessitates the application of tension to hot unset yarn. (Heat setting involves heating to the required temperature and cooling. Heat setting is not complete until the cooling is complete.) The strain applied to hot stuffer box crimped thermoplastic yarns processed through crimping units undoubtedly reduces the degree of stretch and recovery that can be obtained from thermoplastic yarns crimped in this manner. On the plus side, lack of tendency to shrink is an asset in many garments and a reduction in the magnitude of crimp assures greater softness.

Hot Stuffer Box Yarn

The hot stuffer box process of durably texturing thermoplastic yarns makes hard, wiry yarn soft and flexible, increases the hiding power or cover and bulk of the yarns up to several times that of producer twist yarn, depending on the fabric and on the boil-off, dyeing and finishing techniques used in processing the fabrics. Hot stuffer box processing increases the moisture absorption properties of hydrophobic thermoplastic yarns several times by providing minute spaces between filaments that can absorb and hold moisture.

The purchasing public has shown its opinion of this yarn by steadily and continuously increasing its purchases since the introduction of the yarn in 1953. It is anticipated that 30 million pounds will be used in 1964.

Size, Shape, and Frequency of Crimps. As shown in Figs. 28 and 29, photomicrographs of individual filaments and yarn of 70-denier, 32-filament nylon Textralized® yarn, hot stuffer box crimps consist largely of N-shape arcs and bends at random angles from the parallel position of producer twist uncrimped yarn. These photomicrographs necessarily show the fiber and yarn in two dimensions only, having been made by placing the filaments and yarn between a microscope slide and cover glass before photographing to make a sharp picture

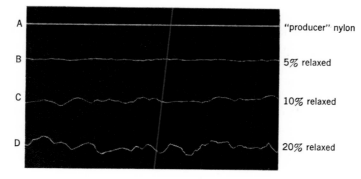

Fig. 28.   Shadowgraphs of four filaments of 70-denier, 32-filament, semi-dull, type-6 nylon taken from a single pirn.   Filament A is from yarn taken directly from the pirn.   Filaments B, C, and D are from yarns Texturized® and relaxed to the extent indicated.

possible.   When not compressed in this manner the yarn is round, not flat, and the filaments arc and bend into the third dimension.

Seventy-denier, 32-filament nylon Textralized® yarn averages 50 to 60 crimps per inch in individual filaments, and 1600 to 1920 crimps per inch in 70-denier 32-filament yarn.   Individual crimps range up to and above fifteen times the diameter of the uncrimped filaments.

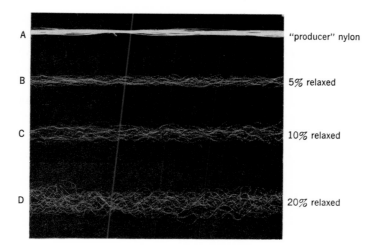

Fig. 29.   Shadowgraphs of four 70-denier, 32-filament, semi-dull, type-6 nylon yarns taken from a single pirn.   A is yarn taken directly from the pirn.   B, C, and D are yarns Texturized® and relaxed to the extent indicated.

Increased Bulk of Yarn. Although individual crimps vary in size, shape, and direction, the crimps are so made in relationship to the yarn itself that the over-all effect is one of uniformity of appearance and hand, particularly when, as is usually the case, a multiple of yarns are plied prior to manufacture into garments.

The increase in bulk created by converting producer twist thermoplastic nylon to Textralized® yarn is in the order of magnitude of 10 to 1. It can be best appreciated by comparing two skeins of equal weight, one consisting of producer twist nylon, the other of nylon Textralized® yarn, both worked gently in a bath of hot water and detergent to fully relax the Textralized® yarn. The volume occupied by the Textralized® yarn is fully ten times the volume occupied by an equal weight of producer twist yarn when both skeins are fully relaxed.

In knitted or woven fabric the increase in bulk is less than when skeins are relaxed, owing to the compressive effect of adjacent and crossing, or overlapping strands of yarn. In fabric made from Textralized® yarns the degree of increase in bulk is controlled by knit, weave, and relaxing procedures (boil-off), as well as by the conditions of texturing.

The increase in bulk produces a very pleasing illusion of lightness or featheriness in the finished garment, as well as warmth and moisture absorptive properties due to the thousands of minute air spaces between crimps.

Increased Covering or Hiding Power. The crimps, at random angles, one to the other, more than 270,000 in one square inch of cloth, woven 80 ends and 80 picks from 70/32 nylon Textralized® yarn, reflect light at random angles increasing covering or hiding power to an extent difficult to understand except in the light of the difficult to absorb number of crimps present in one square inch of cloth. The figure, more than 270,000 crimps in one square inch of cloth woven from 70/32 nylon Textralized® yarn 80 x 80, is calculated as follows:

Crimps per inch, 1 filament		55
Crimps per inch, 70/32 nylon Textralized® yarn	$55 \times 32 =$	1,760
Crimps per inch, warp 80 ends	$80 \times 55 \times 32 =$	140,800
Crimps per inch, filling 80 picks	$80 \times 55 \times 32 =$	140,800
Crimps per square inch		281,600

Denier, filaments, fabric construction (weave as well as ends and picks, the boil-off and dyeing and finishing techniques employed, all affect the degree of increase of covering or hiding power making it impossible to state *how much* covering or hiding power is increased in any generalized presentation. We can say only that the covering or hiding power is increased several times over the covering or hiding power of raw or producer yarn, the degree of increase being dependent on construction, relaxing, and dyeing and finishing conditions, as well as on the conditions utilized in producing the Textralized® yarn.

Increase Denier of Yarn. The apparent denier of Textralized® yarn produced from 70/32 nylon varies, depending on how it is measured. When measured in yarn taken directly from the cone it calculates to approximately 80 denier. When relaxed it calculates to just below 110 denier. As it lies in fabric it calculates somewhere between these two extremes.

Durability of Crimps. The crimps in hot stuffer box crimped yarns are durable throughout the life of the garments into which the yarns are manufactured. They are fully resistant to laundering and dry cleaning and are actually enhanced by these processes. The relaxing that takes place during these operations permits the yarns to return to the position they occupied prior to wearing of the garments.

Although the crimps in Textralized® yarns are durable for the life of garments made therefrom, and durable to washing and dry cleaning, they can be pulled out of the yarn by longitudinal strain. The reason for this is that Textralized® yarn in its crimped position is subjected to heat without the use of longitudinal strain, permitting molecular disarrangement to take place when the temperature is raised above the second-order transition. In this respect Textralized® yarns differ from false-twist torque-crimped yarns that are subject to sufficient strain when heated above the second-order transition to cause the tendency to molecular disarrangement to be used to further align the molecules, substantially precluding any ductility in the cooled yarn.

The ductility of Textralized® yarn does not affect the softness of hand, wear, washability, durability, etc., of Ban-Lon® fabrics and garments made from Textralized® yarns. It has not in any way interfered with the development and public acceptance of Ban-Lon® fabrics and garments. It is conceivable that when mechanical changes are made in equipment to make Textralized® yarn uniform enough to be used in single-end weaving without visible variations showing in the finished goods, this ductility may show up as an increased tendency of fabric woven from Textralized® yarn to muss or wrinkle when used in constructions aimed at reducing or eliminating wrinkling in the finished woven goods.

It is also probable that this ductility will reduce "bounce" or recoverability from pressure when stuffer box yarns are used in other fabrics as, for example, in floor coverings.

Stretch and Recovery. Textralized® yarn is not sold as a stretch yarn, although it does have a degree of stretch and recovery. When the utmost in stretch and recovery is desired in thermoplastic yarns, the torque-crimp type of yarn is used because in properly processed torque-crimp thermoplastic yarns every minute portion of every filament contains latent torque-crimp energy due to its having been heat-set in a helical position while held under constant tension. Textralized® yarn is bent at irregular intervals and to varying extents, and its latent energy is confined necessarily to these bends. In addition it is heat-treated, permitting molecular disarrangement to take place during heat treating, then tension is applied to the yarn before it is cooled, to some extent decreasing crimp and subsequent recoverability.

Despite the above, knitted Ban-Lon® garments or fabrics exhibit more stretch and recovery than unprocessed yarns, and have the very desirable properties of fullness, softness, lightness, opacity, and moisture absorption.

When used as filling in woven goods, Textralized® yarns also exhibit the properties of fullness, softness, lightness, opacity, and moisture absorption. Constructions used, restrictions due to warp and warp size, and the boil-off dyeing and finishing techniques necessary to properly prepare the goods for sale, restrict the filling to such an extent that for the most part they preclude stretch and recovery.

Textralized® Yarns in Weaving. The properties of Textralized® yarns, particularly in respect to high bulk, apparent lightness or featheriness, covering power, softness, and moisture absorption, are such that one would anticipate their extensive usage in the weaving field. Some fabrics have been designed, woven, and sold. It is to be anticipated that one day Joseph Bancroft & Sons Company will decide to open the weaving market to their licensees. Actually all that is necessary is this decision, followed by: production of yarn free from dyeing problems due to contact with the hot metal of the tube, now technically possible; utilization of known constructions, which is actually a matter of choice rather than extensive fabric development; and the application of Joseph Bancroft & Sons Company's merchandising and promotional technique. Sales will follow almost automatically.

Ban-Lon® Promotional Program. All segments of the industry familiar with the Ban-Lon® quality control and promotional program of Joseph Bancroft & Sons Company acclaim it, and consider it to be the primary reason for the present status of Ban-Lon® garments in the eyes of department store buyers and the purchasing public.

Although it is technically possible to make textured yarns resembling Textralized® yarns on false-twist equipment by varying the manufacturing technique, and although such yarns can be used to produce garments resembling garments made from Textralized® yarns, the sale of such yarns (imitations of Textralized® yarns) is so low as to be negligible even though they are offered at prices well below Textralized® yarns.

The reason "Imitation" Textralized® yarns do not sell is the reason for the steady growth of the market for Ban-Lon® garments. Joseph Bancroft & Sons Company chose the fields in which their yarns produce the best results; then in cooperation with their licensees and their licensees' customers, they developed garments that are satisfactory in every way, controlled the quality of these trademarked garments through their quality control and licensing program, and developed the market for the garments by excellent advertising and promotional programs. For further information on this subject see Chapter 15.

Textralized® Yarn and Ban-Lon® Patent and Trademark Position. The strength of the position of Joseph Bancroft & Sons Company in respect to patent and trademark is attested to by the millions of dollars paid as royalties by licensees and by the millions of dollars spent by garment manufacturers and wholesale and retail outlets to augment the excellent job of quality control, merchandising, and promotion done by the company. These endeavors have produced a large and profitable market for Textralized® Yarns and Ban-Lon® fabrics and garments.

5

Crimping of Thermoplastic Yarns
by Drawing Heated Yarn over
a Crimping Edge — Agilon®

The process of edge-crimping thermoplastic yarns by drawing heated thermoplastic yarns over a crimping edge is claimed in U.S. Patent 2,919,534, which issued in January, 1960, and is assigned to Deering Milliken Research Corporation by the inventors, E. D. Bolinger and N. E. Klein. The patent is based on a series of continuation-in-part applications, the first of which was filed on March 1, 1952. Additional application, claiming a method of crimp development, issued as U.S. Patent 3,035,328, in May 1962. Another method of crimp development is claimed by one of the inventors in U.S. Patent 3,021,588, which issued in February 1962.

Many additional patents, assigned to Deering Milliken Research Corporation by various inventors, claiming methods and various apparatus for edge-crimping yarn have issued, and it is assumed that more may be anticipated.

The commercial use of the process has grown slowly and steadily since it was introduced to the trade, first and most important employing 15-denier monofil and 15-denier, 3-filament yarns, to be used in ladies' stretch hosiery, and later employing various heavier deniers for use in many fields including carpets, knitted outerwear, men's hosiery, and many other markets.

Since the issuance of the first license in 1956 more than forty licenses have been granted throughout the world. Many millions of pounds of thermoplastic yarns have been and continue to be edge-crimped, manufactured into fabrics and garments, and sold to the public, much of it under Deering Milliken Research Corporation's trademark of Agilon®.

As with the torque-crimp, stuffer box, and air-bulking processes, the commercially available edge-crimping equipment has been constantly modified and improved, resulting in steadily improved yarns and garments made therefrom.

The newest equipment, employing a 10B downtwister machine provided with added tensioning, heating, crimping, cooling, relaxing, and oiling devices, enables more uniform edge-crimped yarn to be produced at manufacturing costs well below the minimum possible in other processes when low twist multi-ply yarns are required.

This equipment is engineered so well that yarns crimped on it are very uniform with respect to crimp, bulk, etc., from position to position on the machine and within each position. Dyers report less trouble than with yarns crimped by other processes when dyestuffs known at times to produce streaky dyeings must be used.

Agilon® textured yarn was an immediate success in the ladies' stocking industry, where it is recognized as the best yarn for use in producing stretch stockings. Its volume continues to increase at a steady rate despite a very high royalty. Some people in the industry believe that this steady growth is in part due to the high royalty and resultant high price, pointing out that even though there is no quality control program for products made from the yarn, the quality of the yarn itself is controlled and the high price of the yarn assures its use in top quality merchandise.

Heavy denier yarns, carpet deniers, 1000 denier and heavier, are processed on specially built heavy-duty machines. Good progress was made in the continuous filament, textured thermoplastic yarn carpet industry until the advent of producer textured yarns, controlled and promoted by fiber producers, which discouraged additional activity in this field. Although the prices currently charged by synthetic yarn producers appear to leave room for other texturing processes, the hard fact remains that producer costs are so low that synthetic yarn producers, whenever they choose, can reduce prices for the textured yarns below the costs of texturers who must buy the raw thermoplastic yarns from them. For this reason many texturers other than fiber producers have ceased activity in the texturing of heavy denier thermoplastic yarns.

The knitted outerwear and men's and children's stocking industries are logical fields for growth for multifilament edge-crimped yarns, particularly in view of their low costs, uniformity, and extra softness. As additional machines to produce Agilon® textured yarns are installed, and the force of promotion of various textured yarns increases

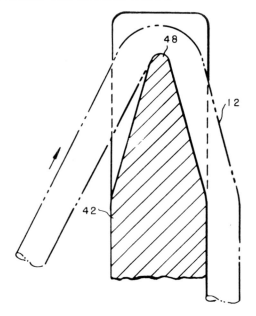

Fig. 30. A reproduction of Figure 4, U.S. Patent 3,025,584 assigned to Deering Milliken Research Corporation. Figure 4 shows how a single filament of thermoplastic yarn, drawn hot over a crimping edge, is compressed in the portion of the filament adjacent to the edge, and stretched in the portion furthest from the edge.

the market for all textured yarns in the knitting fields, it is probable that Agilon® yarn, because of its low cost, full soft hand, and very uniform dyeing, will become a more important factor in this very large market for multifilament textured yarns despite the lack of an end-product quality control and merchandising program.

Early efforts to use edge-crimped thermoplastic yarns in weaving were unsuccessful because early equipment was not as well engineered as current equipment. The unavoidable variations in yarns processed on this equipment produced undesirable visible variations in the finished woven goods. The excellent uniformity of thermoplastic yarns edge-crimped on the new and better engineered equipment should reopen the weaving field to edge-crimped yarns, particularly if sufficient time and effort are devoted to the development of fabrics designed to utilize the special properties of the edge-crimped yarns, and if good promotion is built around controlled quality.

If, as appears likely, low twist yarns can be used in weaving, particularly in the filling, it should be possible to produce edge-crimped yarns for weaving at a very high production rate. Through-put on the modified 10B is controlled by twist and heating time requirements. At low twist, the limiting factor will be time of heating, although higher speeds can be attained by increasing the diameter of the rotating heating and cooling drums, a modification which will increase the length of yarn contact time.

As owner of the edge-crimping process in the United States and of the trademark Agilon®, the Deering Milliken Research Corporation has well demonstrated its ability to use promotion in marketing new and novel items. It would appear that they have thus far restrained their promotional activities until their machines were perfected and installed in sufficient quantity to back up promotion with an adequate supply of high-quality merchandise. It is probable that textured fabric development, yarn manufacture, and promotion of Agilon® yarns will now be increased to take full advantage of the new and improved equipment and resulting improved yarn qualities.

Thermoplastic yarns are edge-crimped by continuously tensioning, stretching, heating, drawing around an edge, shrinking, and cooling, which in some instances may be followed by exposing the filaments to a hot relaxing step to develop crimp and stabilize the yarn. Crimp may also be stabilized after the yarn is formed into fabric or another end product, depending on the particular end use.

Figure 30, a reproduction of Fig. 4 as shown in U.S. Patent 3,025,-584, filed December 30, 1955, issued March 20, 1962, to C. G. Evans, assignor to Deering Milliken Research Corporation, graphically illustrates how the filaments of a thermoplastic yarn, which are relatively uniform before being stretched heated and drawn under tension over a crimping edge and cooled, become varied across the filaments after processing over the edge. The part of the filament nearest the edge, a single filament in the illustration, is sharply bent at the edge, being compressed at the point of contact. At the same time the filament is stretched at the part farthest from the edge, the intervening portions being compressed or stretched in direct proportion to their distance

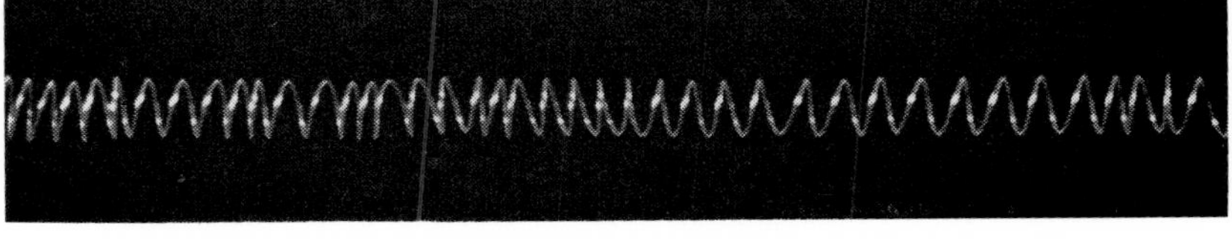

Fig. 31. A photomicrograph of a single strand of 15-denier monofilament nylon properly processed over a crimping edge and relaxed to show the manner in which the coils reverse at intervals.

Fig. 32. A reproduction of Figure 5, U.S. Patent 2,931,089 assigned to Deering Milliken Research Corporation. Figure 5 shows how hot thermoplastic filaments contacting the crimping edge while tensioned become distorted in cross section.

from the edge. Strains are set in the filaments, releasable when the filaments are subsequently relaxed and heated. Release of the strains causes or permits coils to form when the filaments are free to relax, the coils reversing directions at more or less regular intervals, as shown in Fig. 31, a photomicrograph of a 15-denier nylon monofilament, edge-crimped and relaxed under controlled conditions by exposing the yarn to the effect of dry heat.

Tensions and heats employed are sufficient to actually deform the cross sections of individual filaments that contact the crimping edge, as shown in Fig. 32, a reproduction of Fig. 5 in U.S. Patent 2,931,089, filed May 2, 1956, issued April 5, 1960, to C. G. Evans, assignor to Deering Milliken Research Corporation. In multifilament yarns, the filaments contacting the edge are deformed in cross section much more than filaments that pass over the crimping edge while riding on other filaments, rather than directly contacting the edge. Such filaments, though remaining unchanged or only very slightly changed in cross section, are nevertheless stretched, compressed, and partially set by the process, retaining latent crimping energy or force, releasable as minute coils or crimps when the yarn is relaxed and heated under controlled conditions.

The Edge-Crimping Process to Produce Durably Crimped Thermoplastic Yarns

There are two current models of machines offered for edge-crimping, the 2086 and the 2110, both produced by Hobourn Aero Components Ltd., Strood, England. The Model 2086 machine is especially designed for fine denier hosiery yarns, and does not incorporate the crimp development and stabilization steps available in the Model

2110 machine. Though it is not suitable for 15-denier yarns the Model 2110 process sequence will be described below because of its broader application.

From two to six ends of thermoplastic yarns are continuously:

1. Drawn from the supply packages in the creel through guides above a tensioning device that can be an electrically controlled disk tension or a gate tensioner.

2. Guided to a ceramic post guide above a separating comb.

3. Separated on an input comb guide. The purpose of the comb guide is to space the yarns uniformly on the input feed rolls.

4. Passed several times around a set of capstan rolls.

5. Separated by passing through the hot roll comb guide.

6. Drawn to a rotating heated cylinder. The heating cylinder, 4 inches in diameter, that:

a. Stretches the yarn between the capstan rolls and the cylinder. (70/34 type-66 nylon is stretched about 10 per cent.

b. Heats the yarn beyond the temperature of the second-order transition. (Approximately 375°F for 66.)

c. Causes additional orientation of the yarn.

7. Drawn over a crimping edge. The part or side of the hot filaments contacting the crimping edge, or nearest to the crimping edge in the instance of filaments not directly contacting the edge because of intervening filaments, is compressed and molecules are disoriented. The part, or side, of each filament furthest away from the crimping edge is stretched. Intervening portions of all filaments are stretched or compressed the extent depending in part on the distance from the side receiving maximum compression and maximum stretch. Every portion of every filament is strained during the hot pass over the crimping edge, and, after partial setting on the lower side of the edge and on the cool roll following, retains latent crimping energy or force, releasable under controlled conditions.

8. Drawn over cold roll. The cold roll guides the yarn over the crimping edge, cools the yarn, sets the latent crimping energy or force in the yarn, and assists in controlling the tension in the yarn as it passes over the crimping edge.

9. Drawn over a feed roll guide. Necessary to assure that yarns spread properly on the intermediate feed rolls.

10. Drawn over intermediate feed rolls, a pair of capstan rolls. The function of the intermediate feed rolls is to control the degree of shrinkage and tension permitted between the hot roll and the intermediate feed rolls, and feed the yarn for relaxing over the second hot

roller, or for take-up on the 10B bobbins when the second hot roll is by-passed.

11. Guided past static eliminator. Necessary with some yarns to prevent static from forcing ends apart causing erratic and uncontrollable behavior. Static elimination is necessary with some yarns because these yarns do not have sufficient anti-static finish or the finish is vaporized by heating.

12. Reguided over first set of capstan rolls. This brings the yarns to the proper position for separating on the guide comb just prior to passing over the hot relaxing roll.

13. Guided through second hot roll comb. The comb separates the yarns and guides them into the centers of the proper grooves in the hot relaxing or stabilizing roll.

14. Passed over stabilizing hot roll. The yarn is fed to this hot relaxing or stabilizing roll approximately 20 per cent faster than the surface speed of the roll, permitting it to contract by this amount. Crimp is fully developed and then heat-set or stabilized to the desired degree.

15. Passed over output roll guides. The yarn is guided over this ceramic guide to assure the yarn leaving the heater grooves in a straight path and to direct it properly onto the output roll.

16. Advanced by the output capstan rolls that complete control of the per cent of overfeed permitted on the relaxing hot roll, and provide proper tension for oiling and building a package suitable for knitting on the ring-twisting take-up portion of the machine.

17. Drawn over oil roll for application of proper amount of knitting oil.

18. Separated into correct plies and drawn to the ring twister, plied as desired and wound, usually on a disposable paper tube; the wind being so designed that the yarn can be knit, warped, or quilled direct from the tube.

The edge-crimping process sounds complicated. However, because all of the steps, including final wind-up into a package suitable for immediate use, are accomplished in one continuous operation, it is a relative simple operation in production after initial thread-up. Figure 33 graphically shows the units over which the yarn passes in its 4 to 5 second travel from producer supply package to the take-up package. The machine is necessarily very intricate, precision built and assembled, and so designed that thermoplastic yarns processed through this machine are very uniform in appearance and characteristics, this being readily and easily determined when fabric manufactured from Agilon® yarns is dyed. Dyers report that fabrics manufactured from Agilon® yarns are very easy to dye uniformly.

The Edge-Crimping Machine for Producing Durably Crimped Thermoplastic Yarns

Figure 33, a line drawing, shows the most important working parts of an edge-crimping unit. Yarn is drawn from the supply package through disk tension (a), through comb (b) over capstan rollers (c), through comb (d), heated by contacting rotating heater (e), crimped at crimping edge (f), cooled on rotating cooling roll (g), advanced on capstan rollers (h), guided again partly around rolls (c) through comb (i) to heated relaxing drum (j), advanced on capstan output rolls (k), guided over static eliminator (l) guided to oiling device (m), and taken up on a paper board shipping tube on spindle (o) after twist as required through ring and traveler (n).

The yarn is stretched approximately 10 per cent between capstan rolls (c) and hot rotating cylinder (e), heated on rotating cylinder (e), crimped at crimping edge (f), cooled on rotating cylinder (d), shrunk approximately 17 per cent between rotating heater (e) and capstan rolls (h), relaxed on heated cylinder (j), the degree of relaxing being controlled by the differences in distance around rollers (h) and (k); this immediate partial relaxing, usually about 20 per cent, assures the desired amount of crimp in the finished yarn. After relaxing, the yarn is advanced on capstan rolls (k), oiled at (m), and wound on shipping tube at (o).

Note that the yarn is: tensioned; stretched and heated; crimped; cooled; relaxed; oiled; plied, 1 to 6 turns; and packaged for further processing in one pass at speeds of 40 to 200 yards per minute, the primary control of speed being the heating required. The crimp in the yarn is not affected by the normal fabricating tensions. Edge-crimping, in the manner described above, using a 2110 crimping unit mounted on a 10B, constitutes a very economical means of producing textured multi-ply thermoplastic yarns.

Over-all Machines. The new and improved equipment for manufacturing edge-crimped yarns, actually a number of machines varying one from the other to fit specific situations (one model is shown in Figs. 34 and 35), basically consists of a Leesona 10B downtwister, plus an edge-crimping unit, the most recent being designated as

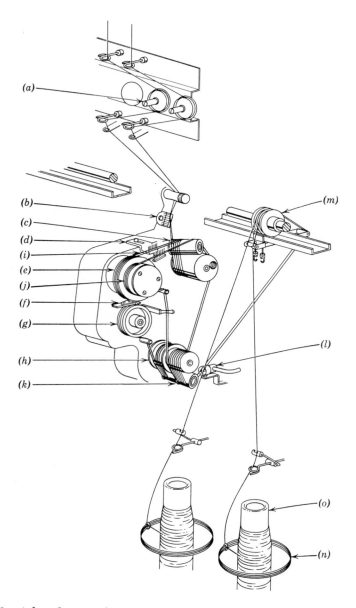

Fig. 33.   A line drawing showing the most important working parts of an edge-crimping unit, and the thread line.

Fig. 34. An Agilon® edge-crimping machine.

Fig. 35.   Close-up of Agilon® edge-crimping units.

Model 2110 edge-crimping machine manufactured by Hobourn Aero Components Ltd., under license by Deering Milliken Research Corporation. Each crimping unit usually serves two spindles and is capable of processing one to six ends of yarn simultaneously, from producer yarn delivery package to an especially designed take-up package generally suitable for knitting without rewinding.

The Yarn Supply Package. Pirns or tubes as desired, so creeled that six ends can be guided to each crimping unit, the creel package so aligned that an extension of its axis passes through the center of the top eye of the double pigtail guide.

Tensioner. An electrically controlled disk tensioner or a gate tensioner, as desired. If a wide range of yarn deniers is to be run, the electro-magnetic disk-type tensioner facilitates necessary tension changes. When gate tensions are used the dead weights used for control must be changed for each change of tension.

Combs. Three combs are used, each for the purpose of spacing yarns properly at critical points in the process as shown in Fig. 33.

Capstan Rolls. Three sets of capstan rolls are used, to accurately control stretching and shrinking where necessary, assuring that the required stretching and shrinking occurs in the prescribed areas.

Hot Cylinders. A two-step revolving heater with steps differing in diameter to cause stretching, relaxing, and shrinking to occur to the desired extent and at the proper times. Two types of electric heaters are available at the purchaser's option, both controlled by two well-regulated voltage circuits, the higher being for operating, and the lower being for maintaining correct temperature when the unit is not running.

The Crimping Edge. A specially prepared edge made of chrome-plated stainless steel, sold and distributed to licensees at a nominal price by Deering Milliken Research Corporation. The edge is sufficiently durable to process $4\frac{1}{2}$ pounds of 70 to 100-denier standard bright or semi-dull yarn through each groove of the hot roller before it is necessary to change edges. At 60 ypm, one edge will last about 80 hours. When dull yarn is edge-crimped the edge must be changed more often because of the abrasive action of the titanium dioxide in the dull yarn.

The Cold Roll. The cold roll assists in guiding the yarn around the crimping edge, controlling the tension, and it further cools the yarn (air, the edge, and its holder cool the yarn to a considerable extent before it contacts the cold roll). The cold roll does not require special cooling. The heat absorbed from the hot yarn is dissipated into the room, the roll itself remaining only very slightly above room temperature.

Static Eliminator. As stated previously, this is necessary only when the yarn finish is deficient in anti-static agent, or when the heat of processing vaporizes enough anti-static agents to cause the yarns to become erratic and uncontrolled.

Oil Roll System. Typical slowly revolving roll, trough and constant level reservoir, speed of the roll being controllable.

Take-up Packages and Spindle Adaptors. Adaptors and tubes, especially a disposable paper tube, have been developed for Deering Milliken Research Corporation and are available to licensees. Wind is such that the yarn can be knit, warped, and quilled directly from the disposable paper tubes.

Edge-Crimped Yarn

Figure 31 is a photomicrograph of a single filament of 15-denier nylon monofil edge-crimped and relaxed under controlled conditions. Note the uniformity of the coils that reverse direction at regular intervals.

Figure 36 is a photomicrograph of a single filament from a 70-denier, 32-filament, type-6 nylon yarn edge-crimped and heat-relaxed without restraint. It is well crimped throughout, though understandably it does not show the magnitude of coil, or the uniformity of coil of a monofil yarn, because the other 31 filaments interfered with the free action of the selected filament, both during crimping and during relaxing.

Figure 37 is a shadowgraph of a 70-denier, 32-filament, type-6 nylon yarn, edge-crimped and relaxed 50 per cent. It is uniformly crimped and very well-bulked.

Edge-Crimped Yarn Royalties

Royalties charged for edge-crimped thermoplastic yarns vary from very high royalties to very low royalties, the entire field being divided in two parts, very, very low denier and all other deniers.

Fig. 36. A shadowgraph of a single filament of edge-crimped nylon. The filament was taken from a strand of 70-denier, 32-filament, semi-dull, type-6 nylon, edge-crimped and relaxed 50%.

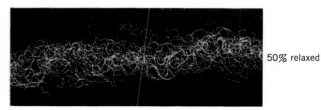

50% relaxed

Fig. 37. A shadowgraph of a single strand of 70-denier, 32-filament, semi-dull, type-6 nylon edge-crimped and relaxed 50%.

Table 1 Edge-Crimping Royalty Schedule

DENIER	ROYALTY
6–13 denier	30% of the cost of the unprocessed thermoplastic yarn, or three dollars ($3.00) per pound, whichever is higher
14–17 denier	30% of the cost of the unprocessed thermoplastic yarn, or two dollars ($2.00) per pound, whichever is higher
18 denier and above	4% of the cost of the unprocessed thermoplastic yarn

6

Air-Bulking Process for Texturing Filament and Staple Yarns — Taslan®

Taslan® is a registered trademark owned by E. I. du Pont de Nemours and Company, Inc. This company licenses their customers and textured yarn licensees engaged in manufacturing textured yarns to use this trademark to designate textured thread and yarn made in accordance with quality standards set by them. Firms throughout the world desiring to manufacture textured yarns of this type must acquire a license from du Pont, which at the present time has 132 commercial licensees.

The license and trademark agreements cover manufacture and sale of the yarn only. The du Pont company does not require that the trademark be used to identify the textured yarn and a substantial quantity of textured yarn is sold under names other than Taslan®. No license is required to weave the yarns or otherwise convert them into fabrics.

The Taslan® texturing process involves texturing continuous filament and spun yarns by air-bulking. When continuous filament yarns are air-bulked a multitude of loops and crimps are formed in individual filaments by exposing the yarn briefly to the turbulence of a stream of compressed air released in a venturi tube while redrawing the yarn, the take-up rolls being operated at a slower speed than the feed rolls.

The loops and crimps greatly increase the bulk or thickness of the yarns, modify the hand, increase the denier, increase the opacity and covering power, and otherwise modify the hand and appearance of the yarns and fabric manufactured thereform.

This process and its product are considerably older than is generally realized, dating back to late 1949. Since that time, work with the process and product has continued at an ever-increasing rate. Technical groups, working within the du Pont laboratories at first, later cooperating with yarn texturers and fabric manufacturers, have produced literally hundreds of new and different fabrics, many of which have been very successfully merchandised throughout the world.

Growth of the use of Taslan® textured yarns, with two exceptions, has been slow and unspectacular. Nevertheless the growth has been relatively steady and is continuing. Currently more than forty firms have active texturing programs and merchandise the yarn into many different and apparently unrelated fields such as upholstery, sewing thread, woven dress and blouse fabrics, double-knit dress and blouse fabrics, shoe laces, rainwear, necktie fabrics, carpets, lace, children's snow suit fabric, and many other equally different and diverse fields.

The two exceptions to the otherwise slow, steady growth in divergent fields are men's shirting fabric of Dacron® and woven glass drapery fabrics, the latter made from Taslan® bouclé and other Taslan® fancy yarns. The men's shirting fabric of Taslan® textured Dacron® polyester fiber, although produced in very great yardages, was short lived in the United States because of poor merchandising. The first production was sold at very high prices. When prices were lowered to broaden the base, purchasing stopped because of falling prices, and the market for the fabric never recovered.

The glass drapery fabrics fared much better. They started off with a rush and continue to be in great demand, with indications that additional slow and steady growth may be anticipated.

It is difficult to understand why the growth of the use of Taslan® textured yarns has been so restrained. The process makes possible the development of endless varieties of yarns from very fine to very coarse deniers. Yarns range from a low degree of texturing, to bouclés, chenilles, nub yarns, and many other types not heretofore existing. Some believe the lack of quantity and quality controls at fabric and garment levels, and lack of promotional funds for specific end-use items have caused growth to be slow.

As with all texturing processes for continuous filament yarns, a considerable portion of the first installed equipment was incompletely engineered. It consisted of converted uptwisters using the lower deck cork rolls as feed rolls, and the upper deck, running slower, as take-up rolls; air jets being inserted between upper and lower decks.

Currently, well-designed and engineered equipment is readily available. This equipment is manufactured by three firms licensed by du Pont for this purpose. These are: (1) U.S. Textile Machine Company, 411 Gilligan Street, Scranton 8, Pennsylvania. (2) Enterprise Machine and Development Corporation, Post Office Box 707, New Castle, Delaware. (3) Muschamp Textile Machinery (Sales) Ltd., Eider Works, Wellington Road, Ashton-Under-Lyne, Lancashire, England.

The Air-Bulking Process of Durably Crimping Yarns

Yarns are continuously:

1. Drawn from a supply package through a light gate tension.

2. Drawn over a rotating positive feeding and tensioning device, also functioning as an overfeeding device.

3. Guided by a small tube, called a needle, to the expanding portion of a venturi tube.

4. Air-bulked, looped and crimped by the turbulence of a stream of compressed air released in a venturi tube.

5. Passed between nip rolls just beyond the jet.

6. Led to a take-up mechanism operated at a linear speed slower than the speed of the feeding rolls.

The Air-Bulking Machine for Durably Crimping Textile Yarns

Line drawing, Fig. 38, shows the principal working parts of a Taslan® texturing unit, the Jumbo Texturizer of the U.S. Textile Machine Company, Scranton, Pennsylvania. Yarn is drawn from supply package (*a*), through gate tension (*b*), around overfeed positive tensioning rolls (*c*), guided to needle (*d*), drawn into same and into the venturi by the expansion of compressed air in the venturi (*e*), air-bulked, looped and crimped, drawn from the venturi by positive tensioning rolls (*f*), and taken up on a headless package (*g*).

OVER-ALL MACHINE

Texturing machines, designed especially for texturing yarns by the Taslan® texturing process, are built around the Taslan® jet, shown in some detail in Fig. 39, an enlarged drawing made from Fig. 4, U.S. Patent 2,958,112, assigned to E. I. du Pont de Nemours and Company. The machine feeds uniformly tensioned yarns into the jet, and continuously removes bulked yarn from the exit side of the jet, guiding the yarn to a take-up unit, a headless package-building device.

Figures 40 and 41 show one model of a complete machine, and a

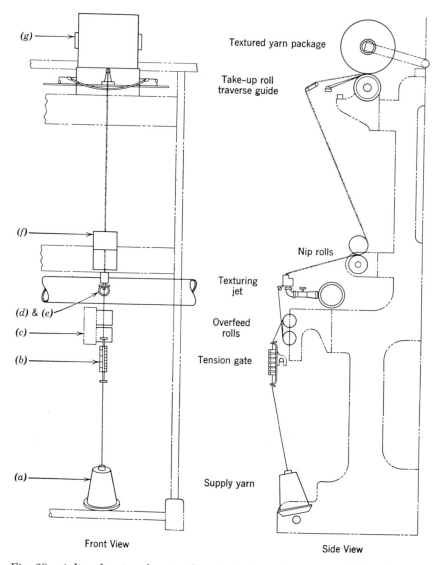

Textured yarn package

Take–up roll
traverse guide

Nip rolls

Texturing
jet

Overfeed
rolls

Tension gate

Supply yarn

Front View   Side View

Fig. 38. A line drawing showing the principal working parts and thread line of a Taslan® texturing unit, the Jumbo Texturizer of the U.S. Textile Machine Company, Scranton, Pennsylvania.

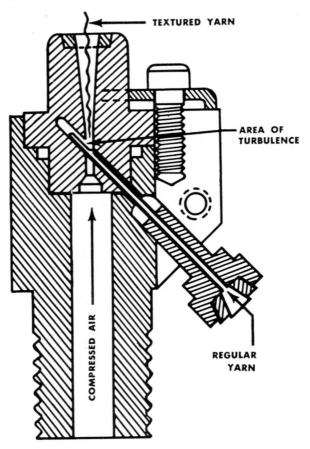

Fig. 39. Enlarged drawing of a Taslan® jet made from Figure 4, U.S. Patent 2,958,112, assigned to E. I. du Pont de Nemours and Company.

bench model of one type of one texturing unit. Specifically the machines are usually built to provide the following units:

1. The Creel. Positioned at the bottom of the machine, space being provided for two full-sized producer packages or large twister spools.

2. Gate Tension. Lightly pretensions the yarn. It is necessary to lightly pretension the yarn to enable the corked roller positive pretensioning device to work properly.

3. Positive Rolling Tension Controlling and Yarn-Feeding Mechanism. Positive and uniform tension and yarn feeding are essential

Fig. 40. A Taslan® texturing unit, the Jumbo Texturizer of the U.S. Textile Machine Company, Scranton, Pennsylvania.

Fig. 41.   One Taslan® unit showing supply package, capstan rolls, jet, and take-up.

to assure uniformity.   The rolling tension eliminates the effect of "plucks" caused by sticking on the supply package due to underwind, ridges, etc., in continuous filament yarns, and fiber entangling when spun yarns are processed.

4. Airlines, Valves, Gauges, Jet Mounts, and Openings for Jets. The Taslan® texturing process requires a very large quantity of compressed air and uniform flow and pressure at each jet.   To assure uniform pressure at each jet a very large pipe is run the length of the machine with a small opening available at each position.   The compressors and reserve tanks for air must be very sturdy, very large, and engineered to supply clean dry air at the jets.

5. *Texturing Jets.* The texturing equipment and operating know-how supplied by du Pont to their licensees is confidential. For this reason reproductions of currently commercial texturing jets are not available. Details of basic jet designs and operating directions are available from issued United States patents. Some of the patents of interest are: U.S. Patents 2,958,112; 2,884,756; 2,869,967; 2,852,906; 2,807,862; 2,783,609.

In lay language these patents explain that compressed air is introduced into the jet, then passed through an internal chamber where considerable turbulence is developed, leaving the jet from a single yarn and air exit. The yarn to be textured is introduced through a second tube and withdrawn at a somewhat slower speed from the yarn and the air exit. The individual filaments of the yarn are rearranged by the turbulent air in the internal chamber to form loops, coils, and whirls at random intervals along the lengths of the individual filaments.

6. *Nip Rolls for Removing Textured Yarn from Exit Side of Jets.* This positive nip removes bulked yarn from the jet at a predetermined rate; it is a necessary unit to assure more uniform through-put.

7. *Take-up.* A headless package type of take-up so designed that the yarns can be used directly from it without subsequent coning.

Operation of Taslan® Machine

Basically the yarn-bulking mechanism of the machine consists of two positive rolling tension devices, the second having a slower surface speed than the first, and a means of bulking yarn by guiding the yarn slack into and through a stream of turbulent air.

The above is a fine example of oversimplification. The equipment must be very well designed and exactly constructed. The air pressures, machine speeds, choice of tube, positioning of tube in the air stream, etc., must be very exact.

The machine may be used to process a single or a multiple of yarns through each jet. When multiple yarns are employed they may be fed at uniform rates or at differing rates. When processing one or more than one yarn, the rate of feeding can be uniform or irregular, *controlled* irregular, to produce nub effects.

When continuous filament yarns are air-bulked the type and number of loops, the type and degree of bulking obtained, and the stability of the finished yarn to longitudinal strain vary appreciably with the twist of the yarn. In most instances it has been found desirable to pretwist the yarn before bulking.

Just a little thought regarding the number of types of yarns available, the deniers, lusters, filament counts, pretwists possible, variations in overfeeds, multiple plies of varying constitution, and nub variations possible by controlled irregular feeds, make it readily evident that the number of different yarns that can be produced on Taslan® texturing equipment calculates to astronomical figures. If each of the above-mentioned variables could be varied in ten ways only, the variations possible calculate to one hundred million! Actually most of the possible variables mentioned can be varied in many more than ten ways.

One final thought regarding operation of the machine. The Taslan® texturing process is the only process for thermoplastic yarns that does not require or utilize heat. Non-thermoplastic yarns can be textured equally well.

Taslan® Yarns

All types of yarns, continuous filament, and spun, natural and synthetic, can be textured by this process provided the twist is low enough to permit the formation of loops and crimps when the slack yarn is exposed to turbulent air.

This chapter is concerned only with Taslan® textured yarns composed of or containing thermoplastic yarns, so constructed that the yarns are suitable for weaving.

Figures 42 and 43 are composite shadowgraphs of single strands of 70-denier, 32-filament, semi-dull, type-6 nylon pretwisted and air-bulked as indicated. Note that the bulk or denier of the textured yarns is directly proportional to the per cent of overfeed used. These nine yarns cover the practical working range of 70-denier, 32-filament, type 6 nylon, air-bulked for weaving as single yarns. More bulk or less twist tend to produce yarns not sufficiently stabilized for weaving. More twist and less overfeed reduce the bulking to such an extent that the modification in yarn properties due to processing does not appear to warrant the extra cost. Much wider variations are practical and are used when composite yarns are produced by air bulking.

Figure 44 is a two-dimensional schematic drawing showing the internal structure of a Taslan® textured multifilament yarn, untwisted.

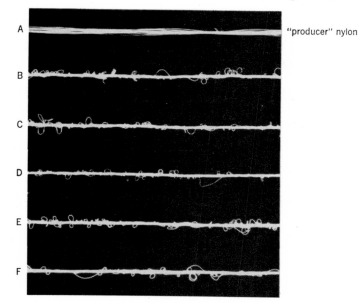

Fig. 42.   Shadowgraphs of 70-denier, 32-filament, semi-dull, type-6 nylon, air-bulked.   A, "Producer" nylon.   B, 18% overfeed, 16 tpi, bulk 83.   C, 18% overfeed, 12 tpi, bulk 83.   D, 14% overfeed, 16 tpi, bulk 80.   E, 14% overfeed, 12 tpi, bulk 80.   F, 14% overfeed, 7 tpi, bulk 80.

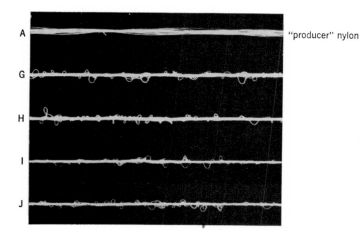

Fig. 43.   Shadowgraphs of 70-denier, 32-filament, semi-dull, type-6 nylon, air-bulked.   A, "Producer" nylon.   G, 12% overfeed, 7 tpi, bulk 78.   H, 10% overfeed, 16 tpi, bulk 77.   I, 10% overfeed, 12 tpi, bulk 77.   J, 10% overfeed, 7 tpi, bulk 77.

Fig. 44. A two-dimensional schematic drawing showing the internal structure of an untwisted multifilament Taslan® yarn. Heavy thread line illustrates the path and appearance of one disarranged filament.

The heavy line illustrates the path and appearance of one disarranged filament. Note that the loops in this disarranged filament are within the yarn bundle (shaded area) as well as on the surface of the textured yarn. Both the internal and external loops in the Taslan® textured yarn contribute to the hand, bulk, and appearance of the yarn.

Figure 45 is a photomicrograph of a number of different Taslan® textured yarns, courtesy of E. I. du Pont de Nemours and Company, illustrating a few of the thousands of fancy effects that can be produced by combining yarns and varying feeds while processing through the texturing jets. In fancy yarns of the type pictured in Fig. 45 the strength of the textured yarns is much lower than the combined strengths of the starting yarns, because all of the strain is applied to only part of the filaments, or one of the yarns when bouclé, chenille, and nub yarns are manufactured. The pleasing and different effects in the hand and appearance of finished fabrics made from these yarns more than compensate for the loss of physical strength due to yarn structure.

Figure 46 is a photomicrograph, courtesy E. I. du Pont de Nemours and Company, of a number of strands of fine denier multifilament du Pont nylon Taslan® yarn showing the manner in which filaments loop and are on the surface of the yarn.

The Taslan® texturing process can be used to vary the appearance and hand of unprocessed yarns in many ways, some of which are listed below.

1. The hand and appearance can be modified in a unique manner unattainable in any other way.
2. Bulk of the yarn can be increased.
3. Denier of the yarn is increased.
4. Elongation of the yarn can be decreased.
5. Tenacity is usually decreased.
6. The opacity or covering power is increased.

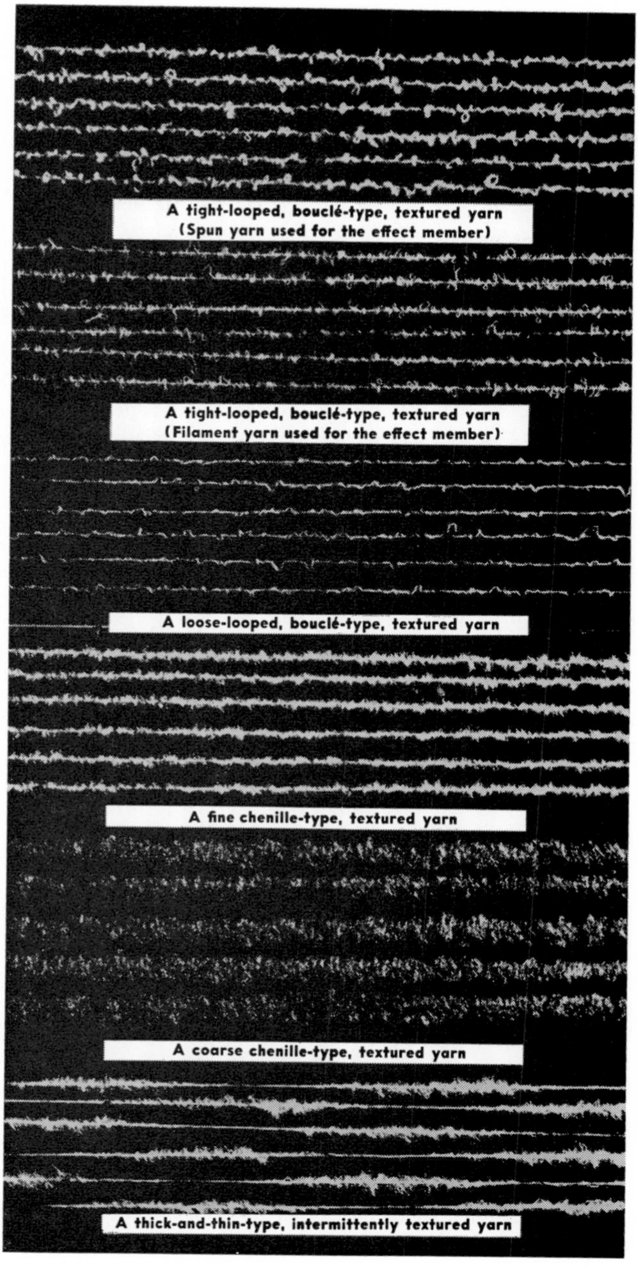

A tight-looped, bouclé-type, textured yarn
(Spun yarn used for the effect member)

A tight-looped, bouclé-type, textured yarn
(Filament yarn used for the effect member)

A loose-looped, bouclé-type, textured yarn

A fine chenille-type, textured yarn

A coarse chenille-type, textured yarn

A thick-and-thin-type, intermittently textured yarn

Fig. 45. A photomicrograph, courtesy of E. I. du Pont de Nemours and Company, illustrating a few of the thousands of fancy effects that can be produced by feeding yarns through texturing jets.

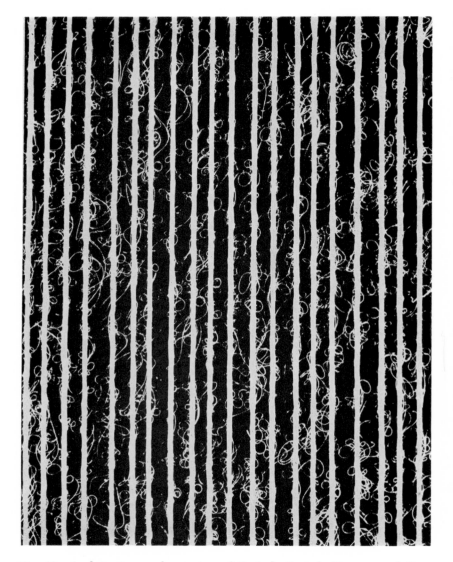

Fig. 46. A photomicrograph, courtesy of E. I. du Pont de Nemours and Company, showing how filaments can be caused to loop and arc on the surface of a fine denier multifilament Taslan® yarn.

7. Pilling is less than in comparable spun yarns.

8. The flexibility of the yarn is increased.

9. The yarns become softer to the touch, yet are crisp and dry as silk when continuous filament thermoplastic yarns are processed.

10. Smooth yarns are reduced in smoothness.

11. Bouclé, chenille, nub, and other fancy effects can be produced.

12. Combinations can be produced with continuous filament yarns of different properties, and with spun yarns.

13. Core yarns can be produced utilizing a high strength, relatively untextured core with a highly textured, relatively weak outer effect yarn to achieve unique effects with adequate total yarn strength.

14. Different colored yarns can be co-textured to achieve multi-colored effects.

Many of the yarns processed through Taslan® texturing jets for weaving are twisted, fine deniers as much as twenty turns, before exposing to the turbulent air, the reason being to promote greater uniformity, strength, and improved running properties. Yarns so processed are sometimes reprocessed with other yarns to provide the rough irregular effects required, particularly in drapery and upholstery fabrics.

Continued slow and steady growth of the use of Taslan® textured yarns may be anticipated, with the ever-present possibility of a style being created and accepted that could create a veritable explosion in its use.

7

Comparison of Various Crimped

Thermoplastic Yarns

Crimping Process Comparisons

In Chapters 2 through 6 we presented the various processes of durably texturing thermoplastic yarns in detail. To review and compare: thermoplastic yarns can be durably crimped by various torque-crimp methods, by post-treating torque-crimped yarns, by stuffer box and gear crimp methods, by scraping hot yarns over a crimping edge, and by air-bulking. This does not exhaust the list of possible methods, or methods that have been proven in laboratory trials. It does cover

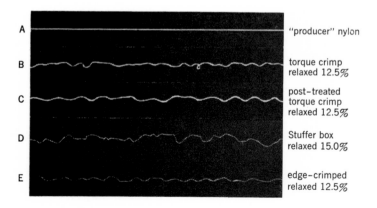

Fig. 47. Shadowgraphs of single filaments of nylon taken from 70-denier, 32-filament, semi-dull, type-6 nylon yarns textured by each of the four continuous texturing processes that use heat to set or partially set the textured yarns. Yarns were relaxed to the extent indicated. Compare with Fig. 48, similar filaments relaxed to a greater extent.

118

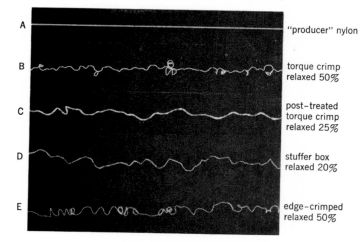

Fig. 48.   Shadowgraphs of single filaments of nylon taken from 70-denier, 32-filament, semi-dull, type-6 nylon yarns textured by each of the four continuous texturing processes that use heat to set or partially set the textured yarns. Yarns were relaxed to the extent indicated. Post-treated torque-crimp and stuffer box yarns were relaxed less than torque-crimp and edge-crimped yarns, because this coincides more closely with commercial practice.

the methods that have been used commercially in multi-million pound quantities.

Figures 47 and 48 are shadowgraphs of single filaments of nylon taken from single strands of 70-denier, 32-filament, type-6, semi-dull nylon, textured by four of the five continuous processes that use heat to set textured yarns, torque crimp, post-treated torque crimp, stuffer box heat-set (Textralized®), and edge-crimped (Agilon®). A single filament taken from a strand of air-bulked nylon could not be included because the process does not "set" individual filaments and a setting process would modify the appearance of the filament.

Figures 49 and 50 are shadowgraphs of 70-denier, 32-filament, type-6, semi-dull nylon yarns from the same cones from which the filaments shown in Figures 47 and 48 were taken.

Below we discuss briefly the filaments and yarns shown in the composite shadowgraphs.

TORQUE CRIMP

The single filaments shown are typical of all torque-crimp yarns, regardless of whether the processing is "conventional" or false-twist,

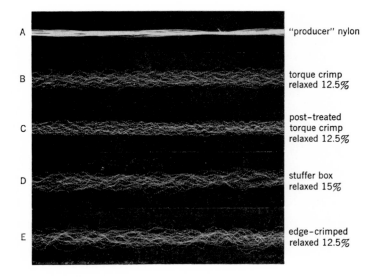

Fig. 49. Shadowgraphs of 70-denier, 32-filament, semi-dull, type-6 nylon yarns textured by each of the four continuous texturing processes that use heat to set or partially set the textured yarn. Yarns were relaxed to the extent indicated. Compare with Fig. 50, identical yarns relaxed to a greater extent.

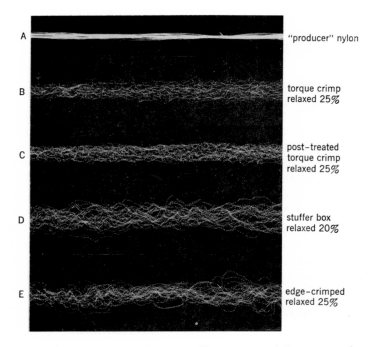

Fig. 50. Shadowgraphs of 70-denier, 32-filament, semi-dull, type-6 nylon yarns textured by each of the four continuous texturing processes that use heat to set or partially set the textured yarn. Yarns were relaxed to the extent indicated.

120

and regardless of the type or speed of the processing equipment. Visual differences observed in pictures of torque-crimp yarns and filaments are due more to processing conditions such as turns of twist, tension, temperature, speed, denier, filament count, luster, degree of relaxing, etc., than to the type or brand of equipment used in twisting, setting, and untwisting the yarn. More specifically, primary differences in the yarns result from variations in the spindle speed, temperature, heater length, tension and underfeed, and overfeed relationships. Visual differences observed in photomicrographs are often due to differences in degree of relaxing, as shown in Figs. 51 and 52.

In order to deform the filaments of a multifilament yarn from their normal parallel relationship, a stress (tension or load) must be used. To facilitate this deforming or changing in shape of the filaments, high temperatures are used to make the filaments more plastic and easier to deform. Within reasonable limits, the longer the time that the stress or load is applied at a given temperature or plasticity, the greater will be the permanent deformation. For this reason a machine having a relatively low spindle speed, which determines the

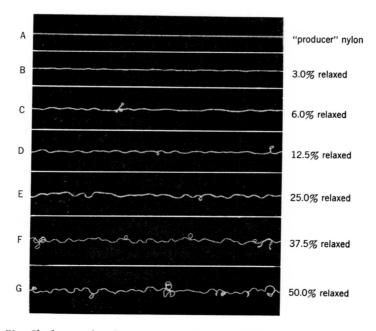

Fig. 51. Shadowgraphs of seven single filaments of 70-denier, 32-filament, semi-dull, type-6 nylon taken from a single pirn. Filament A is from yarn taken directly from the pirn. Filaments B, C, D, E, F, and G are from yarns false twisted 80 tpi on the 553 machine then permitted to relax as indicated.

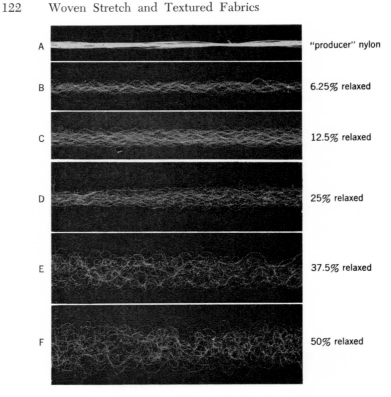

Fig. 52. Shadowgraphs of five single strands of 70-denier, 32-filament, semi-dull, type-6 nylon taken from a single pirn. Yarn A is yarn taken directly from the pirn. Yarns B, C, D, E, and F are from yarns false twisted 80 tpi on the 553 machine then permitted to relax as indicated.

linear speed of travel of the yarn for a given twist, and a relatively long heater, is capable of producing a yarn of optimum torque and crimp. When necessary the very high speed machines may be operated at lower speeds to obtain the optimum of results.

Differences do exist from type machine to type machine, but most of these differences cannot be determined by visual examination of photomicrographs of individual filaments or yarns.

The torque-crimp filaments shown in Figs. 47 and 48, are typical of conventional Helanca®, Fluflon®, Superloft®, A.R.C.T., 553, etc., relaxed as indicated. Appearance changes as the percentage of relaxation is increased or decreased. Figures 51 and 52 show the changes in appearance caused by varying the extent of relaxing the 70-denier, 32-filament, type-6, semi-dull nylon. A decrease in relaxation appears to reduce the crimp. It does reduce the extent to which the yarn can crimp. An increase in relaxation increases the size of the crimps and the number visible in a specific length of relaxed yarn.

POST-TREATED TORQUE CRIMP

Fluflon®, Superloft®, A.R.C.T., 553, or other torque-crimp thermoplastic yarns reprocessed, continuously, or in a separate operation, relaxed a predetermined percentage through a heated zone. This partial relaxing, and partial or complete resetting, controls the release of part or all of the latent torque-crimp memory, accomplishing several objectives discussed in detail elsewhere. The visual effect is to cause each turn of twist in torque-crimp yarns to manifest itself as helical crimp in properly processed post-treated yarns. Note that the post-treated torque-crimp filaments, relaxed to the same degree as the torque-crimp filaments, appear to contain many more crimps and more uniform crimps than single processed torque-crimp filaments. This is because the crimps have been so controlled by the second heat-setting that each turn of twist originally inserted develops into a helical crimp in post-treated yarns, whereas, in the more lively single-processed yarns, fewer crimps show, and many of these are irregular large multicrimps and convolutions.

The helical crimps in post-treated filaments, although much more uniform than the crimps visible in filaments heat-set only once, are not completely uniform throughout long lengths of filaments because the diameter of the helix of individual filaments diminishes; as the filaments near the center of the yarn during false-twisting directly affect the size, but not the number, of individual crimps.

Stated another way, the relative location of a selected filament at any given point along the length of the yarn during the initial twisting in the production of "torque stretch yarn," determines how many filaments of the multifilament yarn the selected filament spirals about. The number of filaments it spirals about, in turn, determines the amplitude or diameter of the spiral in the selected filament at the given point. For example, at one point in the yarn a selected filament may lie in the exact center of the yarn. At this point, the selected filament would not spiral about any other filaments, but would only twist on its axis, the spiral therefore having zero amplitude or diameter. At a second point, the selected filament would spiral about every other filament in the yarn and its spiral at the second point would have maximum amplitude or diameter. Normally, a selected filament will be found in various relative locations along the length of the yarn. For this reason the tendency to untwist varies in amplitude throughout the length of the selected fiber.

After the selected filament is untwisted, by passing around the twist trapper in the spindle, the tendency to crimp when relaxed varies in extent and direction throughout the filament, depending on the location of each portion of the filament in the bundle of filaments at the time of twisting.

When permitted to relax freely the filament pigtails and twists in various directions as the opposing forces adjust, forming single, double, and triple crimps, apparently a lesser number of crimps, and larger crimps than were twisted into the filament. Close examination makes the multiple crimps evident.

Subjecting the selected filament to uniform correlated heat and tensile stress activates both the latent tendency of the filament to assume a spiral formation and the opposed torsional forces, and makes the filament more pliable so as to offer less resistance to the accommodation and equalization of the opposed torque forces.

Figures 53 and 54 show the effect of post-treating on the appearance of individual filaments and yarns. The filaments shown in Fig. 53 were taken from yarn identical to the yarn from which the filaments shown in Fig. 51 were taken, except that the yarn was subsequently post-treated. Similarly the yarns shown in Fig. 54 vary from the yarns shown in Fig. 52 only by having been post-treated. The filaments and yarns shown in Figs. 51 and 52 vary greatly within very short lengths with respect to the magnitude and appearance of the crimp due to the double, triple, and quadruple crimps that form

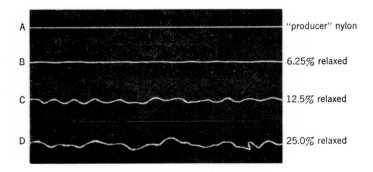

Fig. 53. Shadowgraphs of four filaments of 70-denier, 32-filament, semi-dull, type-6 nylon taken from a single pirn. Filament A is from yarn taken directly from the pirns. Filaments B, C, and D are from yarns false twisted 80 tpi on the 553 machine, relaxed to the extent indicated, and post-treated.

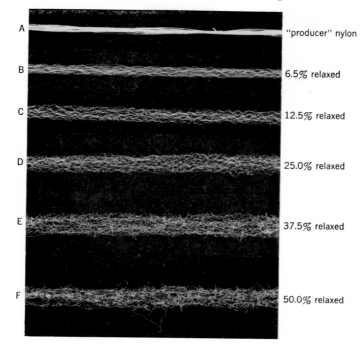

A   "producer" nylon

B   6.5% relaxed

C   12.5% relaxed

D   25.0% relaxed

E   37.5% relaxed

F   50.0% relaxed

Fig. 54. Shadowgraphs of six single strands of 70-denier, 32-filament, semi-dull, type-6 nylon taken from a single pirn. Yarn A is yarn taken directly from the pirn. Yarns B, C, D, E, and F are from yarns false twisted 80 tpi on the 553 machine, relaxed to the extent indicated, and post-treated.

when the degree of relaxation permits. The filaments and yarns shown in Figs. 53 and 54 vary much less in magnitude of crimp, and appear to contain a greater number of smaller crimps. As previously explained when the false-twisting and post-treating operations are correctly performed, each turn of twist inserted in the selected filament becomes an individual crimp. The magnitude of the crimp will vary depending on the location of the selected filament in the bundle of filaments comprising the yarn and on the per cent of relaxing or strain permitted or caused during the second time processing, the reheating and relaxing, or stretching operations.

STUFFER BOX YARN, TEXTRALIZED® YARN

Stuffer box, heat-set, thermoplastic yarns are crimped by crumpling. The filaments are impelled at a high rate of speed against an irregular, constantly changing surface formed by the previously crumpled or crimped yarn being pushed upward through the heated tube comprising the stuffer box. The individual crimps are mostly rounded like a written letter n and arced at differing angles rather than being V-shaped in a single plane as indicated in many places in the literature.

The upward impelling rollers flatten the yarn to a ribbon-like form, leaving each filament relatively free to bend or crumple as it will when it hits the mass of already crimped yarn that immediately preceded it. The surface that it impinges upon is so variable and changeable that it is ridiculous to expect the entire length of each filament to be a series of uniformly bent, reverse V's with straight unbent lengths of yarn between the zigzag, saw-toothed V's.

The crimps, averaging 55 per inch in each filament in a 70/32 nylon yarn, are durably set by passing the yarn slowly through the heated stuffing box, continuously withdrawing heat-set yarn from the stuffer box and winding it on the take-up cone. The yarn retains its bulky, very soft hand throughout the life of the garment, the crimps being sufficiently durable to withstand the heavy, intermittent pressure of the weight of a man while walking.

Though the yarns excellently withstand the intermittent pressure of walking and the steady pressure of standing, as in a man's sock, the yarns do not possess the shrinking power of torque-crimp yarns that have latent torque-crimp memory in every minute fraction of an inch of each filament. Textralized® yarns shrink only a very slight

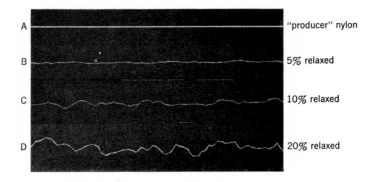

Fig. 55. Shadowgraphs of four filaments of 70-denier, 32-filament, semi-dull, type-6 nylon taken from a single pirn. Filament A is from yarn taken directly from the pirn. Filaments B, C, and D are from yarns Texturized® and relaxed to the extent indicated.

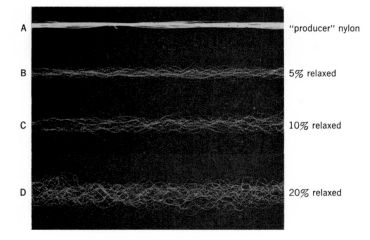

Fig. 56.   Shadowgraphs of four 70-denier, 32-filament, semi-dull, type-6 nylon yarns taken from a single pirn.   A is yarn taken directly from the pirn.   B, C, and D are yarns Texturized® and relaxed to the extent indicated.

extent when allowed to relax freely; they have relatively low resistance to longitudinally applied strain, and very little tendency to shrink when strain is removed because the resistance to strain, and latent energy in strained yarn, is found only at the bends in the yarn, these being rounded and deformed away from the parallel position at irregular intervals only.

Figures 55 and 56 show individual filaments and single strands of yarn, relaxed as indicated, taken from a cone of 70/32, type-6, semidull nylon yarn, processed through a stuffer box machine.

HEATED YARN DRAWN OVER CRIMPING EDGE, AGILON® YARN

Agilon® yarns, produced by tensioning, heating and stretching, crimping, cooling, relaxing, oiling, plying, and packaging for further processing in one continuous operation, are found by dyers to be very uniform with respect to dyeing even when dyed with dyestuffs known to accentuate dye differences between yarns and within individual strands of yarns.

As with torque-crimp yarns, Agilon® yarns require heat to release the latent crimping forces in the yarn, and the yarns can be set in varying relaxed positions by the application of heat under properly controlled conditions.

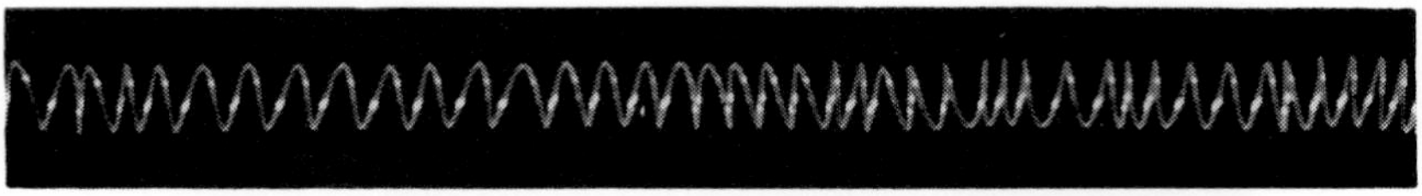

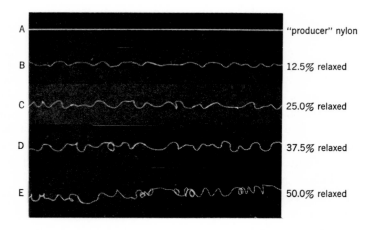

Fig. 57. A photomicrograph of 15-denier monofilament nylon, edge-crimped and relaxed.

Figure 57, a photomicrograph of a single filament of 15-denier, type-66 nylon, edge-crimped and relaxed, shows the degree of uniformity possible on the newer types of edge-crimping machines. Figures 58 and 59 show the degree of uniformity of crimping achieved in individual filaments taken from strands of 70-denier, 32-filament, type-6, semi-dull nylon, edge-crimped, and the appearance of complete strands of this yarn, relaxed as indicated.

AIR-BULKED AT ROOM TEMPERATURE—TASLAN®

The Taslan® yarns shown in Fig. 60, typical of 70-denier, 32-filament, type-6, semi-dull nylon, permitted or caused to shrink to the indicated extent during air-bulking, cannot be considered to be "typical" of all Taslan® yarns, although they are typical of air-bulked, fine denier, multifilament yarns. The Taslan® process is so versatile, applied to so many yarns, continuous and spun, and utilized in so many different ways, that no one yarn can be considered typical.

Fig. 58. Shadowgraphs of individual filaments of 70-denier, 32-filament, semi-dull, type-6 nylon, edge-crimped and relaxed as indicated.

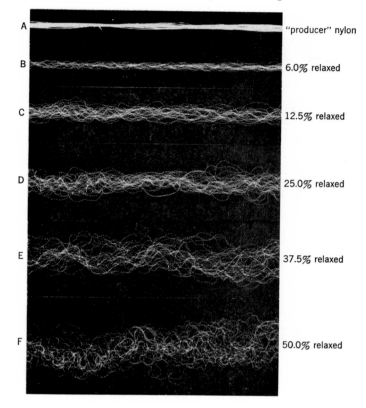

A "producer" nylon

B 6.0% relaxed

C 12.5% relaxed

D 25.0% relaxed

E 37.5% relaxed

F 50.0% relaxed

Fig. 59. Shadowgraphs of strands of 70-denier, 32-filament, semi-dull, type-6 nylon, edge-crimped and relaxed as indicated.

In this chapter we are concerned only with thermoplastic yarns suitable for weaving. The yarns shown in Fig. 60 can be considered typical of fine denier, thermoplastic yarns air-bulked for weaving as singles. More complex weaving yarns, bouclés, chenilles, nubs, and other fancy yarns are produced and improved by air-bulking.

The most noteworthy feature of air-bulked yarns, one that differentiates them from yarns textured by other processes, is the number of very fine loops that give fabrics made from these yarns their typical appearance and pleasingly crisp, dry hand.

Figure 60, shadowgraphs of 70-denier, 32-filament, type-6, semi-dull nylon overfed while air-bulked as indicated, shows the effect of various degrees of overfeed and twist on the appearance of fine denier, air-bulked yarns. Considerably more overfeed is possible, and can

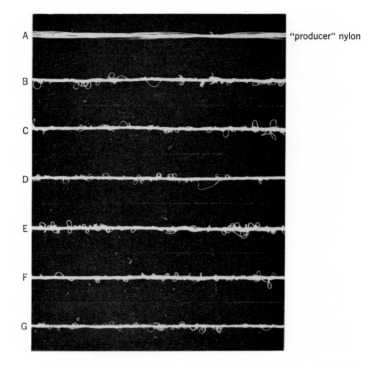

Fig. 60. Shadowgraphs of 70-denier, 32-filament, semi-dull, type-6 nylon, air-bulked. A, "Producer" nylon. B, 18% overfeed, 16 tpi, bulk 83. C, 18% overfeed, 12 tpi, bulk 83. D, 14% overfeed, 16 tpi, bulk 80. E, 14% overfeed, 12 tpi, bulk 80. F, 10% overfeed, 16 tpi, bulk 77. G, 10% overfeed, 7 tpi, bulk 77.

be used in specialized fabric constructions. The figures shown are limited to shadowgraphs of yarns considered sufficiently stabilized to weave well and produce stabilized fabrics.

We will discuss in considerable detail the comparable properties of torque crimp, torque crimp partially relaxed and reset, gear and stuffer box heat-set, hot yarn drawn over a crimping edge, and air-bulked yarn. We must compare the properties of these yarns as they have been observed in commercial production and as they are being produced at this time, rather than how they might compare if produced in improved equipment.

The variations observed from strand to strand in certain of the processes are due primarily to weaknesses or errors of machine design, or to lack of understanding of the nature of thermoplastic yarns by the machine designers, rather than to failure of the basic principles involved. This being the case, it is reasonable to anticipate that in the future, possibly the very near future, improved equipment will be designed and built around the principles of the processes that lack necessary uniformity at this time. Thus what we are presenting in the following pages must be accepted as the situation existing currently, because of the nature of present-day machines, rather than to any criticism of the principles around which these machines and processes have been built.

Torque-crimp yarns produced on false-twist equipment kept in good operating condition are exceedingly uniform from end to end of individual packages, and from package to package, because the machines are designed to permit temperature to be controlled within amazingly close tolerances and, particularly in the newer machines, tensions can be controlled equally well. Ample evidence exists that yarns properly processed through false-twist equipment maintained in good condition are more uniform than the commercial yarns used as starting materials, because the equipment permits differences in strain caused by uneven application of drawing oil components, and other unavoidable variations due to limitations of existing drawing machines, to level out during the pass through the hot zone.

On the other side of the fence we have stuffer box yarns that should be very uniform, and are uniform with respect to crimp, but lack uniformity from the viewpoint of dye affinity. This happens because the major portion of the installed equipment used to process fine denier yarns applies heat through the medium of a heated metallic tube, which is contacted by some of the yarn as it passes through the tube, whereas other portions of the stuffed yarn are contacted only by adjoining yarns and heated air. Obviously the specific heat of metal is much greater than the specific heat of air, thus the amount of energy available to the yarn contacting the metal is greater than the energy available to the yarn contacted by hot air only, resulting in differences in dye affinity that have caused and continue to cause serious defects in hot stuffer box yarns. This is correctable by redesigning equipment, the needed corrections being known to many people working in the field. Until business conditions force a change, all involved are loath to discard the apparent capital value of the existing operating equipment. Use of multi-plies of yarns and the most level dyeing dyestuffs available have minimized this problem, particularly where light fastness is not a problem and where the use of multi-end ply yarns is feasible. The particular variable property of this type of yarn, uneven dyeing, has in large part been negated by the unusually fine quality control and promotional program that has created and maintained the demand for the yarns even though inherent dye variations continue to constitute a major problem.

Early production of heated thermoplastic yarn drawn over a crimping edge was very difficult to dye because of variations from strand to strand owing to the inadequacies of the early machines. The new, very well engineered equipment heats, tensions, crimps, cools, and relaxes the yarn with such precision that dyers claim, and believe, it dyes more uniformly than the producer yarn from which it is made. This new equipment produces not only more uniform yarn, but also softer yarns than heretofore, and at costs well below the cost of producing multiple ply, textured yarns by any other process.

The process of air-bulking multifilament yarns with turbulent air is intriguing because air of itself has no cost and the process would appear to involve a minimum of moving parts. Undoubtedly the principle is good; however, the first equipment utilized was not good. It lacked the necessary controls to enable the production of completely uniform yarns from strand to strand of even one multi-end machine. In addition, the zero-cost air proved to be very costly in terms of power alone when compressed and released. Variations from strand to strand caused by lack of control of the yarn, a function of machine design, produced visible bulk yarn differences and serious dye variations that delayed growth of the process in the weaving field. Some initial success was achieved in a fabric that did not have to be dyed—men's white shirts. Hundreds of samples of fabrics woven from air-bulked yarns, many unique in styling and excellent in appearance and hand, have been produced and shown. Until recently little commercial success was achieved in fine denier woven fabrics because of texture and color variations in the finished fabrics. The improved equipment now available should radically change this situation and cause many of the different and excellent samples already developed to be manufactured in commercial quantities, merchandised, and sold. Designers and merchandisers of blouse and dress fabrics should re-evaluate Taslan® yarn in the light of today's excellent air-bulking equipment, and the very uniform yarns produced by these machines.

A detailed check with manufacturers of textured yarns indicates that well in excess of 70 per cent of all textured yarns woven prior to December 1962 have been textured by torque-crimp processes, and present indications are that this percentage will continue to be maintained. This is a very real tribute to the merit inherent in torque-crimp textured yarns, since woven fabrics based on the texture, stretch, and recovery properties of these yarns have grown steadily in popularity despite the lack of promotional campaigns, and despite the lack of control of the quantity and quality of the merchandise produced from the yarns.

To review, Fig. 48 shows photomicrographs of 70/32, type-6, semi-dull nylon textured by each of the five texturing processes that have become commercially important.

With the exception of air-bulked yarn, Taslan®, the yarns appear surprisingly similar in appearance and bulk. This apparent similarity is deceptive because, as shown in Fig. 47, the filaments differ substantially from process to process in type and number of crimps. Most important, and not visible, is the latent energy built into the yarns by the crimping operations that control the behavior of the yarns during relaxing in fabric form, this in turn controlling the hand and appearance of fabrics made therefrom.

Comparisons are especially difficult because the type of fabrics knitted and woven, and the equipment in and through which the fabric must be processed during dyeing and finishing, are such that yarns produced by different processes can produce similar-appearing fabrics under some conditions and totally dissimilar fabrics under other conditions.

When knit into men's and children's hose, post-treated torque-crimp yarns, Textralized® yarns, and Agilon® yarns produce stockings surprisingly similar in hand and appearance. (When *stretch* hose are desired most knitters use torque-crimp yarns *not* post-treated.)

In the weaving field torque-crimp yarns not post-treated are the most popular when maximum possible amount of stretch is required. It is anticipated that the greater versatility, cover, and softness of thermoplastic yarn torque-crimped and post-treated will lead to their widespread usage as development work continues in the weaving field.

It is difficult to compare air-bulked yarns, Taslan® yarns, with other textured yarns because the air-bulking process of texturing yarns produces such a wide variety of textured yarns that it is practically impossible to describe them generically, other than to use the term that describes their manufacture—air-bulked.

In summation: for the maximum stretch, torque crimp; for maximum softness, torque crimp post-treated, stuffer box and edge-crimped; for bulk with stability and crispness and for a multitude of bouclé, chenille, novelty, and nub effects—air-bulked.

Effect of Chemical Constitution on Crimp Memory of Crimped Thermoplastic Yarns

Type-66 nylon, the first so-called synthetic yarn, as differentiated from regenerated cellulose and cellulose derivatives, was, naturally, the first synthetic yarn to be durably crimped and sold as a durably crimped yarn for use in fabrics based on the benefits derived from durable crimps. Although exact figures are not readily available, it is probable that well over 60 per cent of the entire production of synthetic yarns durably crimped to date have been type-66 nylon.

Type-6 nylon, polyester yarns, polypropylene yarns, and other "synthetic" yarns have been successfuly durably crimped. Triacetate, cellulose acetate, and resin-modified, cross-linked, cellulose yarns have also been durably crimped to various degrees. In this chapter we will first consider the yarns that have been durably crimped and used in substantial quantities. We will compare type-66 nylon with type-6 nylon, polyester, and polypropylene yarns durably crimped by the false-twist, torque-crimp process because well over 70 per cent of all synthetic yarns textured to date have been textured by the torque-crimp process.

Factual numerical comparisons of the durability of torque crimps inserted in the various synthetic yarns cannot be presented at this time because of the lack of recognized tests tied in with actual utilization of the yarns. That they are truly durable cannot be questioned. Manufacturers advertise men's half-hose made from false-twist, torque-crimp nylon claiming that the stockings will last five years, and it has been proven that these claims are correct.

Such evidence as is available indicates that there are no significant differences between the durability and magnitude of the torque-crimp power of type-6 and type-66 nylon, provided that both are processed in the best possible manner for each. There does exist at this time an unresolved question regarding the two yarns and this has to do with required time in the heated zone. Some people active in the field believe that it is necessary to provide an increased time increment when type-6 nylon is processed to compensate for the lower maximum temperature that must be used. This of course is because the melting point of type 6 is substantially below the melting point of type 66. Other workers contend that the claimed need for differences in minimum dwell time is not factual and that future work will prove that type 6 can be processed as rapidly as type 66 when optimum processing conditions are utilized. Be this as it may, it is possible to speak of type-66 nylon as an entity regardless of the specific manufacturer, and it is possible to consider type 6 as different from type 66 but essentially one entity, regardless of the manufacturer because the processing has become very well standardized. Regardless of which manufacturer produces the yarn, and which throwster processes it, torque-crimp memory can be set as durably in type-6 nylon as in type-66, and in both yarns *durable* means years.

Whereas type-66 and type-6 nylons vary from type to type but not from producer to producer in their inherent properties insofar as retention of durable torque crimp is concerned, the same cannot be said for polyester and polypropylene yarns, presumably because, with one exception (Dacron® polyester yarn) polyester and polypropylene yarn manufacture is new and the raw materials and processes vary.

Most dyers who have been called upon to process polyester fabrics from the same manufacturer (Dacron® yarn excepted) at different times and from different manufacturers are convinced that the reaction of polyester fibers to heat varies substantially from producer to producer and in certain instances has varied from time to time from individual producers, causing considerable confusion and trouble in dye plants processing these fibers.

Polyester fibers as a group must be torque-crimped quite differently from nylon in that it is advisable to use more tension in the heated zone, and it is very desirable that the fiber shall be taken up soft on the take-up package. This is accomplished by placing a rotating, positive tension device between the twist trap in the spindle and the take-up package, overfeeding three or more per cent to the take-up package.

When polyester yarns are crimped in the best possible manner, by applying more tension in the heated zone than when nylon is processed, and overfeeding to the take-up, the crimp in the yarn on the take-up package is still not completely durable. Application of slow, steady strain to the yarns will remove all traces of torque-crimp memory and leave in its place straight rod-like filaments. Fortunately yarn, as found on the take-up package when processed into cloth then relaxed or wet-processed with the aid of the various chemicals sold as dye carriers, will regain or increase its memory. When dyed and dried fabrics containing these yarns are heat-set, the memory of the yarn in the finished fabric is as durable as is necessary to last the life of the garment. It is to be regretted that detailed comparisons with nylon regarding permanency of the crimp have not been made or, if they have been made by producers, the facts have not been made known to the purchasers of the yarn.

Regardless of how the ultimate durability of torque-crimp polyester yarns compares with the ultimate durability of torque-crimp nylon yarns, there is no question that the durability is as great as it needs to be and that added durability would not serve any useful purpose.

It is generally recognized that fabrics made from polyester yarns have much greater resilience and resistance to wrinkling than fabrics made from nylon yarns. Some people, active in torque-crimp work, believe that by proper utilization of the controls available in the newest false-twist equipment (Leesona's 553), and by proper utilization of fabric design and dyeing and finishing techniques, an essentially wrinkle-proof nylon fabric could be produced that would be the full equivalent of polyester fabric. Some progressive blouse or dress manufacturer will one day take advantage of this newly developed possibility and market such fabrics, presumably working with a producer of nylon in merchandising the new fabric.

Polypropylene yarns vary even more from producer to producer than do polyester yarns. And as new plants now under construction come into production it is anticipated that the extent of the differences will be increased even more from extreme to extreme.

The average polypropylene yarn is intermediate between nylon and polyester in its ability to accept and retain durable crimp at the time of crimp application. As with polyester the durability can be increased by subsequent treatments, "carriers" or swelling agents during wet processing, and heat treatments before or after dyeing or both.

Polypropylene differs from all other yarns that have been torque-crimped to date in that it requires a substantially longer time in the heated zone than either polyester or nylon. It has been suggested that this is due to the differences in specific gravity between polypropylene and nylon and polyester fibers (nylon 1.14, polyester 1.38, polypropylene 0.92–0.96). This difference, important as it is in providing greater covering power for polypropylene and, apparent lightness in polypropylene fabrics, owing to increased thickness, is scarcely great enough to account for the increased dwell time in the heated zone required by polypropylene. Despite the great difference in specific gravity, the increase in diameter of polypropylene filaments over filaments of nylon is less than 10 per cent, and the increase over polyester is only 23 per cent. The additional dwell time found necessary for polypropylene is much more than these percentages. Regardless of the reason, it is true that polypropylene must remain for substantially longer periods of time in the hot zone than either nylon or polyester fibers in order to produce comparable durable torque crimp.

Similarly, as with polyester, polypropylene should be taken up slack on the take-up package. It should be overfed to the take-up a full 5 per cent by a nip roll or similar tension control device between the twist trap on the spindle and the take-up.

In the opinion of many who are well experienced in determining the degree of softness of fabrics, both polyester and polypropylene, properly processed into fabrics utilizing torque-crimped yarns, produce softer, fuller fabrics than directly comparable fabrics made from nylon yarns. Polyester and polypropylene false-twisted, woven into cloth, and properly dyed and finished, produce fabrics exhibiting much more covering power and apparent bulk than nylon. Polypropylene is far superior to polyester in this respect.

All four yarns, type-66 nylon, type-6 nylon, polyester, and polypropylene, possess a very high degree of durable crimp when properly processed from raw yarn to dyed and finished fabrics, and all possess crimp of sufficient durability to last throughout the useful life of the garment.

Triacetate (Arnel®) yarn has torque-crimp memory comparable to nylon and produces fabrics much softer with respect to hand than nylon, polyester, or polypropylene. All that is required to popularize these fabrics is a promotional campaign properly presenting the fabrics to the buyers of garments and to retail outlets.

Cellulose acetate appears to accept false twist, and does accept it to a degree. Unfortunately the plastic flow of cellulose acetate is such that it gradually loses its memory as torque-crimped garments made from this yarn are worn, washed, and dry-cleaned. The marketing situation being what it is, there is little likelihood of a manufacturer of cellulose acetate yarns being willing to put substantial merchandising effort behind a specialty application of cellulose acetate, and this limits the attraction of this field for the limited number of dedicated workers available. It is entirely possible that modifications in technique could result in sufficiently stretching these yarns to pull out the plastic flow, or that chemical treatments could augment the torque-crimp memory of fabrics made from these yarns, or that other processing could increase the memory to such a point that excellent garments utilizing torque-crimp memory in cellulose acetate might become possible. As pointed out earlier, the incentive is lacking at the moment.

Cotton and rayon yarns, resin-treated, twisted, heat-set, and untwisted, woven, relaxed, and dyed and finished, result in fabrics showing very interesting properties when compared with fabrics utilizing the durable torque-crimp memory of thermoplastic yarns. Incentive exists in this field, particularly the incentive supplied by the United States Department of Agriculture, which has adequate funds available to explore new avenues of outlets for cotton and means of conserving current markets for cotton. Cotton mills have a similar incentive—the desire to continue to maintain their markets in the face of the increasing threat of approaching lower prices of the synthetic yarns. It is impractical to attempt to make a direct comparison at this time because the total amount of work done in this cotton and rayon (combined with resin) field is so much less than the work over the last several years in the torque-crimp, synthetic yarn field that comparisons would be unfair.

All that can be said with certainty is that equipment has been designed and built in experimental quantities that is capable of flash curing and cross-linking resin-treated cotton while it is false-twisted at a high rate of through-put. Cotton yarns resin-treated, false-twisted, and cross-linked on this experimental equipment have been found to have excellent stretch and recovery properties, excellent bulk, and resilience and softness as desired. All that is required to move this development from its present state to commercial practicability is time, proper research brains, lots of money, and good merchandising talent—a grouping difficult to acquire.

8

Design of Woven Stretch Fabrics

Woven stretch fabrics are so new that most of the interrelated factors affecting stretch properties are still in the developing art state. And even those factors that may appear to have reached a relatively stable condition are subject to change because of constantly improving techniques. We are dealing with a surprisingly large number of variable factors, knowledge of each of which is in such an undeveloped state that most of them are necessarily dealt with as arts, rather than sciences. For this reason, we are unwilling and unable to postulate formulae for the guidance of those desirous of designing new and improved woven stretch fabrics.

We will discuss briefly in this chapter, and in greater detail in other parts of this book, each of the many factors affecting the degree of stretch and recovery that may be anticipated by designers active or desiring to become active in this field.

We will start with the factors that must be taken into account in designing only *one* of the many types of stretch fabrics, fabrics consisting of *cotton warps filled with torque-crimp thermoplastic nylon*.

Following this we will discuss the additional factors arising from the use of other yarns and constructions, and will discuss each in relation to its effect on stretch and recovery within the limitations of the current state of the art. The field is very new and rapidly expanding in many directions. The extent to which each can grow can only be a matter of conjecture at this time. Certain branches of the art, for example, twisting, cross-linking, resin-treating, untwisting cotton and rayon fibers to produce latent crimp memory, and utilization of the new aging, washing, and dry cleaning resistant polyurethane stretch yarns are so new that for all practical purposes even an art has not yet been developed.

Factors Affecting Stretch and Recovery of Cotton Warp,
Torque-Crimp Stretch Filled, Woven Stretch Fabric

NYLON FILLING YARN

Type Nylon—66 or 6. In the United States the bulk of stretch
nylon has been produced from type-66 nylon, undoubtedly because
the bulk of the production here is type-66 nylon. In Europe the
reverse is true; the greater part of all nylon produced is type 6. This
has led to development of techniques in processing type 6 that have
produced stretch yarns that are the full equivalent of those produced
from type-66 nylon in the United States.

This would seem to indicate that the type of nylon is important
only in relation to the know how of the throwster processing it. The
combined factor of type nylon and throwster know how must be
taken into account by those designing woven stretch nylon fabrics.

Specific Manufacturer of Nylon. Equal in importance to the type of
nylon used is the manufacturer because differences in raw materials,
equipment, and techniques can produce variations in the properties of
the resultant nylon that in turn affect the manner in which the nylon
responds to the equipment and techniques employed by the throwster.

Spin Finish. There is ample evidence that variations in spin finish
substantially affect the manner in which the finished nylon responds
to false twist. Special spin finishes have been developed that improve false-twist results. Over the past few years several changes
have been made in spin finishes, and there is no reason to suppose
that similar changes will not be made in the future. Thus, changes
in the response of yarns from a specific producer to specific false-
twist techniques can be anticipated and must be taken into account
by the designer and others active in the field, who of course make it
their business to remain in touch with this and other factors affecting
the final results of the fabrics they work with.

Denier. Depending on the weave employed, the count, type, and
size of the cotton yarn used in the warp, the denier of thermoplastic
nylon woven as filling may vary from 2-ply 30's through single 70's,
2-ply 70's, 4-ply 70's, and up to multiple 200's (the latter of course for
upholstery fabrics).

Although denier is an important factor in determining stretch it
should not be assumed that denier and stretch and recovery are directly proportional. They are not. For example a 140-denier, 64-

filament, semi-dull nylon yarn is approximately equal in denier to a 2-ply, 70-denier, 32-filament, semi-dull nylon; yet, if both are processed correctly, the 70-denier, 2-ply, 32-filament, semi-dull nylon will have considerably more stretch and recovery than the 140-denier yarn. This is because denier directly affects the amount of energy that can be put into a yarn by twisting, and thus the latent crimp energy that can be retained by the yarn after heat setting. The optimum twist that can be used in processing 140-denier nylon is 65 tpi, whereas 78 tpi can be used in twisting 70-denier nylon, and *two* ends of the 70-denier yarn must be so twisted for the ply, resulting in 156 turns of twist being inserted in 2-ply, 70-denier, 32-filament, semi-dull nylon, versus 65 turns of twist inserted in the 140-denier, 64-filament, semi-dull nylon. Also, in the 70-denier yarn the helix is smaller in diameter, assuring more retained latent crimp energy per denier.

Other factors being equal, increased denier assures increased torque-crimp energy in thermoplastic yarns and may provide increased stretch and recovery in fabrics, but not always, and not to the extent that might be anticipated because of the effect of other factors. As yarn denier increases retained torque energy increases, but not in direct proportion, because of the effect of the increase diameter of the helix. As yarn denier increases twist per inch decreases, and picks per inch in fabric must be decreased to provide room for the picks and room for the yarn to shrink, both factors reducing the degree of increased stretch and recovery that might otherwise be anticipated.

As explained earlier, use of multiple ends in ply yarns increases stretch and recovery. Unfortunately use of multiple ends of fine denier yarns also increases cost—more expensive yarns, more twist, and extra ply cost.

Diameter of Filaments. Stretch and recovery increase in direct proportion to the diameter of filaments in a yarn of given denier. An oversimplified but valid explanation of the reason coarse filaments retain more torque-crimp energy than finer filaments is readily apparent—more energy is required to deform a coarse filament than a fine filament, thus more latent energy can remain in the filament after it is heat-set in the deformed or strained position.

If stretch and recovery were the only factors to be considered, only coarse filaments would be used. Such is not the case. The purchasing public has learned that woven stretch nylon fabric can be soft, full, and drapy, and has indicated its preference for this type of hand. For this reason it is often necessary for the designer to choose finer filament yarns than he otherwise would employ, obtaining the desired stretch by design of fabric. This often includes use of a larger quantity of expensive stretch nylon than would otherwise be found necessary.

Luster. Of itself luster does not affect stretch and recovery. Because it involves the addition of extra ingredients and blending techniques, either of which may modify the nylon itself before or during spinning, semi-dull nylon retains slightly less latent torque-crimp energy than does bright nylon, and dull nylon a little less than semi-dull.

In most constructions this is of academic interest only, as stretch fabrics of semi-dull yarn are preferred by the majority of all who are active in the field.

Ply Twist and Post Twist. The most controversial subjects in the woven stretch field are the subjects of ply twist and post twist, the need of ply twist, the need of post twist, and the effects and value of each. As stated in the definitions in Chapter 1:

PLY TWIST is twist inserted in a number of ends simultaneously.

POST TWIST is twist inserted in single ends of false-twist yarn.

In both instances the definitions are correct, but neither explains the reasons for, nor the results of, plying and post-twisting.

Designers and manufacturers direct that false-twist yarns be plied, for a number of reasons, one of which appears to be habit. Prior to the existence of false-twist, torque-crimp thermoplastic yarns, when two ends were to be woven together they were plied to assure that they would function as a unit during quilling and weaving, and to prevent friction from causing loops and tight spots at that time. For this reason, to assure better running qualities, torque-crimp thermoplastic yarns made by the false-twist process were automatically plied when they were to be used as a unit, and this practice currently continues in most instances for a number of reasons.

In England, where nylon is more expensive than in the United States, and where throwsters charge much more for false-twisting nylon than they do in the United States, manufacturers experimented with eliminating the expensive plying operation, and found that under some circumstances it could be eliminated. The reason that the plying operation can be eliminated in many instances when torque-crimp yarns are processed is readily evident when two such yarns are placed very close together and relaxed slightly. Both open up and entangle and in effect become one yarn. Thus the danger of tight and loose single ends is greatly reduced.

The technique of running two parallel ends of torque-crimp yarn has not yet been experimented with or utilized to any great extent in the United States. It is anticipated by many that in the near future, as increasing poundages of nylon yarns false-twisted on Leesona's 553 machines are woven, manufacturers will utilize the economies that can be effected by winding parallel ends of S and Z, or two ends of S or two ends of Z twist on a single package, then quilling and weaving directly from this, using Leesona's Unifil loom winder. Both machines have been engineered to permit weavers to realize the savings and improvement in quality made possible by thus eliminating the doubling and coning operations.

In many constructions ply twist must be used to compact the yarn, reducing the tendency of the yarns to pick and pill. Another reason for ply twisting torque-crimp yarns to be woven is that when the yarns are twisted in such a direction that the torque of the yarn is increased, in other words when twist is applied against the torque, the result is an increase in total torque that increases the stretch and recovery properties of fabrics into which they are woven. All of the energy put into the yarn by this true twist remains in the yarn, whereas only part of the energy imparted during false twisting can remain in the yarn, some being lost by plastic flow during the heat-setting operation. For this reason 3, 4, or 5 turns of ply twist produce much more stretch than would utilization of 3, 4, or 5 more additional turns during the false-twist operation. The upper limit of ply twisting that can be so used is the maximum quantity that will permit the yarns to weave without kinking and without other defects usually associated with lively yarns.

It is anticipated that when plying is found necessary in thermoplastic yarns to be woven the doubling step will be eliminated, and large knotless packages will be prepared economically for sequence weaving, by transferring the take-up package from the 553 false twister to the 2 for 1 doubler coner, then to the Unifil Loom Winder.

COTTON YARN IN WARP

Carded Cotton Warp Yarn vs. Combed Cotton Warp Yarn. Though generalizations are dangerous and can lead to errors and misunderstandings, it is nevertheless true that in most instances the type of cotton yarn used in the warp of cotton warp, stretch filled fabrics is very important, primarily because of the differences in diameter and resiliency of carded and combed yarns.

Carded yarns tend to be bulkier and softer than similar counts of combed yarns, and offer a steadily increasing resistance to the shrinking force of the torque-crimp nylon filling, resulting in more of the shrinking force being expended in drawing the warp yarns closely together, thus causing the fully relaxed fabric to be wider than when combed yarns are used.

Cotton Yarn Count. Harold Clarence de Witte Smith, in the mid-1930's, expounded his theory that, other factors being equal, the rigidity of textile yarns increases as the cube of the radius. The absolute accuracy of their theory may be open to argument, but the principle is not. Textile yarn rigidity does increase very rapidly with increases in radius or diameter. Thus, as increasingly coarser yarns are used in the warp of cotton warp, stretch nylon filled fabrics tend to become more and more "lazy" and less and less resilient, even though the ends are reduced. The use of more floats in the construction and of more expensive filling yarns containing more latent torque-crimping power is required to produce stretch fabrics possessing enough stretch and recovery to warrant their initial and repeat sales.

Importance of Twist Factor of Cotton Warp Yarns. Most cotton warp, stretch nylon filled fabrics designed and woven to date have been woven in standard cotton warps in which the twist has been standard warp twist. There are many reasons for this, the most important one being that the warps existed. To start from scratch and prepare two or more warps utilizing increasingly higher twist factors would cause delay and expense, both of which are to be avoided as the plague by weavers, particularly cotton weavers. Despite the loss of time and the unavoidable expense incurred, it is probable that fruitful work would already have been done in this field if the designers, who are well-experienced in cotton weaving but lack similar experience in stretch nylon utilization, appreciated the extent to which it appears that higher warp twists should increase resiliency and stretch and recovery of cotton warp, stretch filled fabrics.

Actually, since the Leesona Corporation withdrew its support of the program that brought stretch fabric into being, there has been no central guidance of a fabric development program and no clearing house for knowledge and ideas. Woven stretch fabrics have just muddled along, and have achieved their current position because the purchasing public has recognized their merit even though many of the fabrics sold to date have been far inferior to fabrics that would have been designed, woven, and finished had a planned program of fabric development and merchandising been available.

To achieve maximum resilience and stretch and recovery designers should utilize warp twists higher than those used to date, the upper limits being yarns too lively to weave well and yarns twisted to such an extent that strength loss or visible variations in the warp yarns become serious factors.

High warp twist compacts cotton warp yarns and permits more of the latent crimping power in the stretch nylon filling yarns to achieve its objective—to produce more stretch and recovery.

Cotton Warp Size in Relation to Stretch and Recovery. Cotton warp, nylon stretch filled fabrics manufactured so far have been mercerized, bleached, and boiled-off utilizing techniques designed to remove as much of the resistance of the warp size as possible while the fabric remains cold. These techniques then continue to remove the remaining resistance at the lowest possible temperature to conserve as much as possible of the shrinking power of the torque-crimp nylon filling yarn until the resistance due to warp size becomes negligible.

Use of a more expensive, cold water soluble, or cold water plus chemical soluble, warp size would make possible utilization of boil-off techniques in finishing plants that would improve the stretch and recovery properties of the finished fabric to a very pronounced degree. It is to be anticipated that some cotton mill will perform the necessary research in this field and that competitive plants will then be forced to follow suit.

THROWING CONDITIONS

Type of Equipment Used by Throwsters. False-twisting equipment varies from type of machine to type of machine with respect to speed, dwell time in the heated zone, kind of heater, mode of applying tension or overfeed, efficiency of tension or overfeed and twist trapper at the input side of the spindle, design and efficiency of the twist trapper in the spindle, means of applying tension at the delivery side of the spindle, type of take-up at the delivery package, and efficiency of the overfeed device just prior to the take-up package when present. Each variable has a definite effect on the physical properties of thermoplastic yarns false-twisted modifying the yarns in degree and permanency of stretch and recovery, rate of dyeing, tensile, elongation, and in other ways.

Temperature in Heated Zone.   One of the most critical factors in producing uniformly crimped thermoplastic yarn by the false-twist process is control of temperature in the heated zone. A study of installed equipment and the patent literature shows the importance attached to control of temperature by inventors, machine designers, and manufacturers active in the false-twist field. All attempt to control temperature within narrow limits, $\frac{1}{2}$ to 2 degrees, and some recognize the importance of relating ambient temperature to the temperature of the heated zone. Even minute variations in the temperature of the hot zone affect strength, elongation, crimp memory, dye index, and other characteristics of torque-crimped thermoplastic yarns. Fortunately manufacturers of the commercially important false-twist machines have installed good reliable heat controls and adequate means of checking and modifying temperature when necessary.

Dwell Time in Heated Zone.   The purpose of applying heat to twisted thermoplastic yarns is to set the twist. It is therefore necessary that the twisted yarns remain in the heated zone long enough for the heat to penetrate to the center of each filament and long enough to effectively set the twist. For this reason, as the speeds of false-twisting machines have been increased, heaters have been lengthened.

Differences of opinion exist about the length of time twisted thermoplastic yarns must remain in the heated zone, and the evidence appears to be quite contradictory when examined casually. It is probable that the reason for the conflicting opinions and apparent conflict of evidence is a lack of understanding of the close relationship between tension and temperature during the heat-setting process.

Unset or very poorly set nylon yarn can be detected readily by applying slow steady tension to the yarn noting its behavior just before the break. If the crimp can be pulled out the yarn is incompletely set.

Tension in the Heated Zone.   Yarns must be tensioned to prevent slippage of twist at the spindle twist trapper. Even overfed yarns are tensioned:— by the contractile or shrinking force released by heat. As tension is increased the stretch and recovery properties of the false-twisted yarn increase. Cover or fullness may be decreased. Tension in the hot zone modifies the denier, decreasing shrinkage in overfed yarns, decreasing denier when sufficient tension is applied.

Tenacity is reduced, this limiting the amount of tension that can be utilized.

Type of Heating Mechanism, Contact, Radiant, or Combination. It is generally conceded that contact heating sets twist slightly better than radiant heating, sets the filaments on the outside of the yarn more thoroughly than filaments on the inside, and, by overheating, discolors the outside filaments slightly. It is also conceded that radiant heating sets the filaments more uniformly throughout and produces a whiter yarn by avoiding the slight yellowing caused by overheating on the contact heater.

The terms contact and radiant are erroneous to a degree when applied to yarns set on the machines that comprise the bulk of the installed false-twisting equipment because contact heaters also heat by radiation (filaments in the center of the yarn cannot contact the heater), and under certain conditions twisted yarns may contact the surface of heaters defined and sold as radiant heaters.

Types of Twist Trapper. Twist trappers in installed and operating false-twist machines, both in the spindle and between the producer yarn package and the spindle, vary greatly in type, size, and efficiency of twist trapping. The initial twist trappers vary from a gate tension, twist trapper device that permits yarn to slip one way, toward the spindle as demanded by the heated zone: through rolling tension, twist trappers that, while effective as twist trappers, permit some slippage of yarn; to rolling tension, twist trapper devices that are also effective as tension controlling devices.

Twist trappers in the spindle vary from wheels that may turn or remain partially stationary, depending on speed and tension employed, to pins that are quite efficient twist trappers in some instances and permit considerable slippage in other instances depending on the yarns, twists, speeds, and tensions involved.

Slippage at the spindle twist trapper constitutes good practice when it is uniform, produces good quality false-twisted yarns, and permits the through-put of yarns to be higher than would otherwise be possible. Variable slippage at the twist trapper, when permitted, causes variations in stretch and recovery, strength, elongation, dye index, and other troubles leading to the eventual production of inferior merchandise when yarns produced in this manner are woven into fabrics.

Turns of Twist. As pointed out under the heading "Types of Twist Trapper," turns of twist imparted to the yarn are not always identical with the turns that theoretically should be imparted by calculating twist from spindle speeds and yarn speeds.

The turns per inch have a very great effect on the stretch and recovery of the resultant yarn and an even more pronounced effect on the surface interest of the fabric when it is woven in constructions that permit the release of latent torque crimp under controlled conditions to produce surface interest. It is absolutely essential that the same number of turns of twist are inserted in and removed from false-twist yarns to be used in weaving.

Seventy-denier, 17-filament nylon is usually false-twisted 75 to 78 turns for weaving when the objective is to produce the maximum attainable amount of stretch and recovery. New and novel results in woven fabric constructions can be produced by varying the turns of twist appreciably from the relatively standard 75 to 78 turns. It is probable that as the art progresses and knowledge of and markets for woven false-twist fabrics grow, designers will add this tool to their repertoire.

The optimum number of turns of false twist necessary to produce maximum stretch and recovery in nylon yarns of various deniers, filament counts, lusters, etc., have been determined by various throwsters who are prepared and willing to furnish such yarns to the weaving industry.

Post Twist, If Used. At the outset, when thermoplastic yarns containing latent torque crimp were made by the conventional or Helanca® process, it was relatively easy to produce a balanced plied yarn containing S and Z latent torque-crimp yarns.

For example, a 2-ply balanced yarn can be produced on conventional equipment as follows:

1. Twist one yarn 92 turns Z, set the twist, redraw and back twist so as to leave 12 turns Z in the yarn.
2. Twist another yarn 68 turns S, set the twist, redraw and back twist so as to leave 12 turns Z in the yarn.
3. Double 1 and 2.
4. Ply twist 12 turns S.

To produce a similarly balanced, false-twist yarn the procedure would be to produce a Z torque yarn with 80 turns false twist and an S torque yarn with 80 turns false twist, then redraw and single-end twist each 12Z, double, and ply turn 12S.

Throwsters make this type of post-twisted yarn in small quantities on order, but would be unable, currently, to produce really large poundages on existing equipment because of the scarcity of installed uptwisters in throwsters' hands.

Use of post-twisted yarns should be avoided when possible because each handling or processing of the yarn is an added potential source of trouble. The uptwister, at best, builds unevenness into yarns because of tension differences between full and steadily emptying bobbins during uptwisting, and because most uptwisters now available are not as precisely built as the most recent false-twist machines.

Leading throwsters, working closely with their customers, have found that results equaling or bettering the best that can be done by post-twisting can be obtained by plying two ends, one S and one Z, torque. Depending on customer choice they ply $2\frac{1}{2}$ to 5 turns in an S direction to assure better running qualities from the quill during weaving for filling stretch. For warp stretch the twist choice might be 5 to 12 turns S.

Conventional and false-twist yarns can be made with single ends of the same torque to produce post-twisted yarns known as unbalanced plied yarns, which produce results different from balanced yarns, necessary to achieve results required in certain fabrics.

Tension at Take-up Package. Fluflon® and Superloft®, slow and high speed machines, were designed and built to provide tension between the twist trapper in the spindle and the take-up package, producing hard wound bobbins of false-twisted nylon. Fortunately the memory of false-twisted nylon tightly wound on large ironheads is excellent.

Polyester and polypropylene yarns gradually lose their memory when tightly wound on ironheads. These yarns are greatly benefited by overfeeding 3 or more per cent to the take-up package. This is accomplished by providing positively driven feed rolls between the spindle and the take-up package, the surface speed of the feed rolls being faster than the surface speed of the take-up rolls. This type of mechanism is provided on the newer types of false-twist machines, of which Leesona's 553 is a good example.

QUILLING AND WEAVING

Tension and Uniformity of Quilling. One of the many critical areas in the production of uniformly woven stretch fabrics is tension, uniformity of tension, and general uniformity of quilling.

Fortunately the nature of false-twisted thermoplastic yarn is such that they tend to open, making possible the utilization of quilling tensions much lower than is possible when low or high conventional twisted nylons are quilled. False-twisted yarns open slightly, holding the yarn in place on the quill and preventing sluffing off when necessarily low quilling tensions are used.

It has been successfully demonstrated that stretch nylon is most uniformly quilled on the Unifil Loom Winder and that use of this machine is very helpful in minimizing the effect of such minor variations as may exist from package to package of stretch yarn. Their operation is such that quills are woven within a few minutes of the time they are quilled, before variations from quill to quill have been magnified by standing. When stretch nylon is quilled on multi-spindle quilling machines and allowed to stand a number of hours, variations in firmness, not noticeable when the yarns are quilled, become serious. Some quills soften on standing causing readily apparent visible variations in finished fabrics.

Another important advantage is that though there will inevitably be differences in yarn and tensions from unit to unit, these variations will not cause variations within individual cuts as each cut is filled with yarn quilled on the same unit. If a quilling tension gets out of adjustment or a bad package of filling yarn is encountered, although it can produce many yards of faulty cloth in one cut the problems will be confined to one cut and not spread over the entire production of a mill. This alone warrants use of the Unifil Loom Winder when woven stretch filled fabrics are to be produced.

Because of sequence weaving, and because the Unifil Loom Winder quills faster than the loom can weave, there is no need of or advantage to be gained by winding more yarn on a quill than can be woven to best advantage. The quiller should be so set that the taper is as long as 1½ inches. This produces a small quill and a quill that varies less in tension from beginning to end than is the case when shorter tapers and larger diameter quills are woven.

The tension of quilling, measured as near as is practical to the actual quilling itself, should be 10 to 12 grams for 2-ply, 70-denier stretch yarn, and slightly higher for heavier deniers. Quills wound with this light tension appear to be too soft to be woven, particularly to cotton men unfamiliar with stretch nylon. Although soft, the quills do not sluff off because the yarn relaxes slightly, "opens" a little, permitting the yarns to intermingle just enough to hold the yarn together firmly enough to assure good weaving.

Quills used for stretch yarns should be free from defects that might pick or snag the yarn and, preferably, should be unvarnished. This is because some oils used in coning tend to soften varnish, causing very serious trouble. Oil-softened varnish causes yarn to stick to quills and creates intolerable tension variations. Oils are available that will not soften varnish; such oils should be chosen when stretch yarns are oiled for weaving. Stretch yarns prepared for weaving should be oiled, preferably with an oil rich in anti-static ingredients, to minimize tension problems and to reduce or eliminate static due to friction between thermoplastic yarns and the guides and tensions these yarns must contact during quilling.

Shuttle, Type, Tension, Furring. The preferred shuttle is a synthetic yarn shuttle with an adjustable clip tension designed so that the yarn can be uniformly tensioned on both sides of the tension clip.

As seen in the July 1961 bulletin on weaving prepared by the Leesona Corporation, proper furring of the shuttle is important. Fur is desirable to control the ballooning of stretch yarn woven from the top quarter of quills. After that fur can do no good and may do harm. For this reason it is advisable to use very soft fur, and to apply it to the front end of the shuttle only, not more than approximately 4½ inches back on each side, and to taper the fur slightly from the front end towards the back. The fur should be glued with the grain toward the front of the shuttle.

Weaving Tension. The clip tension in the shuttle should be so set that yarn can be withdrawn from the quill with a minimum of tension, definitely less than the tension used in quilling.

Warp Tension. Warp tension should be as low as possible consistent with good weaving. It is desirable that the filling yarns interlace with the warp rather than having straight rigid warp ends with the filling doing all of the bending. This condition is very difficult to attain when weaving sized cotton warps, which have to be at least moderately stiff, and oiled, soft torque-crimp filling yarn, which by its nature cannot avoid being soft.

As the count of warp yarns diminishes and the rigidity increases this preferred interlacing position becomes more and more difficult to attain and, in many fabrics, cannot be attained.

BOIL-OFF AND DYEING

Conditions of Mercerizing. Most if not all cotton warp, stretch filled fabrics are mercerized at or slightly above room temperature, using 20 per cent caustic soda as the first step in the wet-processing operation. This is done on a pad, the padding operation being followed within the next hour by a neutralizing and rinsing operation to remove the caustic prior to further processing.

The caustic modifies the individual cotton fibers, and sets the warp yarns to a degree, thus assisting in preventing the development of shrinkage problems thereafter. It is very important to note that the caustic modifies the starch and/or starch derivatives used to size the warp in such a manner that it is more readily removed afterwards. In some instances, particularly when starch ethers and other starch derivatives are used, the solubilizing by caustic is quite complete.

It would of course be desirable for this causticizing operation to be done in a continuous unit or, through using more soluble warp sizing materials, to be delayed until after removal of size and relaxing of the stretch filling with accompanying shrinking of the fabric.

Some of the shrinking power of the stretch filling is inevitably lost when the fabrics are treated with caustic on the pad.

Method of Bleaching. Bleaching methods and materials used on cotton warp, stretch nylon filled fabrics must take into account the action of bleaching chemicals on nylon. In general two methods are now used: one is padding with peroxide and silicate, cold; the other is the use of sodium chlorite, starting at room temperature and gradually raising it to the minimum that will bleach the goods the required amount, which depends on whether the goods are to be dyed in light or dark shades or finished white. Generally speaking the maximum temperature necessary is 180°F.

Speed of Dye Reel. Most finishing plants dyeing cotton warp, stretch filled fabrics have found it expedient to reduce the speed of the reels to a minimum to prevent warp yarns from being pulled into a straight line position with the filling doing all the bending. When the dye reels are permitted to run so fast that the warp yarns are pulled straight, a papery type of hand, generally considered undesirable, is evident in the finished fabric.

Time in Kettle. During dyeing the crimp of the filling yarn increases slightly from the condition noted when the goods first reached the boil to a maximum attained in the neighborhood of one to three hours after the goods reach the boil. When fabrics are boiled longer a small reduction in crimp occurs, and finished fabrics stretch less and less when, as sometimes becomes necessary, they are boiled for more and more hours to attain a match.

It is especially desirable that the goods should not be hurried at the outset of the kettle operation. It was found to be best to start the goods at room temperature and raise to the boil in not less than one hour, holding the goods at about 140°F on the way up, while removing the last of the starch with enzyme if the warp size is such that application of enzyme is mandatory.

Extracting.   Cotton warp, stretch filled fabrics are opened and squeezed free of excess water on the quetch or passed over a vacuum extractor, the rolls thus formed being ready for drying.

Drying.   Cotton warp, stretch filled fabrics are dried most often on air lay or loop dryers, assuring maximum shrinkage in the filling.   In many cases this filling shrinkage amounts to as much as 5 inches. Cans have been used and in rare instances drying has been done on the frame even though this results in actual stretching of the goods when heavy wet goods are so processed.   The stretching occurs because stretch nylon has much less recovery when wet, and the weight of the water added to the weight of the fabric causes the goods to stretch on the frame.

Chemical Finishing and Resin Treating.   With rare exceptions cotton warp, stretch filled fabrics, even though resin treated, are softened with cationic softener to such an extent that the goods have a hand which is best described as "silky," rather than the typical dry hand normally associated with cotton.   This chemical finishing augments the softness and fullness due to the use of the crimped thermoplastic yarns and provides a hand that has come to be accepted as standard for this merchandise.   Surprisingly the combinations of resins and softeners used augments rather than diminishes stretch and recovery in the finished fabric.

Heat Setting.   This operation has to be of great interest to designers of cotton warp, stretch filled fabrics because it has a very great effect on the stretch and recovery of the finished goods.   Actually the temperatures and times used in heat setting are such that the nylon must shrink in length, thus gaining denier or becoming stretched. Without going into greater detail at this point it is obvious that both shrinking and stretching can take place when a fabric is completely heat-set.   Both shrinking and stretching of the yarn because of its inability to shrink in the fabric, depending on construction, reduce the width to which the finished fabric may be stretched, thus reducing the stretch and recovery of the finished goods.   This reduction amounts to as much as 3 inches in 45-inch goods in extreme instances.

For the above reason it is good practice to so design cotton warp, stretch filled fabrics that after proper boil-off and dyeing and drying operations the fabrics are within 1½ inches of the desired finished width. Resin application will cause them to be slightly wider after drying, and the final framing operation stretches them a little more, thus making it possible to bypass the heat-setting operation.

As previously discussed and as can be readily understood from consideration of the effects of various operations to which the yarn and fabrics must be subjected, it is impractical to attempt to design cotton warp, stretch filled fabrics "by formula." There are too many variables, and too few known and accepted methods of measuring and determining the effects of these variables. It must be done by the trial and error method, backed up by experience. It requires close cooperation between designer, throwster, weaver, and finisher.

Other Finishing Operations. The various other finishing operations used to provide special effects and results, such as calendering and decatizing, have little effect on stretch and recovery.

FABRIC DESIGN

Denier and Count. In this section we are dealing with cotton warp, torque-crimp thermoplastic nylon filled fabrics only. The warp yarns used vary from 60/1 combed to 8/1 carded, most being twisted and sized as for more conventional fabrics. It is anticipated that special twists, higher than standard, and special warp sizes, more soluble than standard, will be utilized as the art progresses.

In most instances fillings vary from 30/2 through 200/2, there being a loose relationship between the count of the warp yarn, and the denier and ply of the filling.

Ends and Picks. All designers seek to produce the desired end result in fabrics at minimum cost; this has a direct bearing on the ends and picks used in each construction. Obviously the low limit is where the fabrics slip. Cotton warp fabrics filled with torque-crimp thermoplastic stretch yarns must be picked and filled with a lesser number of ends and picks than when all cotton fabrics are woven to provide room for the stretch yarns to swell laterally as they relax; for the warp ends to move closer together to provide the shrink that makes subsequent stretch possible; and to assure good stretch and recovery properties in finished fabrics by allowing a considerable proportion of the latent torque-crimp energy to draw the warp threads closer together, rather than being wasted pulling against warp threads that already press closely against each other.

Type of Weave. The sketches in Fig. 61 slightly exaggerate but nevertheless graphically show why plain weave fabrics cannot stretch and recover beyond a very limited extent and why stretch and recovery increases as the length and number of floats increase. Note that the size, number, and spacings of the warp threads are shown as identical in Fig. 61, that the spaces between threads shown in sketches (b) and (c) provide room for the warp threads to move, one against the other, thus allowing the latent torque-crimp shrinking power of the filling to draw the threads together during the relaxing operations.

For the reason illustrated in Fig. 61 stretch fabrics are, in a manner of speaking, "float" fabrics and depend on the judicious use of floats to provide necessary space between adjacent threads. When the float structure used creates a "face" and "back" effect as in a sateen, the normal tendency of such fabrics to develop tight selvages or selvage roll is greatly increased and causes very serious problems in finishing unless eliminated by design in the greige goods.

As all designers know, tight selvage and selvage roll can be completely eliminated by proper fabric and selvage design. When possible, as in many fancy weaves, it is best to utilize floats on the face to balance the floats on the back, thus maintaining a flat or at least a balanced condition in the fabric. When, as in the production of

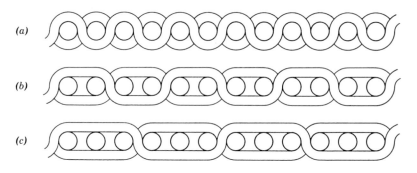

Fig. 61. Sketches showing in an exaggerated manner why filling floats are freely used to increase the stretch and recovery of filling stretch fabrics. The warp ends, round circles in the sketch, are indicated as being equal in size and spacing in all three drawings. Note that very little shrinkage during relaxing is possible in the plain weave (a), and that weaves (b) and (c) provide spaces between warp ends that permit necessary shrinkage to occur during relaxing.

cotton face, stretch filled fabrics so popular in 1961, fabrics must be designed with the preponderance of floats on one side of the fabric, special attention must be given the selvage, to prevent tightness. Unless the selvage is actually slightly slack and woven soft it will roll or fold when the goods are relaxed in rope form.

Excellent results have been obtained by weaving the first selvage ends two as one, without otherwise changing from the weave of the body of the fabric, then weaving the rest of the selvage two as one in a simple 2 x 2 basket weave, ½ inch wide.

When possible, wide looms are used for cotton warp, stretch filled fabrics, the fabrics being reeded 62 to 67 inches to produce goods that can be finished at 45 inches with 20 to 30 per cent stretch and recovery. Designers can save their mill organizations lots of money and produce better fabrics and more stretch by working with finishers closely enough to end up with fabrics 43 to 43½ inches after boil-off, dyeing, and drying. This would eliminate the heat-setting operation that, if used, necessitates a wider reed setting, or less stretch in the finished fabric due to the shrinking effect (with correspondingly increase in denier) of the heat-setting conditions on nylon. Narrower fabrics are also woven as narrow as 50 inches in the reed to finish at 36 inches.

Although there has been a modest number of fancy cotton warp, stretch filled fabrics produced, most utilizing dyed yarns, the bulk of the cotton warp, stretch nylon fabrics woven to date has involved the use of simple weaves such as oxford, basket, sateens, twills, and broken twills. This is because the first major use of cotton warp, stretch nylon filled fabrics has been in sportswear and the fabrics mentioned above are suitable weaves for that market. More recently, in this same field, stretch corduroy has been produced and marketed.

Originally it was anticipated that cotton warp, nylon stretch filled fabrics would first find application in the blouse field because by taking proper advantage of the properties of heat-set, torque-crimp nylon combined with cotton and resin treatments, it is possible to produce unusually good cotton-appearing fabrics that will not muss or crease (these latter properties having kept nylon from the blouse field to date). So far none of the principals involved have seen fit to present these facts to the proper people in the blouse industry, backing up the facts and fabrics by an intelligent promotional and merchandising campaign. It is difficult to understand why this is so because the field is such a natural for torque-crimp nylon combined with cotton, and could produce substantial sales and profits for its backers if there were such backers. Possibly the lack of action may be due to the shortage of nylon and the shortages of installed torque-crimp producing spindles that make immediate expenditures unnecessary. Those who are in a position to view the situation dispassionately anticipate that the competition of polyurethane spun yarns blended with stretch inert yarns and cotton that is given stretch properties by a proper blending of twist and resin will force attention on this presently neglected field.

The dress field, like the blouse market, has been neglected by designers and merchandisers of stretch fabrics most likely for the same reasons, and if, as it seems likely, the one market becomes active, it is to be anticipated that activity in the other must follow.

It is further anticipated that stretch fabric will be developed for and marketed in many other fields, for example, contour sheets and upholstery.

Factors Affecting Stretch and Recovery of Stretch Fabrics Other Than Cotton Warp, Stretch Filled Fabrics

As stated near the beginning of this chapter, we have covered cotton warp, stretch nylon filled fabrics in some detail by touching on all the important factors affecting stretch and recovery in this one type of construction, but we have not attempted to weigh each factor in relation to the others; for, as we have already said, the industry currently operates, and will for some time continue to operate, as a number of arts rather than as a science.

We shall present other factors affecting the stretch and recovery of stretch fabrics, again of necessity discussing each factor only briefly in this chapter. Most of the factors will be covered in greater detail in their respective parts of this book.

CHEMICAL CONSTITUTION OF YARN

Polyesters. The very first stretch fabrics produced in the United States were made from a polyester yarn, taking advantage of its special properties and promotion. When properly used, polyester yarns produce fabrics that are extremely resistant to creasing and mussing and are thus especially useful in the blouse field. Polyester yarns cover much better than nylon, giving an impression of lightness or featheriness in constructions properly utilizing torque-crimp yarns.

Polyesters currently manufactured and sold elongate more and will retain torque-crimp memory to a noticeably lesser degree than nylon processed through the same torque-crimp twisting machines. It is possible, although difficult, to pull all the crimp from polyester yarns that appear to be well set after their passage through false-twist equipment; this cannot be done with completely set nylon. This factor is less serious than might be anticipated because the incomplete set condition can be rectified by the proper use of carriers during dyeing and by heat-setting in fabric form, the period of fabric heat-setting being many times longer than the period of setting during false-twisting.

Because polyester yarns elongate more than nylon at the temperatures necessary to produce torque-crimp yarn, machines must be adjusted when polyester yarns are processed. It is advisable to apply more tension to polyester yarns while they are in the heated zone, thus stretching the yarn, and reducing denier and residual elongation at the break. It is also advisable to wind polyester yarns on take-up packages slower than the yarn is drawn from the spindle by the tension rolls between spindle and delivery package. This overfeeding to the take-up permits the yarn to relax and crimp slightly, thus retaining much more of the imparted crimp than when the yarn is tightly wound on delivery packages.

As additional production of polyester yarns becomes available it is probable that these yarns will again become important in stretch fabrics especially if and when price competition brings them in line with nylon.

Polypropylenes. The question as to the ultimate position of polypropylene fibers in the over-all picture is far from resolved as this is written. There are many who believe that one of the principal effects of polypropylene on the yarn and fiber market will be to reduce the selling price of nylon and polyester fibers to a level more in line with the profit picture of the rest of the textile industry. At the same time this should bring polyester and nylon closer to their respective costs of manufacture than they were in 1963.

Others feel that chemical manufacturers other than fiber producers already have so much money invested in polypropylene that they must follow through with promotional activities equaling or exceeding those which have been made and are being made by nylon and polyester producers. The same people believe that this effort will have its effect on and capture a large part of the fine denier market for polypropylene.

Polypropylene has one property that will assure its use in many fabrics; its low specific gravity causes it to be much bulkier for any given denier than either nylon or polyester. This bulkiness gives the fabrics an appearance of lightness and softness that is most desirable in fabrics planned for feminine apparel.

It could well be that the fiber may eventually be underpriced by polyester fibers and nylon; this can be seen from a realistic appraisal of the basic costs of the chemicals and processing involved in all three fibers.

With respect to torque crimp, polypropylene reacts somewhat similarly to polyester in that it is not completely set when processed through false-twist spindles run at the linear speeds that permit the full setting of nylon. Again, as with polyesters, this situation can be corrected in part by taking into account when the fabrics are wet-processed and heat-set.

Polypropylene yarns must remain longer in the hot zone to set sufficiently to prevent excessive loss of crimp in subsequent processing.

The unique properties of polypropylene yarns, a unique hand, much more cover than the other thermoplastic yarns, and its very low density assure it a place in the large and growing family of stretch fabrics, as it becomes commercially available in quantities in fine deniers.

Triacetate. Triacetate (Arnel®) retains its "memory" and latent torque crimp fully as well as nylon. It can be wound tightly on ironheads during the false-twisting operation and will retain its memory even after being stored on ironheads for months.

Woven fabrics utilizing triacetate have the benefit of the normal soft hand of triacetate itself, and the additional softness due to the multi-crimp condition of the yarn after relaxing. Designers and merchandisers have not yet taken proper advantage of the combinations of exceedingly soft hand, texture, and stretch that can be obtained from torque-crimp processed triacetate. The most logical explanation for this is that the yarn has been in such short supply that an insufficient quantity has been available to fill the marked demand created by the promotional and merchandising activities.

It is to be anticipated that triacetate will one day enjoy a substantial position in the torque-crimp field. It only requires that some manufacturer or merchandiser adopt a promotional program built around garments based on properly designed and manufactured torque-crimp triacetate, and that triacetate be made available for the program.

Cellulose Acetate. It is possible to impart good torque-crimp characteristics to cellulose acetate yarns, and by proper fabric design, manufacturing, and wet processing to produce fabrics showing the benefits of the torque-crimp process. So far no one has come up with a means of processing cellulose acetate that will produce a truly permanent effect. Garments made from this yarn appear unchanged after one washing, but they gradually lose their drape, hand, recovery, etc., and become stretched when subjected to a series of washings and dryings. It is doubtful that workers in the field have by any means exhausted the possibilities in cellulose acetate yarns because the incentive to work actively in this field has been lacking. There has existed a shortage of torque-crimp spindles and, part of the time, a shortage of nylon. These shortages preclude the spending of money by throwsters and weavers in a field that would require market development following successful technical development. This is particularly true since major market developments of this sort have been underwritten by synthetic yarn producers in recent years, and the major producers of cellulose acetate yarns have other newer developments that are expected to have first call on marketing and developing funds; logically so because the new developments are inherently very profitable, whereas cellulose acetate yarn manufacture has dropped to the general profit level of the textile industry.

Polyurethane and Other Elastomers, Blended with Inelastic Fibers. At first it would appear that du Pont's U.S. Patent 3,007,227 has the market for spun yarns consisting of blends of elastomeric fibers and "stretch inert" fibers so completely sewed up that there is no room in the field for other manufacturers. Actually it is rather generally understood by those in the field that many other manufacturers are currently working on the production of blends of elastomeric fibers spun with inelastic fibers, and that more than one is producing better than pilot plant quantities as this is being written. Whether or not the patent ever has to be defended, it is unlikely that du Pont will attempt to create and maintain a monopoly in the field. It is more likely that, as with nylon, properly qualified firms will be able to obtain a license or licenses permitting them to operate in this new field that promises to be very lucrative and productive of entire families of new and unique stretch fabrics.

By using relatively small quantities—5 to 30 per cent—of elastomeric fibers in spun blends, designers can produce good stretch fabrics from all conceivable blends, provided that the design of the fabric itself leaves room for the yarns to shrink.

It is anticipated that when elastomeric spun fibers are available in quantity, promotions and merchandising built around these new fabrics will not only create markets for these but will also substantially increase the market for stretch fabrics made by other methods.

Twisted, Cross-Linked, and Resin-Set Cottons. The Southern Regional Research Laboratories of the United States Department of Agriculture has proven conclusively what has been obvious since the development of the market for stretch fabrics, that resin can be applied to cotton yarns before or after twisting, chemically combined with the fibers, as in cross-linking, and/or mechanically present in the pore space of the fibers. These resins are heat-set while the fibers are in a tightly twisted condition, thus causing the combined resin-fiber unit to have latent torque-crimp memory after part of the twist is removed from the yarn.

The Leesona Corporation, assignee of U.S. Patent 3,025,659, issued to N. J. Stoddard and Warren A. Seem, March 20, 1962, covering their method of thermally processing non-thermoplastic yarns, has developed a false-twist machine capable of twisting, heat-setting, and continuously untwisting, at a high rate of through-put, resin-treated cellulose (cotton and rayon) yarns, producing in one pass finished yarns with good latent torque-crimp memory. Resin can be applied in a separate operation in raw stock or yarn form, or it can be applied continuously as part of the false-twisting operation.

This process is technically feasible and should be especially attractive to cotton mills as it can enable them to produce stretch fabric with no change from their normal operations other than replacing part of their older, slow producing, twisting equipment with more modern, high through-put, better-engineered machinery, weaving more open constructions. This in turn assures them of increased through-put and higher prices for part of their production.

The more troublesome parts of the operation, relaxing, boil-off, dyeing and finishing, will become problems of commission finishers rather than problems of weaving mills. Actually there should be no serious problems in the processing of stretch filled goods. The remaining problems in the stretch warp field must, in any event, be solved for other stretch warp fabrics before these fabrics can be finished in volume without undue variation in stretch and recovery in the finished goods.

This field of activity still requires a rather considerable volume of work in designing, resin-treating, dyeing and finishing, and fabric testing, all of which must follow manufacture and delivery of enough of these special false-twist machines to enable the necessary work to be done. More important, cotton mills desiring to take advantage of this new development must budget adequate funds for the work and acquire the services of experienced and capable personnel to develop merchantable fabrics quickly and cash in on the first wave of high profits from this new development.

Wool. Woolen fibers have a very substantial amount of crimp, and woolen yarns can be made that possess a degree of stretch and recovery based on this crimp. By using the best wools for the process, properly designing the yarns and fabrics in such a manner that room is left for the swelling that takes place when the fibers, temporarily straightened by weaving, are permitted to relax, and space for yarns to be drawn together by this relaxing, it is possible to produce stretch fabrics from woolen and worsted yarns having a useful amount of stretch and recovery.

The Raeford and Pacific Divisions of Burlington Industries, Inc., demonstrated a fabric made in this manner at the February 11–14, 1962 meeting of the National Association of Retail Clothiers and Furnishers held in Washington, D.C.

It has been postulated that it should be possible to augment the stretch and recovery of fabrics made from well-chosen natural wool fibers properly built into fabrics prepared for stretch by increasing the natural crimp inherent in the woolen fibers, with chemicals applied during the wet finishing portion of finishing plant operations.

FINISHING TECHNIQUES

Processing of Stretch Warp Fabrics. This subject will be dealt with in proper detail in a separate section. The growth of stretch warp fabrics has been restrained in the United States because of lack of special equipment for processing lightweight stretch warp fabrics, and lack of interest on the part of commission finishers. These finishers are not familiar with stretch fabrics and have little interest in accepting the risk and trouble involved in processing stretch warp fabric samples in equipment not primarily designed or fully satisfactory for the work. Partial and total failure of samples that obviously should have produced good finished fabrics have discouraged designers and manufacturers from being more active in creating new stretch warp fabrics.

Finishing machinery manufacturers, who are thoroughly capable of designing the needed equipment, either do not know of the opportunity that presents itself or have not been contacted by the proper interested parties capable of describing the exact function that the needed finishing equipment should perform. Until finishing machinery especially designed for the processing of lightweight stretch fabrics exists, it is doubtful that there can be much activity in this field because of the very serious problems caused cutters when stretch warp fabrics vary in degree of stretch and recovery from cut to cut.

ADDITION OF ELASTOMERS TO NON-STRETCH FABRICS

This means of producing stretch in properly designed fabrics made from stretch inert fibers, compacted and combined with elastomers in this compacted position, would appear to be the cheapest way of building stretch into fabrics. It can make stretch fabrics from all fibers woven on all types of equipment requiring only proper design of the goods and proper treatment in the finishing plant. There is always a place for inherently meritorious articles, made available to the public at low prices, and it is probable that this method of producing stretch fabrics will find its nitch in the volume market.

It is possible to be adversely critical of this chapter because it does not spell out in detail exactly how stretch fabrics should be designed. We have attempted to present each of the many factors having an effect on the stretch and recovery of finished fabrics, and to present pertinent information in areas in which the art is reasonably well developed, believing that this limited amount of information, all that is currently available, should be of help to those faced with the problems of designing new and different fabrics in a new and rapidly developing field.

9

Weaving of Stretch Fabrics

This chapter will be confined to the weaving of stretch fabrics based on the latent torque-crimping power built into thermoplastic yarns primarily by the false-twist process because, other than elastic fibers woven from rubber and synthetic rubber, covered and uncovered, used for foundation garments, bathing suits, etc., the only stretch yarns that have been used to date in the production of the fabrics known as stretch fabrics are torque-crimp thermoplastic yarns.

We are eliminating woven fabrics containing rubber and synthetic rubber yarns of the types woven prior to the development of fine filament elastomers such as the polyurethanes, because they are a totally different class of fabrics, designed, woven, and dyed and finished, in a different manner and serve a limited specialty field. The large diameter of these yarns limits them to heavy fabrics, the utility of which is such that they are highly prized for garments where firmness is an asset rather than a liability, and the need for special handling, as in cleaning, is more than offset by their specialized merit.

In due time stretch fabrics woven from yarns other than torque-crimp thermoplastic yarns such as continuous filament polyurethane yarns—spun in blends with other fibers, cotton and viscose-process rayon-twisted, resin-treated, and heat-set and untwisted—will be manufactured in substantial quantities and techniques will be developed for relaxing, boiling-off, and dyeing and finishing them in a commercial manner. Once these developments are complete, the growing pains over, and there is a reasonable degree of standardization of processing fabrics from these yarns, it will be possible to present the then existing facts in an orderly manner. As of now it would be the purest conjecture to state what special problems will arise in the processing of these fabrics and how these problems will be solved.

Stretch fabrics currently being manufactured have followed the

164

usual path of items new in synthetic textiles but not controlled by yarn supply or patents. Good fabrics and processes were developed in an orderly way. The fabrics met with stiff price resistance, followed by a breakthrough in a higher than average bracket. This initial success was followed by converter designing of fabrics to meet their pricing desires, and manufacturers producing these fabrics to please individual converters. The result was the production of a very considerable quantity of very poor merchandise, giving stretch a black eye, followed by the usual leveling off in sampling, the continuation of development efforts by the stronger houses with the usual final result; development and production ended up in strong, capable hands. Now that the problems caused by lack of control of the development have run their course the continued growth of markets for these fabrics based on their merit and on sound orderly development and merchandising seems assured.

The fabrics we will be concerned with in this chapter are stretch filled fabrics utilizing cotton, rayon, acetate, wool, and various blended yarns in the warps, and stretch warps mostly utilizing wool and blends of wool with other fibers such as Acrilan® in the filling, these being the fabrics that have been and are still being produced in quantity.

NON-STRETCH WARPS FOR STRETCH FABRICS

We will start with consideration of warps made of conventional non-stretch yarns, filled with stretch nylon, and containing latent torque-crimp energy built into the yarn by false-twist processing. These warps must vary from the general run of warps with respect to the number of ends per inch used in specific constructions. It is necessary to reduce the number of ends sufficiently to provide room between ends crossed by floats to permit these ends to move close together during the relaxing operation. Otherwise too much of the latent torque-crimp energy of the stretch filling yarns will be uselessly dissipated pushing against warp yarns that cannot be moved enough laterally to enable the fabric to shrink as it should during relaxing. This dissipated energy results in the loss of a considerable part of the elastic or recovery properties of the filling yarn, producing a "lazy" fabric.

When continuous filament or spun rayon warps are used the ends must be reduced still further, and the need of this extra reduction of ends must be taken into account during designing to prevent warp slippage in the finished fabrics. The reason for reducing the number of ends in a rayon warp below the number used in other warps of similar yarn counts is the well-known fact that rayon yarns, spun and continuous filament, swell laterally much more than cotton and other fibers when wet. Currently, relaxing of stretch fabrics takes place in an aqueous medium. Certain of the newer cross-linked rayons swell much less than regular rayon when wet, and should be used when added ends are necessary to produce the required weight or effect in finished fabrics.

Much has already been written regarding the manner in which non-stretch warps filled with stretch yarns should be woven. With one exception, we will eliminate all discussion of this part of the weaving of these fabrics because it is reasonably safe to assume that mills currently manufacturing and selling woven fabrics know how to weave and do not need any guidance or suggestions for weaving regular warps with less than the ordinary number of ends. The one exception is tension. Thermoplastic yarns highly twisted, heat-set, and untwisted become very soft when permitted to relax, whereas the warps in which they are woven are for the most part much stiffer owing to twist and warp size. It is, therefore, advisable to tension the warps as lightly as possible to provide as much interlacing of warp and filling as can be achieved with such different yarns.

We do want to point out that many of the fabrics could be improved, and we anticipate that in the near future this will be done by utilizing increased turns of twist to compact the warp yarns, thus creating more room for shrinking, giving more stretch and especially more recovery to the finished fabrics. We want to stress that whereas most of the fabrics already woven have come from warps sized with the sizes normally used in their respective mills, these very properly being for the most part the cheapest possible sizing materials that will give good weaving; in stretch fabrics particularly there is real merit in utilizing sizing materials that can be readily removed by water at or below room temperature containing normal scouring materials. Use of such warp sizing ingredients will produce more stretch and recovery in the finished goods. These ingredients should be used whenever stretch fillings are woven in non-stretch warps. Sizing materials readily soluble in water at room temperature are so well known that it is neither necessary nor desirable to list them here. All involve higher sizing costs, and slightly higher greige goods cost, but all are very cheap when considered in relation to the waste incurred when expensive latent torque-crimp shrinking energy pushes vainly against rod-like groups of firmly bound fibers instead of soft flexible individual fibers.

Whereas, with one exception, tension, we eliminated all discussion of how to weave non-stretch warps on the grounds that weavers know how to weave, we intend to cover all details regarding the weaving of stretch yarn as filling in non-stretch warps. Stretch filling yarns require handling totally different from the handling of non-stretch yarns.

STRETCH FILLING YARNS

We will start with the yarn. Nylon from one individual manufacturer, identical in merge, luster, denier, filament count, and form of put-up, will vary appreciably in its latent torque-crimp energy as delivered by two different throwsters even though both use identical false-twisting equipment. This happens because each throwster has his own ideas as to how to process nylon best through false-twist machines to produce the best results in weaving. Differences in speed of through-put, temperature in the heated zone, tension in the heated zone, number of turns of twist utilized, overfeed to the take-up bobbins, etc., all affect the strength, elongation, dyeing properties, shrinking properties, and stretch and recovery properties of the resultant thrown yarn.

For the above reasons stretch nylon yarns used as filling in a single style of fabric should be purchased from one throwster, or, if it becomes necessary to obtain the yarn from more than one throwster, care should be taken to keep the finished fabrics as well as the thrown yarns separate; and the fabrics containing these differing fillings should be identified by different code numbers. Otherwise fabrics apparently identical in construction and stretch properties will reach the finishing plants under one code number and will be mixed indiscriminately by the finisher. Given one dye lot containing fabrics identical in construction but woven with stretch nylon filling from different throwsters, it is to be anticipated that the dyed and dried fabrics will vary in depth of shade, width after drying, per cent of stretch, and especially rate and extent of recovery after stretching. Differences in color within a lot make redyeing mandatory. This in turn reduces the stretch and recovery properties of all the fabrics still further and very likely still produces a color difference after redyeing, requiring another segregation and another redyeing of part of the lot.

Differences in width alone after dyeing and drying can be as much as 4 inches, and differences in extent and rate of recovery can be even more serious. When such differences are noted in dried and unfinished fabrics, finishers will process for the widest fabrics in the lot, unavoidably creating an incompletely set condition in the narrower goods which causes creep during storage, on the cutting table, after cutting, and very serious trouble in finished garments, particularly when such fabrics are used in different panels in a single garment.

When otherwise identical fabrics, filled with nylon textured by different throwsters, are identified as being different by code number, finishers should maintain segregation of the goods, heat-set both the wider and the narrower goods properly, and deliver each lot properly set to assure uniform behavior at the cutting table. Although not normally encountered in properly designed and finished goods, a slight difference in filling shrinkage from different lots of stretch fabrics is actually much less troublesome than a similar difference in non-stretch goods for obvious reasons. The stretch properties overcome what would otherwise be problems due to minor differences in shrinkage. However, even minor shrinkage differences cause major problems when present within one individual dye lot.

Nylon textured by the torque-crimp process for weaving purposes should be oiled to reduce variations in friction due to contact with guides and tensions during quilling and weaving. It is probable that the oil on the yarn functions primarily by constantly lubricating the guides and tensions over which the yarn must be drawn during quilling and weaving. In any event, oiling is a "must" and the type used is very important.

The oil should not be of the "paint remover" type. Oils developed specifically for high penetration, used in soaking ironheads and other packages in blends of oil and solvent such as Varsol (a common practice with some throwsters), and oils especially designed to be bland in their effect on long standing on cut and spun rubber and synthetic rubber yarns are in most instances of such a nature that they will mutually dissolve in and with varnishes and paints, causing very serious trouble when varnished quills are used. Such oils should be avoided.

The oil should be non-oxidizable, readily removable during scouring, and, very important, should be extremely rich in anti-static ingredients, to reduce problems due to static during weaving to an absolute minimum. Fortunately oils stable to storage, non "paint remover" in character, readily removable during dyeing, and rich in anti-static properties are available and used by throwsters experienced in the preparation of stretch yarns for weaving.

Cones of false-twisted nylon purchased for weaving should be uniform in density to prevent variations in quilling tensions, should be as large as can be produced on throwsters' equipment, and should be knotless even though this involves delivery of smaller cones and cones varying in size.

QUILLING

As stated in Chapter 8, quilling is unquestionably the most sensitive area in the manufacture of stretch filled woven fabrics.

It is possible to produce good quills by carefully adjusting tensions and speeds of any installed quilling mechanism, modifying the wind to produce quills smaller in diameter than is otherwise found necessary, and weaving these quills in sequence and within a very short time of quilling, utilizing only those in a near perfect condition. But it is obviously impractical to attempt to manufacture substantial quantities of stretch fabrics in this manner because of the difficulties in maintaining a relatively uniform time lag, particularly when this time lag must be of short duration, and the difficulty and expense of weaving in sequence when large quantities of fabric are to be produced.

A uniform time lag and sequence weaving would be mandatory if a serious attempt were to be made to produce completely uniform, stretch filled fabrics using quills wound on multi-unit quilling machines. This is because quills of stretch nylon tend to soften on standing, some more than others, creating visible differences in dyed and finished stretch fabrics. Also, regardless of the type of quiller used, it is obviously impossible in practice to maintain every unit at exactly the same tension. When quills are produced separately and mixed indiscriminately on quill boards minor variations in quilling tensions, unavoidable from unit to unit, will produce visible variations in finished stretch fabrics.

When quills are wound on the Unifil Loom Winder, variations of the same magnitude from unit to unit will not show up as variations in the finished fabrics because each individual cut is quilled with quills made on one unit only and, therefore, barring mechanical breakdown, is quilled at the same tension. In this manner minor tension variations may produce minor variations from cut to cut, where they are not noticeable, but cannot produce variations within cuts.

Use of the Unifil Loom Winder, Fig. 62, makes it possible to: quill economically at slow speeds; weave with quills much smaller in diameter than are found necessary when yarns other than stretch are woven; weave in sequence without incurring added costs; and maintain a relatively uniform time lag between quilling and weaving with-

Fig. 62.

out conscious effort or extra expenditure of time by weaving personnel.

For the above reasons, and others so familiar to weavers that they do not need stressing here, use of the Unifil Loom Winder in weaving stretch fillings has become almost universal when stretch filled fabrics are woven in the United States.

Quills of torque-crimp thermoplastic yarns should never contain knots. When present on quills knots cause serious tension variations during weaving that show up as dye bars that are usually 1 to 4 inches wide in finished goods. To prevent the occurrence of such dye bars in finished goods yarn packages purchased for use as filling yarns should be knotless even though this may necessitate accepting some packages of less than the desired size. Fortunately use of the 553 false-twisting machine for preparing stretch thermoplastic yarns makes it possible for throwsters to deliver very large packages of one end each of S and Z, or two ends of S or two ends of Z as desired. These large packages are designed to fit on the Unifil Loom Winder and can be used directly from the false-twisting machine when constructions permit. When ply twisting is desirable or mandatory to reduce picking and pilling (the tendency to pick and pill varies greatly with construction) or to produce increased torque in the yarns by applying ply twist against the torque, it is possible to obtain large knotless packages of such yarns by utilizing Leesona's two for one twister that can simultaneously twist and cone very large units of torque-crimp thermoplastic yarns.

Use of knotless packages is a must in the production of uniform-appearing, finished, stretch filled fabrics. It would obviously be ridiculous to go to this extreme and then tie knots at the loom. Each package of stretch yarn should be threaded individually into the quilling machines rather than running continuously using knotted tails. When for any reason yarn breaks, partial quills should be woven rather than knotted at the quill.

Inasmuch as shuttles used during the weaving of stretch yarns are limited to the synthetic type and quills are limited to those that can fit these shuttles and that will operate well in the Unifil Loom Winder, the choice of quill becomes partially limited. The type of quill chosen should be one that has not been finished with varnish or lacquer because of the danger of sticking if oil capable of softening lacquer or varnish on long contact should be encountered. If there is any question regarding the suitability of a specific type of quill a check should be made with the supplier of the Unifil Loom Winder regarding its suitability for use with stretch thermoplastic yarns.

There is no advantage to be gained by the use of oversized quills, nor is there any advantage to be gained from producing quills containing the maximum possible quantity of yarn. Quills wound with a long taper and having a small diameter are preferred for stretch yarns, and produce more uniform cloth. Very good results have been obtained with quills $7\frac{3}{8}$ inches long with number five butt adjusting the stroke to produce a $\frac{3}{4}$ inch diameter.

Detailed studies made with the aid of a Brush Tension Analyzer encompassing the production of hundreds of quills, some being checked for tension variations while drawn at the average rate of weaving from quills placed in shuttles, and others woven and dyed and finished, have conclusively proved that stretch yarns should be quilled at the minimum tension that will assure delivery of yarn from the quills in furred shuttles in such a manner that no sluffing-off takes place at the start of a fresh quill. The reason for utilizing this absolute minimum tension is that the tension of yarn drawn from quills placed in shuttles increases in percentage as well as in quantity from the beginning to the end of a quill as the tension of quilling increases. As explained previously, tension variations that would be considered minor in producer twist and conventional twisted yarns can produce visible variations in finished fabrics made from false-twisted yarns. It is obviously impractical to attempt to pinpoint the proper tension for all types and deniers of stretch yarns, particularly when the processing conditions of the yarns varies from throwster to throwster. It has been found that 2-ply, 70-denier, 16-filament, torque-crimp nylon quilled at a measured tension of 6 grams gives very satisfactory results. Most weavers prefer to use a tension nearer to 12 grams to provide what they feel is a margin of safety against sluffing-off during weaving. From this, a low of 6 to a high of 12 grams for 2-ply, 70-denier nylon, a reasonably intelligent starting point should be indicated for other deniers and plies.

Stretch yarns relax and "open" readily upon release of tension and can catch or snag much more readily than conventional yarns. For this reason it is very important that the quills used be completely free from defects; and it is especially important that the surface be completely smooth throughout.

As stated above, the safest way to be assured of not having trouble from oil softened varnish is to avoid varnished quills.

Choice of quill is automatically limited to those that can be used in the Unifil Loom Winder and to quills that can be used in shuttles satisfactory for weaving synthetic yarns, as the Unifil Loom Winder should be used for the quilling and synthetic type shuttles for the weaving. Should there be any question with respect to any specific quill it is a simple matter to check with the suppliers of the Unifil Loom Winder.

SHUTTLES

Shuttles designed and used for the weaving of producer twist and high twist synthetic yarns are quite satisfactory for the weaving of stretch yarns. It is advisable to choose a type of shuttle that controls tension by a positively controlled clip tension device. It is mandatory that the shuttle be smooth throughout and that the quill center properly in the shuttle.

The primary problem here is the furring of the shuttle. It should be furred at the front end only, just enough to prevent ballooning of full quills and to apply a light tension to yarn drawn from full quills. As the quills weave and the yarn draws from further and further back on the quill the yarn tends to hug the barrel, replacing the fur as a means of applying light tension.

The fur should be soft, extending from the top of the shuttle only $4\frac{1}{2}$ inches toward the base of the quill, and the guard hairs should be tapered from the top of the quill toward the back; the fur being so mounted in the quill that its grain is toward the front of the shuttles.

The lighter the tension that can be used in the shuttle, the better will be the uniformity of the finished fabric. The yarn should be tensioned as lightly as possible, this being the minimum tension that will permit the building of a proper selvage. In 2-ply, 70-denier this is usually found to be in the neighborhood of 6 grams per denier. Detailed studies made with the Brush Tension Analyzer, using properly wound quills and properly furred shuttles, indicate that it is possible to produce a quill so perfect, and to have the quill so well-centered in the shuttle, the tension properly applied, and the furring properly tapered to such an extent that yarn drawn from the quill at the average speed of weaving will not vary more than 2 grams from the beginning to the end of an individual quill.

WEAVING

As stated previously it would be presumptuous of the author to attempt to tell weavers how to weave. With stretch yarns certain precautions should be taken, these being adjustment of the center fork spring in order that it will work at the light tensions employed in weaving stretch yarns; inspection of every part of the raceway to make sure that it is smooth and straight; inspection of the temples, sand rolls, and let-off, to assure uniform warp tensioning and fabric take-up; and a checking of the selvage to make sure that it is a trifle slack compared with the body of the fabric and shows no tendency to roll. If a rolling selvage is detected the fabric should be rechecked for design (see Chapter 8) to prevent production of yardage that may be difficult or impossible to finish.

STRETCH WARP FABRICS

Stretch warp fabrics were developed in Europe for the ski trade. These fabrics used stretch nylon yarns given latent torque-crimp memory by the conventional batch process: twist, heat-set, and reverse twist techniques, developed and patented by the Heberlein Patent Corporation and merchandised under the tradename of Helanca®. Although expensive, and subject to variables that cannot be completely controlled (variations in heat setting on ironheads), the process makes possible the production of balanced ply twists having any desired number of single end and ply turns without incurring extra steps in the process. This assures maximum possible stretch and recovery and maximum resistance to picking and pilling, especially important in fabrics subject to the rigors of skiing. The built-in resistance to picking and pilling, inherent in torque-crimp yarns, twisted, heat-set, untwisted, and ply twisted in such a manner that the single ends have torque due to single-end true twist in addition to latent torque-crimp memory and high ply twist, enabled European designers to utilize longer floats, which contributed additional stretch and recovery to the finished fabrics.

European ski fabrics were marketed at very high prices, and their quality was such that the prices held and the market grew. As a result European designers and manufacturers did not skimp on twist, ends, or picks. They built stretch fabrics for maximum beauty, stretch, and utility, then priced them to show a good profit. The fabrics had enough latent crimping power to draw the filling picks closely together and held them so throughout dyeing and finishing operations.

When fabrics were produced in the United States, similar in weight, single-end and ply twist, ends, and picks, the results were comparable and highly satisfactory. The fabrics had enough margin of safety in stretch to permit careful dyers to produce satisfactory results even though available dyeing and finishing equipment was far from ideal as far as assuring the finishing of cut after cut with uniform stretch and recovery properties.

Soon it was found that false-twist yarns containing less than one turn of true twist could be plied a number of turns, for example, 6 turns in 70-denier, 2 ply, producing fabrics essentially similar to the European fabrics. Such fabrics continue to be manufactured, although in decreasing quantities because of the inadequacy of existing dyeing and finishing equipment (see Chapter 11), and to utilization of wool and worsted warp, stretch filled fabrics that can be properly dyed and finished on existing equipment.

The European ski fabrics and their American counterparts are heavyweight fabrics, expensive, suitable for skiing, but for the most part limited to this field by their weight.

Almost immediately after the introduction of heavyweight ski fabrics, lighter weight versions appeared, intended for casual wear, after-ski wear, etc. These fabrics were designed lighter in weight, to obtain the desired result economically, by using fewer ends and lighter weight filling yarns rather than by using finer denier nylon yarns. Use of finer denier filling yarns reduced the length of floats. The necessity of avoiding slippage in lighter-ended goods reduced the length of floats still further. All these factors combined to reduce the available latent shrinking power far below the shrinking power of the heavier ski fabrics.

The problem was compounded by existing business practices; heavy woolen fabrics are usually dyed and finished by the firms that weave them, whereas lighter weight women's wear fabrics are more usually sold in the greige, purchased by converters, and dyed by commission dyers. For this reason many samples of women's wear stretch fabrics, some well-designed and some poorly designed, were dyed and finished by a surprisingly large number of commission dyers specializing in the dyeing and finishing of synthetic fabrics. All professed to know how to process the goods, but none had equipment as suitable as that possessed by woolen and worsted dyers. The installed equipment in wool and worsted dye plants can be used to produce satisfactory heavyweight stretch fabrics only because these fabrics have an excess of shrinking power and because the integrated plants, less pressed for high production and low costs, are more willing to dye "by formula," assuring a shorter time in the kettle and more uniform dyeing time from lot to lot.

The problem of producing good-quality, lightweight, stretch warp fabrics was further compounded by the rush of each converter to be first with a cheaper version, leading to the weaving of many samples that could not in any event have been satisfactory.

Many pleasing samples were produced, being very carefully processed as samples by dyers seeking additional business. Unfortunately when attempts were made to reproduce the samples in quantity, variables, which were unforeseen by the weavers and the dyers, appeared and caused very serious differences in stretch from piece to piece within lots, and from lot to lot, leading to serious losses in many instances and causing the fabrics to be very poorly accepted by the public.

One of the reasons for the uneven shrinkage in the finished goods was sizing. Many of the fabrics were woven without sizing, leading to differences in shrinking power from loom to loom because the normal loom to loom differences in tension, acceptable in conventional warps, will cause variations in stretch in finished goods when unsized stretch warps are woven.

Other warps were sized, some correctly, some too heavily, some at temperatures so high that part of the crimping power was lost, each variable contributing to the ultimate problems encountered in stretch warp fabrics.

The primary cause of the variations in stretch, however, was not sizing variations or lack of sizing, but variations in wet processing and lack of existing equipment in which to properly process the goods.

Variations in stretch and recovery from lot to lot, serious as they are, cause less trouble than variations within lots. When garments are sewn using panels differing in shrinkage properties, one panel can shrink more than another causing visible distortion of the garment before it is sold, or distortion that develops during the first wearing or dry cleaning.

At this stage in the development, because of lack of specialized equipment for the wet processing, overfeeding, and controlled heatsetting, it is impossible to know whether lack of this equipment, overzealousness of commission dyers to produce the maximum possible amount of stretch and recovery in each sample without consideration of the ultimate end use of the fabric, or improper design of stretch warp fabrics has contributed most to the problems that have beset the production of lightweight stretch warp fabrics.

Incompletely set and unset stretch warp fabrics and fabrics finished in a partially stretched condition have caused untold customer dissatisfaction. This has led to the return of entire shipments of garments in many instances, and to temporary abandonment of stretch fabrics by many cutters. The fear of trouble in lightweight stretch warp garments has slowed down development to such an extent that many dyers are afraid to handle these fabrics. Those who are willing to process the fabrics have not yet dared to gamble on expensive equipment especially designed to do the job properly.

Incompletely set lightweight stretch warp fabrics, "woke up" when worn, have caused shrinkage that creates discomfort in women's slacks held taut by under-arch straps. The use of the straps permits latent shrinkage, in incompletely set or unset partially stretched, stretch warp fabrics, to pull the slacks tight at the strap and uncomfortably low in the waist. In men's slacks, which are held more firmly in place by belts, shrinkage causes chafing at the groin and raises the cuff too high from the ankles.

At this point we want to stress that many of these problems would have been prevented had the fabrics been designed properly, or expensively. Use of more ends of finer denier yarns, twisted a greater number of turns, would have produced sufficient shrinking power to draw the filling picks tightly together and hold them in this position throughout carefully controlled dyeing and finishing procedures as with properly designed heavy ski fabrics.

It is equally true that less expensive fabrics woven with fewer ends of coarser yarns could be properly finished if special equipment and more adequate know-how were available.

The actual weaving of stretch warp fabrics presents little difficulty. Warp preparation, sizing, and uniformity of tension during weaving are the critical areas. In warp preparation it is necessary that tensions be maintained even more uniformly than when true twist yarns are woven. Tensions should be low, 8 to 16 grams for 2-ply, 70-denier stretch nylon or polyester yarns, but cannot be so low that relaxing or bulking can cause yarn intermingling or soft beams.

It is advisable that the warps be given a light slashing, and it is mandatory that the temperature of drying should be low: 200°F being an absolute maximum, 160°F as a top temperature being preferable, even though this does reduce slasher through-put. There is no reason for modifying the warp size formulation except that the quantity used should be low and only soluble materials should be used. Polyethylene emulsions, successful for many polyester fabrics, should be avoided when stretch warp yarns are woven. Loom tensioning should be as low as possible without interfering with weaving and, more important, should be maintained as uniform as possible throughout each warp and from loom to loom.

IO

Boil-Off and Dyeing
of Stretch Filled Fabrics

Cotton warp, stretch filled fabrics ranging from 8's to 40's in the warp and 70/4 to 70/2 stretch nylon in the filling constitute the bulk of all stretch filled fabrics woven to date. The problems of wet processing these fabrics without undue loss of stretch are softening and removing the starch at the lowest possible temperatures and in the fastest manner, destroying and removing the bits of seed and leaf in the cotton, and bleaching the cotton without injury to the nylon. In some instances the weaver has used carboxymethylcellulose and partially solubilized starched and starch ethers that greatly facilitate removal of the warp size. When the warps are sized in this manner superior stretch results. The finisher faced with the problem of through-put cannot check the warp size and vary his boil-off procedure accordingly. He must set his boil-off procedure to remove corn starch that has had no treatment other than a simple boiling in the slasher kettle. This treatment cannot in any way hurt cotton warp fabrics containing more easily removed sizing materials, nor will its use in any way detract from the maximum stretch development in fabrics sized with easier to scour sizing materials.

Cotton warp, stretch filled fabrics can be processed with the maximum amount of retained stretch and recovery by a basic procedure discussed below. Depending on the available equipment and the nature of the warp size this basic procedure may be modified, in the direction of economy, in various ways. With the exception of the beaming operation we will discuss each step in the procedure in whatever detail appears necessary.

1. Beam.

2. Pad through Cold Caustic. Depending on equipment available and quantity of goods to be processed this can be done on the pad as indicated, through a small or large tank containing caustic or on the jig.

The concentration used is in the neighborhood of 20 pounds of dry caustic, or its equivalent in a total of 100 pounds of treating solution, the remainder being water with a sufficient quantity of wetting-out agent, caustic soluble, to facilitate penetration of the caustic to the center of the sized cotton yarns. Twenty per cent caustic or a concentration near this amount is used because it is the optimum concentration of caustic for producing the greatest possible effect on the starch and on the cotton in the time available. The caustic is used cold because this concentration of it is actually more effective on cotton cold than hot.

When the operation is performed on a jig, usually for sampling purposes only, there is always the danger of a "torpedoing" or "telescoping" a sudden sliding of the goods to one or the other ends of the jig due to the very slippery nature of 20 per cent cold caustic. When the operation is performed on the pad, warp tensions are such that there is no danger of the goods failing to make a good roll; and the goods contain less caustic to be removed during the rinsing and neutralizing operations.

When Williams units and "drowning" units are available, as in a vat dye range, they can be very advantageously utilized for caustic treating, neutralizing and rinsing in one continuous operation.

When a caustic tank is available equipped with a refrigerating unit the goods can be submerged for as much as one minute while running continuously, then rinsed free or substantially free of caustic by passing it continuously through a series of water sprays and squeeze rolls. When available this constitutes an excellent unit in which to process cotton warp, stretch filled goods.

The caustic swells the starch, softens it, and converts it in part to materials much more readily removed by rinsing. The caustic also modifies the cotton fiber itself, very substantially sets the fabric assisting in preventing shrinkage in the finished goods, starts the solubilizing of and removal of bits of seed, twig, burr, and leaf present in the cotton yarn, brightens the fabric, and modifies difficult to dye neps sufficiently to cause them to dye at the same rate and to the same depth as the body of the cotton yarns.

3. Remove Caustic by Rinsing, "Neutralizing," or Both. When the initial caustic treatment is performed on the jig the goods are given two ends and the bath dropped or the goods transferred to a second jig if more than one roll is to be treated. In any event the caustic-containing goods are given two ends in a cold bath containing 2 pounds of sodium bicarbonate per pound of caustic determined by calculation to be present in the goods. This requires more bicarbonate than can be dissolved quickly in the jig bath. It is usual to add the bicarbonate to cold water, agitate vigorously for 4 to 5 minutes, run one end, reagitate 4 to 5 minutes to dissolve most if not all of the remaining bicarbonate, then given a second end. This is followed by four ends through running cold water, two ends through weak (2 to 4 pounds, 84 per cent acid) acetic acid, followed by two additional ends through running cold water.

When the goods are caustic treated on a unit consisting of Williams units and rinse boxes it is possible to apply the caustic on the pad and Williams units, drown in bicarbonate in the first rinse box, and use the remaining rinse boxes for continued rinsing of the carbonate formed and removing unconverted caustic.

When the caustic treating is done in a large, temperature-controlled tank followed by a series of squeeze rolls and water sprays, bicarbonate becomes superfluous.

When the goods are caustic-treated on the pad they can be transferred to the jig, neutralized, and rinsed, or, if volume warrants, continuously drowned in an open width rinsing unit set up between the pad and the beck.

4. Process Cold on Beck—15 Minutes. Depending on the degree of rinsing, if any, prior to being run on the beck the goods should be cold-rinsed on the beck until the caustic is gone. In the case of goods well-rinsed, as goods pretreated on the jig, no further rinsing will be necessary. Such goods should be given a 15-minute cold run, then the steam valve should be cracked. In the case of goods run through the pad, a drowning tank, and direct into the beck in a continuous string, the goods should be continuously cold-rinsed while being loaded and then a sufficient number of cold rinses or overflowing rinse to remove all the caustic.

5. Raise to 140°F during 45 Minutes. It is important that the temperature be raised slowly and steadily to permit the maximum amount of shrinking to take place at the lowest possible temperature. In the case of goods sized with CMC and starch ethers, it is possible that the strong caustic will prepare the goods in such a way that practically all the size will be removed before the goods reach 100°F. In the case of goods sized with cheaper ingredients, such as pearl starch, the strong caustic will still have modified the starch to such an extent that much of the starch will be removed at low temperatures; and the remaining starch will be soft and much less of an obstacle to shrinkage than it would be if the caustic had not been used.

6. Add Enzymes and Run 45 Minutes in the Cooling Bath. This treatment is not necessary for fabrics sized with CMC and many fabrics sized with dextrinized and etherized starches. It is often necessary for low count cottons sized with unprocessed starches. Forty-five minutes should remove all traces of residual starch.

7. Cool and Rinse.

8. Add Chlorite Bleach. It is possible to do an excellent bleach job on cotton containing stretch nylon by padding with cold peroxide and allowing the pad roll to stand overnight, rinsing out the spent liquor on the following morning. This procedure is utilized by some plants and constitutes good practice. However, nylon is also resistant to sodium chlorite bleach, at least sufficiently so to permit its use. When chlorite is used the starting bath contains ¾ gpl of sodium nitrate, ¾ gpl of sodium chlorite, and ¾ gpl of formic acid, the nitrate being added first to prevent gassing. The goods are run in the cold bath for 5 to 10 minutes, then raised to 180°F during one hour, as stated in step 9 below.

When peroxide is used the goods are padded or given two ends on the jig, covered and allowed to stand overnight, then rinsed free of spent liquor on the beck. If the goods are to be finished white, or dyed a light pastel shade, they are slack dried prior to bleaching. (This is preceded by a light rayon scour in the kettle, raising temperature from room to 180°F during 1 hour.) When padded dry the goods can be bleached to a good white with 30 pounds of peroxide, 12 pounds of silicate, ¾ pound of chelating agent, 1¾ pounds of petroleum solvent, and 9 pounds of ethoxolated nonyl phenol per 50 gallons of liquor. When medium to dark shades are to be dyed the goods can be vacuum extracted or partially extracted on quetch or pad, then padded or jigged through double strength bleach solution, covered, allowed to stand overnight, and beck rinsed.

The purpose of the solvent and ethoxolated nonyl phenol is to soften and remove waxes and heat set drawing oil from the cotton and nylon. Some dyers believe this more expensive peroxide bleach provides a better bottom for dyeing, resulting in more uniform dyeing of the stretch nylon filling.

9. Start Cold and Raise Temperature to 180°F during 1 Hour. By proceeding in this manner when sodium chlorite is used as the bleaching agent the greater portion of the bleaching takes place at lower temperatures, reducing possible adverse effects on the strength of the nylon. It is necessary to use enough bleaching material to destroy the bast-type material already weakened by the action of the caustic, regardless of the color to be dyed. In many instances a full bleach bottom is desirable because the cotton and stretch nylon fabrics have been largely used in sportswear and the present styles require the use of extremely bright colors. When a full bleach is required the quantity of chlorite used should be increased and sufficient acetic used or added during bleaching to maintain a pH of 4 throughout the entire bleaching operation.

10. Cool and Rinse.

11. Dye. Disperse colors are used when fastness requirements permit because of their level dyeing properties on nylon. When faster results are called for, the more level dyeing members of the acid dye group are used. The cotton is usually dyed with fast directs except when brightness of shade requires use of the brighter reactive colors.

When the floats used in design are long, ply twist low, and when the bulk of the stretch nylon is on the back of the fabric, there is a tendency for the goods to pick during dyeing. This condition when encountered can usually be corrected on the next lot by reducing the speed of the dye reel. It should be corrected in greige goods as soon as possible by notifying the manufacturer to take the necessary steps to reduce this tendency of the goods. This can be accomplished by adding ply twist and/or slight design modifications that do not need to change the character of the fabrics.

Up to a total kettle time in the dye of 3 to 4 hours, stretch will not be adversely affected and in some instances may be slightly improved. After this time there is a very gradual progressive decline in the stretch and recovery properties of the finished merchandise. Because of this the dyer should be quite certain of his formula before starting and should make every effort to hit the shade in not more than 4 hours actual dyeing time.

Early in the development of woven stretch fabrics, polyester yarns were torque-crimped and woven. When fabrics containing polyester yarns were dyed it was found necessary to use carrier in the dye bath to obtain the desired depth of shade on the polyester yarns. In this manner it was discovered that the use of the carrier in conjunction with the dyeing of torque-crimp polyester yarns increases the crimp in direct proportion to the amount of carrier used and time in the kettle above 170°F up to 10 grams per liter of carrier and 6 hours kettle time. The improvement or increase in torque crimp caused by the carrier is so great that even when light pastels and whites are to be dyed it is necessary to use the carrier for the gain in crimp, texture, etc., regardless of whether or not the carrier is necessary for aiding dye penetration and depth of dyeing.

The carriers necessary for Dacron®, in the quantities used, have a very bad effect on nylon, causing excessive shrinkage and loss of crimp. It is anticipated, however, that workers in the field will develop additives to the dye bath, much milder in their action on nylon than are the Dacron® carriers, and that use of the proper quantities of selected additives will increase the stretch and recovery of stretch nylon fabrics.

12. Cool and Rinse. When maximum softness or "silky" type finish is required cationic softener is applied in the kettle immediately after the rinse.

13. Remove from Kettle.

14. Extract—Quetch or Vacuum. The goods will not stand running over a beater to open. They should be skied to open, then extracted over a vacuum extractor or squeezed through a quetch.

15. Slack Dry and Batch Roll. This is usually done in an air-lay dryer, although a loop dryer can be used when necessary. The goods should be batched on a roll for further processing. Many fabrics shrink as much as 5 inches in width during this drying operation. All show much better stretch and recovery properties after drying.

16. Heat-Set If Necessary. It should not be necessary to heat-set. Proper fabric design followed by proper wet processing treatments should produce a fabric 1 to 1½ inches narrower than the desired finished width as the goods come out of the slack dryer. This eliminates need for heat-setting as the goods will widen a little bit when resin-treated and will gain a little more during framing. When fabrics are encountered that are so narrow after drying that they must be heat-set, width will be sacrificed. The heat-setting operation shrinks the nylon, reducing the final width to which the fabric can be stretched by hand or machine after heat-setting, although of course the fabrics will come out of the heat-setting unit wider than prior to heat-setting. When it is necessary to resort to heat-setting, trials should be made on short lengths—2 to 3 yards each—with end cloths to determine the proper setting of the unit to insure the goods coming off at the desired width. Some fabrics, those weak in recovery power, will come out of the heat-setting unit wider than fed in and others possessing high recovery power may pull in as much as 2 inches after leaving the clips.

It would be desirable to modify the covered frame on which heat-setting is done to reduce the velocity of air at the venturi when stretch fabrics are heat-set, especially when the fabrics are inherently low in recovery power. In practice this is not done.

Type-66 nylon, when heat-set, is set at temperatures varying from 380° to 420°F, depending on the amount of heat-setting found necessary. Finishers have learned that the lower the heat-setting temperature the better is the hand of the finished goods; and for this reason they keep the temperature as low as possible to produce what appears to be properly set goods.

It is possible that improperly designed fabrics coupled with insufficient heat-setting have been responsible for much of the trouble encountered in excessive shrinkage of finished garments during wear and dry cleaning. The art is too new for the establishment of a recognized technique for determining the permanency of heat-setting, correlated to wear, and as explained above, the tendency exists to keep heat-setting temperatures low to provide softer hand in the finished goods.

When type-6 nylon fabrics must be heat-set, temperatures must be much lower because the melting point of type 6 is lower than the melting point of type 66. The thermometer reading on heat-setting units is usually 360° to 380°F when type-6 fabrics are processed.

The actual time of exposure to the top temperature is 20 to 40 seconds, this being accomplished by running the machine at 33 to 50 yards per minute.

17. Apply Finish on Quetch. Regardless of whether the fabrics are finished direct from the slack dryer or after heat-setting, they are given an application of resin and softener in which the softener component is usually two to three times the concentration used on other fabrics. This is because the trade has come to expect a "silky" type of hand on the cotton and stretch nylon fabrics. The quantity of resin used is average to slightly below average for the weight of cotton in the goods and should be of a type that will not produce an

undesirable harsh hand on the nylon. Other than the ratio of softener to resin and avoidance of resins that produce an undesirable
hand on nylon, the application of finish is identical to cotton fabrics
similar in weight.

18. Slack Dry.

19. Cure.

20. Cold Frame to Straighten.

21. Calender or Decatize. Owing to the use of resin to increase
the wrinkle resistance of the fabric it is usually necessary to calender
in order to break up the resin hand. Occasionally the fabrics are
decatized to increase fullness.

Warps Other Than Cotton

SPUN RAYON

Spun rayon warp, stretch nylon filled fabrics, similar in appearance to cotton warp, stretch nylon filled fabrics, have been designed
and woven in sample and limited production quantities. It usually
develops that these fabrics are lazy with respect to recovery and in
most instances their manufacture has been abandoned at the sampling
stage. This is undoubtedly because at the time of designing, proper
attention was not paid to the effect of water on rayon. Regular
rayon swells laterally much more than cotton. This is disastrous in
stretch fabrics because the rayon yarns become very thick while wet,
limiting the shrink of the stretch filling yarns during relaxing, and
resulting in loss of recovery in that the latent energy in the stretch
nylon is wasted pushing against swollen rayon warps.

This defect can be readily remedied by substituting the newer cross-
linked rayons for the older style rayon. The cross-linked rayons swell
to about the same extent as cotton and can be utilized to produce
more stretch and recovery in stretch fabrics than when non-cross-
linked rayon is used. It is anticipated that such fabrics will be designed and woven and will find a place in the stretch fabric family.

The rayon warp, stretch filled fabrics sampled to date have been
entered into the dye beck dry, processed in a mild scouring bath 10
to 20 minutes at about room to hand temperature, then raised slowly
to the boil during 1 hour, cooled, rinsed, and dyed. Finishing procedures parallel those used for cotton warp, stretch filled fabrics.

Depending upon construction, and available equipment, it is probable that fabrics using cross-linked rayons in the warp can be advantageously processed through the Henniken-type, continuous boil-off machines. It is also readily possible to conceive of constructions that may require this processing to avoid cracks, crows feet, and other defects that can occur when the balance of shrinking or creping power and total warp resistance is such that the shrinking or creping power tends to be released too fast.

ARNEL®

Many fine samples of Arnel® warp, stretch nylon filled fabrics have been produced and offered. None have been merchandised, probably because the Arnel® itself has been channeled in other directions.

With respect to relaxing, boiling-off, and dyeing and finishing, the fabrics in general are processed in the same manner as spun rayon warp fabrics, with due attention being paid to the Arnel® itself when heat-setting is involved.

Arnel® warp, stretch nylon filled fabrics have been produced in which the total resistance due to warp and warp size was so low that the fabrics tended to crack even when wet processed through the Henniken. To control the relaxing of these fabrics, and to prevent them from cracking and pulling in so far that framing became very difficult, it was found necessary to partially preheat-set the fabrics by processing them through the heat-setting unit at a temperature of approximately 260°F. In effect the Fluflon®-type filling yarn is converted to Saaba®-type yarn, reducing the total shrinking power in the fabric and thereby preventing cracks and undue shrinkage from developing.

Arnel® warp, nylon stretch filled fabrics, properly designed, and properly relaxed and dyed and finished, have an unusually fine hand and appearance and may yet find a place in the stretch fabric field.

ACETATE

Cellulose acetate yarns swell much less than rayon; this enables designers to produce acetate warp, stretch nylon filled fabrics possessing much more stretch and recovery than when regular rayon is used in the warps. This of course does not apply to cross-linked rayon warps, as these swell laterally only to a limited degree. Many acetate warp nylon stretch filled samples have been made with very fine stretch and recovery, surface appearance, and hand. None of these fabrics has won a substantial place in the market presumably because acetate warp, nylon stretch filled fabrics have not been merchandised and promoted.

As with spun rayon warp and Arnel® warp fabrics, in some instances the fabrics can be entered into the kettle dry, and slowly relaxed, producing excellent stretch and recovery and pleasing surface interest effects. Other constructions require a preliminary partial setting in flat form by running through a Henniken boil-off machine, partially heat-setting at moderate temperatures in a covered frame, or preliminary calendering with high pressure and relatively low temperature.

Once the fabrics are properly relaxed and scoured they are handled as cotton warp, stretch filled fabrics, with one exception. Due attention must be paid to the effect heat-setting temperatures would have on acetate, preventing heat-setting and making it necessary that the goods be so designed, and wet and dry processed, that the relaxed dry fabrics are just slightly narrower than the desired finished result.

POLYESTER AND COTTON

Stretch filled fabrics woven in polyester and cotton warps have a fine hand, excellent resistance to wrinkling, and excellent stretch and recovery properties when properly designed and processed. Presence of the three fibers, polyester, nylon, and cotton, in a single fabric creates a problem for the dyer but not an insurmountable one. It has been found practical to boil-off, relax dry, and heat-set these fabrics, dye the polyester first by the thermosol method, and then return the goods to the kettle and dye the cotton and nylon by conventional methods.

Depending on count of the warp yarns and the amount of debris in the cotton itself the fabrics may be handled as cotton warp, stretch filled fabrics or as rayon or acetate warp, stretch filled fabrics. This gives a very wide latitude in the relaxing and boil-off procedures. A decision as to how to proceed with any specific fabric can be made easily by subjecting it to laboratory or plant preliminary relaxing trials.

With the exception of the dyeing, discussed above, the fabrics are processed as though they were cotton and stretch nylon fabrics.

WOOL

As discussed in detail in Chapter 9, troubles encountered with lightweight stretch nylon warp fabrics, because of improper design, improper dyeing and finishing techniques, and lack of available finishing equipment especially designed to handle these fabrics, have resulted in the production of so much inferior and defective merchandise that many cutters have currently, though not necessarily permanently, abandoned lightweight stretch warp fabrics in favor of lightweight wool warps filled with stretch nylon.

Wool is very soft while wet and wool warps offer less resistance to the latent shrinking power in stretch nylon filling than other yarns, resulting in the development of excellent stretch and recovery properties in finished wool warp, stretch nylon filled fabrics.

Wool warp, stretch nylon filled fabric dyeing and finishing procedures vary only slightly from straight wool dyeing and finishing procedures, as the techniques used for wool are, for the most part, very satisfactory for stretch nylon.

As with cotton warp, stretch nylon filled fabrics, design is very important. The fabrics should be so designed that after relaxing, and dyeing and finishing, the fabrics are approximately 1 and 1½ inches narrower than the final desired finished width. Because of the difference in wool and worsted yarns, the stretch nylon yarns, the results desired, and the equipment available in dyeing and finishing plants processing these fabrics, it is not practical or possible to attempt to lay down hard and fast rules for their designing or dyeing and finishing procedures, nor is it possible to process all of these fabrics in the same manner.

To provide for the necessary shrinking power during relaxing it is necessary that the fabrics be woven with multifloats, in weaves that might be considered sleazy if the fabrics were not to be shrunk, using very soft flexible warp size when sizing is necessary. For these reasons certain of these fabrics tend to crack during relaxing, a situation that may call for modified techniques in processing.

Crabbing is sometimes mandatory and can give good results. Crabbing can so seriously reduce the latent shrinking energy in the yarn that the final fabric is lazy. The difference lies in the merchandise, conditions of crabbing, and in subsequent treatments. The crabbing process should be avoided when possible.

When size is to be removed from the warp yarns the fabrics should be processed at or below room temperature 15 to 30 minutes, then gradually raised, permitting the filling to relax as the warp size is removed. This slow temperature rise tends to prevent development of surface irregularities because relaxing takes place too fast.

The ideal situation of course is the designing of a fabric that can be entered dry into the dye kettle, processed at approximately 100°F for 15 to 20 minutes in a mild scouring bath, raised to just under the boil during 1 hour, cooled, rinsed, and dyed.

Mills having a Henniken available can advantageously process some constructions, those that tend to relax too fast through the Henniken before beck boil-off.

The dyeing of wool warp, stretch nylon filled fabrics presents no particular problems over and above the problems of dyeing wool and nylon in a single bath. There is of course the problem of getting sufficient color on the nylon, a situation that can be helped by the use of type-6 nylon that has a greater dye affinity than type 66.

After dyeing and rinsing the fabrics are extracted, preferably flat, then dried slack. It is necessary that the fabrics be dried slack to permit the final shrinkage to take place. Under no circumstances should they be dried on a frame as this prevents the goods from relaxing and causes the nylon, in effect, to become stretched.

Heat-setting should be avoided by fabric design and use of proper boil-off and dyeing techniques. When necessary, heat-setting should be done without subjecting the goods to a strong blast of hot air as this will stretch the nylon, reduce crimp, and produce a lazy fabric.

OTHER WARPS

Obviously various fibers and fiber blends other than those discussed earlier in this chapter can be used as warps for stretch filling yarns. Acrilan® and Acrilan® and wool blends have been used with excellent results. Many other blends have been sampled, and it is anticipated that many more will be commercialized as the development continues.

The wet and dry dyeing and finishing procedures used to process stretch filled fabrics utilizing various fibers and fiber blends in the warp should be along the following lines:

1. Size Removal and Slow Relaxing. With the exception of fabrics requiring or benefiting from a preliminary treatment in a Henniken boil-off machine, the initial treatment should be at or below 100°F, in the beck 15 to 30 minutes, followed by a slow rise (during 1 hour) to or near the boil in a bath containing detergents and mild alkalis

suitable for the specific fibers present. When the Henniken is used it should be followed by a beck boil-off identical to the procedure outlined above to be used when the Henniken treatment is not necessary. At this point the goods should be completely desized and the bulk of the relaxing and shrinking of the filling should have been accomplished. The goods are cooled and rinsed preparatory to dyeing.

2. Dyeing. In most instances stretch filled fabrics will continue to shrink somewhat during dyeing and will, in any event, show better stretch and recovery properties after a 2 to 4 hour boil than before this treatment. After 4 hours, however, depending on the specific stretch yarn used, and on the construction of the fabric, there is a gradual reduction in stretch and recovery properties noted after finishing. For this reason it is wise to reach the shade in 3 to 4 hours; this requires preliminary laboratory trials particularly when new samples are processed.

3. Slack Drying. After dyeing and flat extracting, on the vacuum or by processing through a quetch or pad, the goods should be dried completely slack to permit the development of the maximum amount of shrink in regard to filling.

4. Heat-Setting. The fabrics should be so designed that heat-setting is unnecessary; this requires the dyed and dried fabrics to be approximately 1½ inches narrower than the final finished width for safety's sake and to allow for a slight widening after curing, and another slight widening after finish framing. When heat-setting must be resorted to it should be preceded by trials where each sample has long end cloths. This is necessary because some fabrics will come out of a heat-setting unit wider than when they enter, and others tend to pull in as they come off the clips, both conditions indicating improper fabric design or processing during boil-off, or improper dyeing or finishing prior to heat-setting.

II

Boil-Off and Dyeing
of Warp Stretch Fabrics

Heavyweight ski fabrics, nylon stretch warp fabrics filled with fine worsted yarns, originating in Europe and copied with minor modifications in the United States, have given, and continue to give, excellent service. These fabrics continue to be manufactured in increasing quantities and for the most part are excellent with respect to stretch and recovery throughout a long, useful life.

Many attempts have been made to manufacture and market lighter weight versions of stretch ski fabrics aimed at other markets, such as men's slacks, women's stretch slacks, casual wear, etc. Although some fabrics have been sold, most of these attempts have produced finished garments found unsatisfactory by the public for many reasons—lack of stretch, residual shrink, and lack of aesthetic appeal being the primary problems.

In every instance the basic problem is lack of sufficient stretch and recovery in the fabric, augmented by lack of the existence of specially designed dyeing and finishing equipment that might help overcome the low stretch and recovery inherent in most of these lightweight stretch warp fabrics.

The poor stretch and recovery properties of many lightweight stretch fabrics are due to improper designing. Loss of stretch during dyeing and finishing occurs because of improper techniques, lack of specially designed or specially modified equipment, and improper use of existing equipment. In most lightweight stretch warp fabrics sampled and manufactured, the yarns used have been the same as those used in heavier ski fabrics. Lightness has been achieved by using a lesser number of ends of stretch nylon in the warp and finer count yarns in the filling. Actually the maximum possible stretch

191

and recovery in these fabrics has been reduced in three ways: by reduction of ends, by reduction of float length with the use of finer yarns in the filling, and by design change; designs being modified in many instances to produce smoother, thinner fabrics. Each modification has somewhat reduced the possibility of stretch, and all three have reduced the recovery factor to such an extent that it is very difficult to finish the fabrics in existing equipment, installed and available under one roof, in such a manner that the stretch warps can pull the filling threads together and hold them in this condition throughout the wet and dry dyeing and finishing operations, and throughout the life of the fabric.

Shrinkage during wearing has been fully as much a problem as stretching during wearing because of the inadequacies of the equipment available in plants doing the finishing, primarily synthetic finishers rather than worsted finishers, thus, especially limited with respect to the equipment needed for processing stretch warp goods. In such plants fabrics have been partially set in a partially extended condition, this "set" being subsequently "woke up" during wearing and/or dry cleaning, causing the fabrics to shrink slowly during wearing or rapidly during dry cleaning. Latent shrinkage primarily caused by lack of specialized equipment or lack of knowledge of proper techniques has caused return of entire shipments of garments by merchandisers and return of individual garments by the public. Both have led to abandonment of stretch warp garments by many cutters.

Other lightweight stretch warp fabrics, possessing less inherent stretch and recovery than those partially set in a partially extended condition, regardless of whether they were set or unset, have slowly stretched during wearing. Sometimes they were stretched just by their own weight while hanging in closets, becoming unsightly, ill-fitting, baggy, and essentially worthless.

Lightweight stretch warp fabrics should be capable of retaining their initial dimensions after many more flexings than are found necessary in ski fabrics because these lighter weight fabrics are worn on many more occasions than are ski fabrics, and can retain their original pleasing appearance only as long as they maintain their dimensional stability.

Regardless of whether stretch warp fabrics are heavy or light, designed to withstand the stresses and strains of skiing or a much greater number of lesser stresses and strains as in men's slacks or women's boudoir garments, the fabrics should be so designed that during the initial relaxing operation the warp threads can pull the filling picks closely together. Also, there should be sufficient shrinking power in relation to the resistance offered by the filling to hold the filling threads tightly adjacent throughout the entire dyeing and finishing operation, and throughout the useful life of the garments made from the finished fabrics. This requires an excess of shrinking power in the fabric over the amount that might theoretically be considered necessary, although it is probable that future improvements in, and modification of, boil-off and dyeing and finishing equipment for these fabrics will enable them to be successfully produced from fabrics possessing a lesser amount of shrinkage than is now required.

Ski fabrics that stand up so well are actually worn a very limited number of hours when compared with the wear expected from slacks and other garments not designed for highly specialized end uses. For this reason if the stretch properties are to be utilized they must be adequate to stand many more flexings than ski fabrics, and the fabrics should have "dimensional stability" after thousands of stretchings and release of stretch, both with respect to stretching and shrinking.

In terms of grams per denier resistance to stretch and ability to recover, lightweight stretch warp fabrics should have more stretch and more efficient recovery than ski fabrics as the strains applied to the fabrics will be as great in many instances and of longer duration, for example, when slacks are worn by a person sitting for long periods of time. In skiing the goods are flexed many times for a very short while, but are not subjected to hours of steady strain as when lightweight stretch slacks are worn for hours in cars, trains, or planes, strain being applied steadily at the knees and buttocks.

As stated previously most lightweight stretch warp fabrics have had less recovery power than heavy ski fabrics for three reasons: reduction of ends; use of finer yarns in the filling, reducing float length; and design change to produce more "feminine" appearing fabrics. Another reason is cost. Twist and finer denier yarns cost money. Added ply twist costs money. By utilizing finer denier yarns it is possible to build extra recovery into lightweight stretch fabrics. It is also probable that one day this will be done and that the resulting fabrics will be well promoted and earn their developers and merchandisers a suitable return for their efforts and risk.

Below we show an oversimplified costing of warp yarn in three stretch fabrics, the weight per yard of warp yarn in each, and the denier turns of false twist used in 1 square inch of warp in each fabric. When design of fabric permits, the extra denier turns in the No. 3 fabric will assure superior long-lasting recovery to repeated strains, over and above that of No. 1, the ski fabric.

WARP YARN	FORMULA	WEIGHT PER YARD GREIGE	THROWSTER YARN PRICE	WARP YARN COST PER YARD GREIGE	WARP YARN COST PER YARD, 40% WARP SHRINK
	Ends per inch and inches in reed				
	Yards per pound				
(1) Ski fabric 160 ends 70/2	$\dfrac{160 \times 50}{31,000}$	0.258 lb $\times$	\$2.50 =	\$0.65	\$1.08
(2) Typical lightweight fabric 120 ends 70/2	$\dfrac{120 \times 50}{31,000}$	0.193 lb $\times$	\$2.50 =	\$0.483	\$0.802
(3) Possible lightweight fabric 210 ends 40/2	$\dfrac{210 \times 50}{54,500}$	1.92 lb $\times$	\$3.75 =	\$0.72	\$1.20

TOTAL DENIER TURNS FALSE TWIST PER SQUARE INCH GREIGE GOODS

Formula—Ends per inch $\times$ denier $\times$ number ply $\times$ turns false twist =

(1) Ski fabric 160 ends 70/2	160	$\times$	70	$\times$	2	$\times$	80	= 1,792,000
(2) Typical lightweight fabric 120 ends 70/2	120	$\times$	70	$\times$	2	$\times$	80	= 1,344,000
(3) Possible lightweight fabric 210 ends 40/2	210	$\times$	40	$\times$	2	$\times$	120	= 2,016,000

At this stage in the development of the art no one can say definitely how much a stretch fabric should stretch, what should be its recovery power, or how many flexings and recoverings it should be expected to possess to be considered satisfactory.

No one can say to what extent the fabric should stretch because various people in various branches of the industry have different ideas and these differences have not yet been resolved. Then too what is required of a ski fabric is not necessarily desirable in a sport jacket or a pair of men's slacks. Another problem also unresolved is what should be the initial resistance to strain and what should be final resistance as the fabric nears its maximum stretch position. There have been many comments by people in a position to know to the effect that one of the outstanding advantages of stretch fabrics made from torque-crimp thermoplastic yarns is that they give easily when strain is initially applied and gain in resistance as the stretch increases. This permits the garments to be comfortable when worn yet supplies the necessary resistance to assure their returning to their initial shape after being subjected to greater than average strain.

It is inevitable that in due time testing laboratories such as the United States Testing Company, working in conjunction with, and determining the needs and desires of, the trade, will devise tests to measure resistance of stretch fabrics to specific percentage stretching, for example, 10, 20, 30 per cent and maximum. The tests would also measure the number of times the fabrics can be stretched to these specific percentages and relaxed without being permanently distorted from their initially relaxed position more than an acceptable amount; this, in turn, being determined by trade discussions.

The many problems encountered in lightweight stretch warp fabrics have been caused primarily by the lack of a centralized clearing house for discussion of the problems, swapping of information, guided study of the problems, and steady effort to overcome them to the greatest possible extent in existing equipment, as well as to develop needed specialized machinery to make the handling of the goods simpler, more economical, and relatively foolproof.

That lightweight stretch warp fabrics already manufactured can be very satisfactory with respect to stretch and recovery is thoroughly proven by the fact that entire lots of finished garments have been returned by retailers because they shrink too much. They could not shrink too much if they lacked inherent recovery properties. Obviously such fabrics have been properly designed from well-made false-twist yarns but improperly processed in the dyeing and finishing operations. Further proof exists in the very slow, steady shrinkage some stretch garments have undergone to the dismay of the purchasers who eventually were forced to discard the garments for reasons of comfort.

Just as it is inevitable that proper tests will be developed so it is inevitable that detailed studies will be made of heat setting, and conditions will be arrived at that will very materially improve the fabrics. Polyester fabrics, finished textured rather than stretched, were studied in a centralized program and conditions were determined and utilized that resulted in properly set polyester textured fabrics from rather poorly set polyester textured yarns. More specifically, the yarns after processing through the false-twist equipment were so poorly and incompletely set that application of steady strain would remove all of the latent torque-crimp memory from the yarn leaving each filament in a completely straight, rod-like condition. Fabrics manufactured from these yarns, properly wet processed with the aid of carrier, then properly heat-set to give permanency to the set, were so well set that no amount of strain short of actually breaking the yarns could cause the yarn to lose its torque-crimp memory.

It is easy to understand how this can come about when one considers that the maximum exposure in the hot zone in false-twist equipment is 2 seconds, whereas the fabrics are exposed to the maximum temperature for 20 to 40 seconds when heat-set in finishing equipment.

Development of methods of "waking up" and increasing the torque-crimp memory of nylon during dyeing and finishing by using chemicals in the dye bath affecting torque-crimp nylon in the same manner that properly chosen carriers affect torque-crimp polyester yarns, followed by maximum utilization of heat setting, will make possible the production of lightweight stretch warp fabrics having all the properties necessary to make finished garments practical, more aesthetically desirable, and economically feasible.

Dyeing and Finishing of Ski Fabrics

Heavyweight ski fabrics, utilizing high-sley, 70-denier, 2-ply stretch nylon and long floats, possess sufficient shrinking power to enable these goods to be processed in existing equipment in such a manner that during the initial relaxing the stretch nylon in the warp shrinks to such an extent that the filling threads are pulled tightly one against the other and remain in this position throughout the entire dyeing and finishing operation and throughout the life of the garments made therefrom. Below we will briefly discuss a procedure successfully used in the production of very substantial yardages of very high-quality ski fabrics.

Dolly Washer. Depending on type of wool used in the filling, and the construction, the goods are given a light crabbing or are entered dry in the dolly washer, the speed being considerably slowed down to prevent undue strain in the warp, and the machine being filled to maximum height as another means of reducing strain during relaxing. The scouring agents used vary appreciably from plant to plant as would be anticipated. Use of solvents that can soften nylon should be avoided. Otherwise scouring agents normally used for wool are satisfactory. With the exception the slower speed, and making sure that the machine is full of liquor while the goods are running, the goods are scoured exactly as though the fabrics contained wool only.

During scouring, part of the latent torque-crimp energy is released and a considerable portion of the crimping and shrinking takes place. The balance develops in the dye kettle as the goods are dyed, and in the dryer as loss of moisture increases the crimping power of the yarn.

Beck Dye. As with the dolly washer the beck is slowed down as much as is feasible, bearing in mind the need of moving the goods often enough to assure level dyeing. After additional rinsing to make sure that all scouring ingredients are removed, the goods are dyed with the time and temperature regulated as if wool alone were present in the fabric. Combinations of dyes are used that will produce a good union on the wool and stretch nylon, or wool-Acrilan® or another blend and stretch nylon, always starting with a proven laboratory or plant formula and checking closely to remove the goods from the kettle at the earliest possible time. Excessive running in the dye kettle can reduce stretch, causing stretch variations from lot to lot which are very troublesome to cutters and the ultimate wearers of the garment. Every attempt should be made to process each lot as closely as possible to the same time and temperature conditions in the kettle. When dyestuffs used and shades required permit, temperature should be kept down to 180°F. Of course this is not always possible.

When black is required the nylon used should be solution dyed, thus making it necessary to dye only the wool portion of the fabric, and ensuring rapid processing through the dye kettle.

After dyeing, cooling, and rinsing the goods should be removed to a box taking the precaution to run the reel slower than when all wool fabrics are processed, again to prevent undue and unnecessary strain on the warp.

Open. Fortunately the goods possess much more resistance to strain when cold than when hot; for this reason the opening operation is not likely to cause trouble. Nevertheless, the goods should be opened by hand, or if skied should be run over the sky reel slowly.

Squeeze. The excess moisture must be removed. One successful way of doing this is to run the goods from a box to a box through a quetch. This removes much of the excess moisture without undue warp tension.

Loop Drying. The loop drying operation is a very questionable operation because the goods hang in rather long loops, are quite heavy when wet, and temporarily lose their resistance to strain when hot. A net dryer of the type formerly used in the silk industry would be preferable but is not available in most plants processing ski fabrics. It is possible to modify the length of the loop, shortening it as much as is practical. It has been found desirable to reduce the speed of the machine and the temperature, the speed reduction being necessary to make temperature reduction possible. Some fabrics are improved by a second pass through the dryer, also with short loops, exposing the dry fabric to a higher temperature than that used in drying, but not above 420°F.

It is desirable to run the goods through the loop dryer from box to box to avoid the strain that would otherwise take place if the goods were to be rolled, although they can be batched on a roll at the dry end if the roll is made sufficiently soft and if ball-bearing rollers are available when the goods are subsequently run into the compactor.

Compacting. This unit makes it possible to correct to a degree of variation inevitable from lot to lot because of unavoidable variations in length of time in the dye kettle. The goods are run one, two, three or more times through the compactor as necessary, producing fabrics that cannot shrink in wearing. This eliminates one very serious danger, and assures that the goods will stretch to the same extent from the fully relaxed position to maximum stretch, this being a plus value. The compactor cannot make up for torque-crimp shrinking power lost in dyeing so its use, while assuring the complete absence of shrinking problems and delivery of uniform maximum stretch, cannot assure uniform recovery from the extended position or after hundreds of stretchings and relaxings.

Decatizing. In some instances it is desirable to decatize to improve hand and surface appearance.

Detailed Discussion of Each Step in the Wet Processing of Stretch Warp Fabrics

Below we will discuss, step-by-step, the various processes through which both heavy and light stretch warp fabrics must be passed. The variations possible in each step using equipment existing in different plants, though not necessarily all under one roof, will also be discussed. It will be noted that adequate machinery exists for every step in the operation with the exception of heat setting. Modifications in units currently used for heat setting, or better, manufacture of heat-setting equipment especially designed for stretch warp fabrics, would enable finishing plants to produce fabrics with more stretch and more uniform stretch and recovery from lot to lot.

Crabbing. Some stretch fabrics are so designed with respect to the weave and wool used that they must be given a crabbing operation to prevent creasing, etc., during relaxing. When mandatory the crabbing should be as mild as possible, this being determined by running short lengths of new fabrics before processing a lot. Crabbing definitely reduces stretch and recovery though it is unavoidable in certain constructions.

Relaxing and Scouring. Proper relaxing can substantially benefit fabric and result in superior finished merchandise. There is no method or machine best for all fabrics. Each style must be tested by trial and error to determine which method and which piece of equipment can be used to produce the best possible stretch and recovery without adversely affecting the fabric by distorting the face, unduly felting, or permitting cracks and creases to develop.

Scouring agents used during scouring and relaxing are for the most part used for wool alone. Use of nonionic detergents such as ethoxolated nonylphenol and petroleum solvents including toluol and xylol assists in removal of partially heat-set drawing oil components from the false-twisted nylon.

Relaxing and scouring can be done in dolly washers, dye becks, tumblers, Henniken, or similar continuous boil-off units, or combinations of these units as, for example, the Henniken followed by the beck. In this manner a light crabbing effect can be given to best advantage when crabbing is unavoidable, the temperature of the bath determining the degree of set of the fabric.

Relaxing is a very important and critical step in the processing of stretch warp fabrics. Its importance and the need for careful attention to choice of the proper relaxing method for each fabric cannot be overestimated.

Dolly Washers. Depending on the constructions and wool used in the filling, some fabrics can be relaxed and scoured in the dolly washer with scouring agents normally used for all wool fabric, preferably augmented by the ethoxolated nonylphenol type of detergents and petroleum solvents, and strengthened with xylol to help soften and remove partially heat-set drawing oil from the torque-crimp nylon. When used the dolly washer should be filled to the overflowing level, and the speed of the rollers should be reduced to lessen strain on the stretch warp.

Tumbling. At best tumbling is considered to be a makeshift, troublesome, and dangerous operation by all who, for one reason or another, have resorted to this technique over the years. Although troublesome, especially when the goods tangle, the tumbler is a good unit for certain operations, one of which is the relaxing of stretch warp fabrics, particularly when fabrics low in inherent shrinking power must be processed and when their construction is such that the surface effect is not hurt by tumbling.

Many of the problems blamed on tumbling should be blamed on specific tumbling machines and their misuse, especially with respect to speed. When properly used on fabrics benefited by tumbling, the tumbler is a very good machine. Stretch warp fabrics low in shrinking power can be very effectively shrunk by tumbling in a slow-moving multipocket tumbler, the pockets being long enough to take full width fabric. Another technique that can be used successfully with some fabrics is a pass through a Henniken followed by bagging each cut after it is folded out of the Henniken, one cut to a bag, each bag tied tightly, a number of bags being tumbled as a unit, separated only by the seam and a one-half to three-quarters of a yard of goods. As with multipocket machines, a large tumbler containing a number of bags connected one to the other by the goods should be run slowly.

The make-up of the scouring bath used in the tumbler should be somewhat similar to a dolly washer scour, but milder with respect to alkali.

Henniken. This is a very good machine for the initial processing of goods inclined to crack and crease. The treatment can be mild to strong as required by the fabric. The advantage of the Henniken over crabbing when partially setting stretch warp goods is that in the Henniken the goods hang loose, no warp tension is applied except the weight of the goods suspended under water. Henniken treatments as low as 110°F have proved very helpful; creases are prevented yet shrink is not reduced. Other fabrics must be processed at higher temperatures, some just under the boil to avoid subsequent injury to the face. Because even lightweight stretch fabrics are relatively heavy for a Henniken, the rack should be used. Scouring cannot be completed in the Henniken so there is no reason to be concerned with trying to scour while partially setting. Use wetting-out agents only, with lubricant added (amine condensates make good lubricants) and scour on the beck before dyeing as part of the next step.

Beck. Some fabrics can be relaxed on the beck during the scouring operation without the development of cracks or creases and without injury to the face of the fabrics. When such fabrics are to be processed there is no need of, or benefit to be derived from, subjecting them to an extra operation. When used in this manner the goods should be run at or about 70°F for 15 to 20 minutes before raising the temperature. Alkali, if used, should be dropped and a fresh bath prepared before the goods are raised slowly to high temperatures during 1 hour to complete the relaxing while completing the scouring. When the bath is changed in this manner the second bath should be alkali free; nonionic detergent and solvent will be sufficient.

Dyeing. Although important, the dyeing process is not nearly so important or critical as the relaxing process. Assuming that the goods are fully scoured and rinsed as part of the relaxing operation, and tacked prior to or after an intermediate step during partial setting relaxing operations, when the construction is such that tacking is required, the dyer should be concerned with four factors:

1. The goods should be raised from room temperature to the boil during 1 hour. This may appear to limit somewhat the choice of dyestuffs as it does not provide for a waiting period or slow raise at the striking point with dyes having a sharp strike. Such is not the case because the goods will not be harmed by holding at an intermediate temperature to permit sharp striking colors to go on levelly at their striking temperatures and the goods will, if anything, be benefited by using a longer period to raise from room temperature to the boil.

2. The goods should always be processed as closely as possible to a standard time, the objective being set somewhere between 3 and 5 hours depending on the goods, the dyer, etc.

3. A good formula proven in the plant or at least checked closely in the laboratory should be available to the dyer to reduce to the minimum the number of dye adds that may become necessary, to keep as closely as possible to the time schedule.

4. The reels should be run as slowly as possible consistent with level dyeing. The shrinking and opening of the warp assist tremendously in promoting level dyeing and make possible the slower operation of the machine, which of course is desirable to reduce strain on the warp.

After dyeing the goods are cooled and rinsed as usual. The unloading reel should be run more slowly when other types of fabrics are dyed.

Opening. Opening presents no particular problems because the fabrics are cold and have much more resistance to strain than when hot. Opening can be done by hand or over a reel.

Extracting. Excess moisture can be removed from the goods by running through a quetch—running from box to box, never to a roll.

Drying. The drying operation is very critical, as much so as the relaxing operation. The weight of wet or partially dried cloth, hanging in loops, hot, is sufficient to prevent the extra shrink that should take place during drying from having its full effect with constructions that do not possess an excess of shrinking power.

In many mills loop dryers must be used as no other equipment is available. When loop dryers are used the loops should be not more than half the length normally used, the speed of the machine should be reduced to compensate for the shorter loops and for the lower than average temperature that is also advisable. Maximum drying temperature should be 230°F. This is because torque-crimp stretch nylon yarns increase in crimp as temperatures are raised. Advantage should be taken of this property particularly when lightweight stretch fabrics partialy deficient in shrinking power are processed. The goods can be repassed through the loop dryer at a higher temperature, or in extreme cases twice each pass, being at an increasingly higher temperature. Again, depending on construction and fabric, it may be advisable to pass through the compactor to shrink and straighten before repassing through the dryer for additional shrinkage.

A far superior machine for drying stretch warp fabrics is a modified net dryer of the type used so successfully by the silk industry in processing fabrics requiring shrink. The net dryer should be so modified and set that the fabric can be pushed or dropped *overfed* on the first net and continue to be overfed on subsequent nets until dry. This enables the maximum possible shrinkage to be obtained and prevents waste of shrinking power. The speeds of each net should be controllable to enable the machine to be so operated that the goods are slack throughout the length of each net, to assist in obtaining the maximum amount of shrinkage and recovery in the finished stretch warp fabrics, particularly in lightweight goods.

The first or outside feeding net should not run up at an angle as is customary with silk drying operations because the weight of the goods would cause them to slide back on the net, defeating the entire purpose of the initial overfeeding. The first net, as in the drying compartment, should run parallel to the floor; this creates a problem of feeding that is readily solvable by the dyer and plant engineer.

The temperature of the dryer on the initial or drying pass should be at or below 230°F because a second pass at a higher temperature will increase the shrinkage and build additional resistance to stretch into the fabric.

It is often necessary to straighten the fabric on a steam frame, and it is sometimes advisable to follow this by a pass through the compactor to get the most out of a second pass through the nets and end up with a good smooth face. The goods can be taken up at the exit end on a roll, provided that the roll is run exceedingly soft.

Stretch yarns, fabric design, available equipment, preliminary techniques, etc., are necessarily so varied that it would be ridiculous for any one to attempt to state just exactly how an unknown fabric should be processed through drying, heat setting, and compacting. Different fabrics often must be handled by different techniques. Nevertheless one fact should be kept clearly in mind: as the temperature goes up, torque-crimp nylon will shrink, or, if it cannot shrink it will in effect become stretched. This property can be used to build extra stretch into fabrics partially deficient in shrinking power. Whether this "extra" shrinkage is permitted to take place on a net dryer, or on an overfed pin frame, and just how the compactor should be used to best advantage in any specific fabric must be determined for this fabric by trials based on experience. This "extra dividend" can be obtained only in fabrics that, after drying at low temperatures, have not pulled the filling picks firmly together, one against the other.

Compacting. Use of the compactor is a must for all fabrics which do not possess an excess of shrinking power and for fabrics varying in stretch after dyeing because of variable times in the dye kettle. The compactor can assure delivery of fabrics that will not shrink during wearing and dry cleaning, and fabrics that will stretch to the same maximum point from lot to lot; but it cannot build back into the goods recovery power lost during previous processing.

As previously discussed, there are instances when the compactor can be advantageously used as an intermittent step in drying. In the same manner, particularly when heat-setting equipment and/or the overfeed mechanism is partially deficient for the processing of stretch fabrics, it may be found advantageous to use the compactor between heat-setting passes when multistep heat setting is used.

The compactor, shown as a picture in Fig. 63 and as a line drawing in Fig. 64, is one of the best tools available to a finishing plant processing stretch warp fabrics.

Heat Setting. With the exception of certain European-built equipment, heat setting is done on equipment designed for drying. The

Fig. 63.   A compactor.

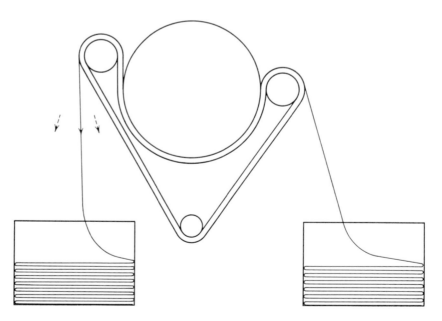

Fig. 64.   A line drawing of a compactor.

overfeeding devices used were designed for goods with relatively stable warp, rather than goods that can stretch 40 per cent in a warp-wise direction. Most pin frames and overfeed devices are capable of uniformly overfeeding 5 to 6 per cent only; beyond this point the goods will not stay on the pins. Stretch warp fabrics of the light-weight variety often can shrink much more than 5 per cent during heat setting. The impossibility of overfeeding more than this on most available equipment causes the goods to become stretched during heat setting; this in turn permits the goods to develop shrink during wearing and destroys part of the recovery power built into the yarn at high cost during the torque-crimping operation. It is possible to avoid this unfortunate degrading of stretch warp fabrics by processing them through the heat-setting unit a multiple of times raising the temperature approximately 30°F for each pass. This, of course, is feasible and desirable only when fabrics lacking full shrinking power are processed through equipment that cannot be overfed more than 6 per cent.

Most machines used for heat setting are converted dryers or slightly modified copies of dryers and are so arranged that high-velocity hot air is blown on the fabric through a venturi. This is excellent practice when fabrics are to be dried because the high-velocity air substantially increases the drying rate, making it possible to run the machine faster thereby increasing through-put. It is very poor practice when used in conjunction with stretch fabrics because the stretch nylon yarns lose temporarily resistance to strain at high temperatures. This high-velocity air blowing directly against the fabric stretches the goods during heat setting. Inasmuch as the temperature also shrinks the nylon, this stretching that takes place may not be observed visually when the operation is watched, but its effect can be measured by checking the length to which a premeasured pre-heat-set section of fabric can be stretched. Reduction in the velocity of the air will produce benefits in terms of stretch and recovery of heat-set warp stretch fabrics.

The maximum temperature of heat setting will vary with the fabric; it is usually in the neighborhood of 420°F unless type-6 nylon is used, or the filling contains fibers adversely affected by this temperature.

Decating. Occasionally fabrics are benefited with respect to hand and surface appearance by decating as a final step in the finishing operation. When decating is done the goods should be fed to the decater from a box, and the box should be mounted in such a manner that it can be raised as emptied to prevent a substantial lift of fabric from the box to the decater.

Tubing. The tuber should be operated much more slowly than when other fabrics are tubed; and it will pay to slide the fabric along a rather long table to the tuber by hand. This step is costly but prevents the tubing operation from stretching the goods enough to cause troublesome variable shrink of 1 to 3 per cent on the cutting table.

12

Design of Woven Textured Fabrics from Thermoplastic Yarns

The shadowgraphs show why well-designed fabrics made from properly textured thermoplastic yarns, dyed and finished in suitable equipment and using the best-known techniques, are so soft and silky to the touch, and why they drape so well. One strand of 70/32 nylon, false-twisted 80 tpi, and properly post-treated contains 80×32 or 2560 crimps per inch, on the basis of producer delivery, and 3200 crimps per inch if permitted to relax 20 per cent in the finished fabric. Each crimp adds its bit to the softness and drape of the finished fabric; and the interstices between crimps provide space for moisture, creating moisture absorption properties where none were thought to exist. The softness or "give" of the yarn due to the crimps increases tear strength far beyond the amount that might be anticipated, because the softness and flexibility imparted to fabrics by the crimp spread stresses and strains over a number of threads. Surprisingly, when one yarn is textured and relaxed, for example, torque-crimp yarn or torque-crimp yarn post-treated, and the opposing yarn, warp, or filling is a low or medium twist yarn, the tear strength of the fabric is increased in both warp and filling owing to the "give" of the fabric that spreads strain in both warp and filling.

Fine denier, fine multifilament continuous filament yarns, textured by any process that inserts thousands of minute crimps in the yarn, can be woven and finished, design permitting, into soft, supple, drapy fabrics, full and light to the touch. When the yarns are thermoplastic, and the crimps durably set, these soft, supple, drapy properties, and the illusion of lightness, remain throughout the life of the fabrics.

The initial work in designing woven fabrics from thermoplastic yarns textured by the torque-crimp process utilized the softness and

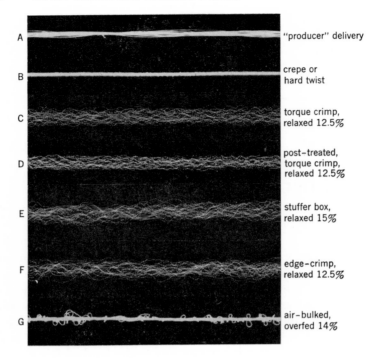

Fig. 65. Seventy-denier, 32-filament, semi-dull, type-6 nylon, producer delivery, and twisted and textured as indicated.

drape possibilities of these yarns rather than the stretch characteristics. Literally hundreds of fine fabrics were produced, some totally new in concept and some following the lines of the crepe-type fabrics so popular during the 1930's.

A peculiar set of circumstances seemed to conspire to prevent these fabrics from being properly merchandised and promoted when they were first designed and sampled. These were the understandable self-interest of synthetic yarn producers who confine the expenditure of their promotional funds to processes and constructions they can control; the lack of similar funds from the inventors of the two texturing processes, torque crimp, and torque crimp partially relaxed and reset, that were uniform enough to produce salable textured woven fabrics; and the existence of an artificial price ceiling of $1.00 per yard, which is what the cutters were willing to pay for woven synthetic fabrics at the time that these soft supple, drapy full fabrics were produced.

One weaving mill had the courage to produce one of these fabrics in quantity and offer it, with promotion, to the blouse trade at a price consistent with its high quality and uniqueness. It was an immediate success and was followed, one at a time, by two minor variations, also very successful. The manufacturer promoted the fabrics by tradename only; no attempt was made to create an image of a totally new and different fabric concept.

Shortly after the showing of the first samples of woven fabric made from torque-crimp thermoplastic yarns, similar fabrics were made from the stuffer box type of crimped thermoplastic yarns, and promotional funds were made available for the merchandising of these fabrics. As explained earlier, the stuffer box yarn then available was made by heat setting in a hot metallic tube the portions of the yarn contacting the tube, which were affected by the heat much more than the portions of the yarn contacted by hot air only. This resulted in variations too great to warrant major merchandising efforts even though funds were available. A moderate amount of certain of the fabrics were produced and sold; these were very soft to the touch, well covered, and dimensionally stable. Their growth was substantially hampered by the variations inherent in yarn unevenly heat-treated. Improvements in machine design have since improved the uniformity to such a point that it is probable that the improved yarns will again be sampled and offered. If promotional funds are again made available and the merit inherent in the fabrics made known to the public, immediate and widespread acceptance should be anticipated.

Woven fabrics textured by air-bulking thermoplastic yarns could not be promoted because of variations from strand to strand in bulk, cover, etc., and because of very serious differences in dye index caused by variations of stresses and strains applied to the yarn during texturing in the equipment then available. In certain heavy fabrics the opacity was so great that the bulking variations were of less importance, and under some specialized situations, such as in the making of woven glass fabrics, the application of the color was such that the dye affinity of the yarn was not involved. For these reasons the air-entangling method of bulking continuous filament fibers was immediately commercially successful in the glass fabric industry, but not in fine denier woven thermoplastic fabrics. Improved equipment has since eliminated the early problems, and fabrics made from bulked yarns are steadily increasing in number and yardage.

If, as now appears likely, fine denier thermoplastic yarns textured by synthetic yarn producers are made available, and fabrics designed and woven from these yarns are properly promoted and merchandised, the market should thereafter become receptive to numberless new and different fabrics woven from thermoplastic yarns textured by the torque-crimp and torque-crimp post-treated processes, finished "textured" and finished "stretch." Even without promotion, the merit of these fabrics and the versatility inherent in the processes should result in the development of many new and different fabrics by alert designers, after promotion of "producer textured" yarns opens the door and breaks the artificially low price ceilings on blouse and dress fabrics imposed by the cutters.

A parallel development, of equal or greater importance, in stretch fabrics only, is the anticipated immediate development of woven stretch fabrics from fine filament, spun polyurethane fibers, blended with various elastically inert fibers. Activity in fabrics woven from cotton and rayon yarns twisted, resin-set, and untwisted should follow in short order.

The composite effect of all the foregoing activities in stretch and crimp textured woven fabrics should stimulate immediate and substantial activities in the designing and sampling of fine denier lightweight stretch and textured fabrics—not stretch as in ski pants but stretch combined with texture and drape—suitable for use in blouse, lingerie, dress, and other "feminine" type fabrics. Once this happens a whole new era of new fabric development and design should begin, resulting in increasing profits for the industry and increased beauty and comfort in fabrics for the women of the world.

Designers would do well to consult the fabric libraries of producers of continuous filament viscose, acetate, and cuprammonium yarns, paying special attention to the crepes of the 1930's and the many improvements on these crepes developed subsequently by the fabric development departments of rayon and acetate manufacturers. These are beautiful serviceable fabrics that should have been merchandised when developed.

All of these fabrics can be improved upon by taking proper advantage of the properties of fine denier thermoplastic yarns durably crimped by torque-crimp processes, and at costs far less than might be anticipated because the higher through-put and lower floor space requirements of the new high-speed, false-twist machines make the purchase and operation of these machines by weavers feasible, substantially reducing the cost of torque-crimp yarns to weavers. One machine can produce in excess of 1000 pounds per week of 40-denier yarn; this is enough to produce 20,000 yards of cloth per week or 1 million yards per machine per year. The increase in cost over producer twist yarns amounts to not more than 8 cents per yard; this includes writing off the machine in 2 years' time with full tax considerations.

In Chapter 8 we discussed factors important to the designing of one typical stretch fabric. We suggest a review of this chapter by those interested in combining stretch with texture or in producing dimensionally stable textured fabrics from continuous filament thermoplastic yarns, durably crimped.

In this chapter we are primarily concerned with texture. Immediately following is a discussion of the more important factors affecting texture; as in Chapter 8, we will discuss each factor within the confines of the current state of the art.

Factors Affecting Texture of Woven Fabrics Filled with Fine Denier Multifilament Torque-Crimped Thermoplastic Yarns

CONSTRUCTION OR TYPE WEAVE

As discussed in Chapter 8, construction should provide room for torque-crimp yarns to relax, otherwise the available latent crimping power exhausts itself pushing against the total resistance of the warp with the result that crimping cannot take place, and the desired texture cannot develop in the fabric. In fabrics designed to have good stretch and recovery properties, floats must be used quite freely to provide a long enough length of unhampered torque-crimp yarn for the yarn to pull the opposite yarns close together. In fabrics intended to utilize texture only, the designer has much more latitude. Many excellent textured fabrics have been produced in plain weaves, and others in more involved weaves, that produce excellent textured goods but could not possibly be used in stretch fabrics because of the reasons explained in proper detail in Chapter 8. Some fabrics using torque-crimp yarns have been produced in which the weave would appear to be much too tight to permit crimping to take place, yet the fabrics when finished are different in hand and appearance from similar weaves using plain yarns. This difference in hand, appearance, and particularly wrinkle-resistant properties warrants the use of torque-crimped yarn even though only a portion of the crimping power appears to be used.

As discussed earlier in this chapter, designers interested in producing new, different, and superior fabrics from torque-crimp yarns would do well to consult the excellent fabric libraries of the producers of acetate, viscose, and cuprammonium yarns, not with the idea of copying but of very substantially improving upon and creating fabrics somewhat similar but different, and superior, particularly in hand and drape.

Crepe fabrics depend upon the latent energy in highly twisted yarns endeavoring to cause the yarns to untwist; this distorts the opposing yarns in the fabric in an interesting manner and produces the type of hand, excellent drape, and interesting surface appearance that constitutes crepe fabrics as existing heretofore.

Torque-crimp yarns do not depend upon the latent energy of a high twisted yarn trying to untwist but upon the opposite force—untwisted yarns attempting to twist. The force is similar, but in the one instance we have a relatively hard, wiry yarn and in the other instance a very soft, flexible, drapy yarn. The properties of the latter are similar to the properties of a crepe yarn only in that the latent energy in each is released in a manner which disturbs the opposing yarn, producing pleasing effects when design, fabric manufacture, and dyeing and finishing operations are carried out as intended.

For the above reasons it is possible to produce from relatively hard, dense, individual filaments finished fabrics that are softer than similar fabrics made from natural fibers and from cellulose and cellulose-derivative continuous filament yarns. Textured thermoplastic yarns have brought into being an entirely new family of fabrics, the possibilities of which have not yet been fully comprehended by various segments of the industry. Most of these people have come to rely on the promotional activities of synthetic yarn producers rather than on their own judgment of fabrics and the manner in which these fabrics will be received by the purchasing public.

It is possible to use the textured yarns in either a warp or filling direction, but it is more practical to use them in the filling unless extra softness and drape of a two-way textured fabric is desired. Two-way textured fabrics have been designed, woven, and sold in very substantial quantities at very pleasing profit situations to the manufacturers.

Although in general textured yarns constitute 50 to 60 per cent of the total weight of yarn in the fabric, this is by no means always necessary. Excellent soft, drapy fabrics depending on textured thermoplastic yarns for their special merit have been made with as little as 20 per cent of textured yarn. This is accomplished by using floats (as in an 8-shaft satin) and using a very low twist multifilament yarn in the warp, producing an unusually excellent fabric consisting of a triacetate warp filled with stretch nylon.

One unexpected phenomenon was encountered—the reaction of

single-shuttle fabrics, plain weave, lightweight warps, 30's, 40's, and 50's filled with 70/1, 100/1, and 70/2 stretch nylon and polyester yarns. Under proper relaxing conditions such fabrics duplicate in appearance, and surpass in hand and drape, results heretofore thought possible only by weaving S and Z crepe yarns alternatively in box looms. Now, using torque-crimp yarns, single-shuttle looms equipped with Unifil Loom Winders can produce crepes which are pleasing in appearance and more uniform than earlier box loom fabrics. Only one problem has developed with these single-shuttle fabrics; they have a tendency to curl slightly after cutting. Curling tendency can be corrected by heat setting and other finishing operations to an extent that makes the weaving of this type of merchandise feasible.

One of the necessary steps in the boil-off, dyeing, and finishing of these single-shuttle fabrics is a preliminary heat treatment before relaxing to control the release of the torque-crimp energy to such an extent that the surface effect of the fabric is a fine uniform pebble rather than a very coarse, irregular pebble that in turn would produce a harsh hand.

The technique of partial heat setting prior to boil-off of these fabrics actually converts the Fluflon® or Superloft® type of torque-crimp yarn to Saaba® type torque-crimp yarn in the piece, instead of as a single treatment.

Still better control, more uniform fabrics, better drape and hand, and a wide variety of variations in appearance, hand, drape, etc., can be produced by using torque-crimp yarns, post-treated instead of one-time processed torque-crimp yarns. As discussed in full in Chapter 3, when the yarns are to be used as ply yarns the post-treating operation does not in actuality consist of a separate operation since the yarn can be reheat-treated while plying. Even in singles the treatment is relatively inexpensive, consisting of a single pass over a heated plate. One pound of yarn can fill up to 20 yards of cloth in light constructions.

Post-treated yarns can be varied during the post-treating operation by varying the percentage of relaxing and the resetting temperature. This produces a whole family of post-treated yarns from just one false-twist yarn. Relaxing can be varied from zero to well above 35 per cent, producing widely varying results.

We have stressed this group of fabrics—lightweight, low twist, continuous filament thermoplastic warp yarns filled with single and ply torque-crimp yarns woven in single shuttle looms—as the easiest manner of illustrating the broad scope of effects that can be produced by modifying standard construction fabrics slightly with respect to picks and ends, and replacing relatively inert filling yarns with torque-crimp thermoplastic yarns containing latent crimp memory.

Torque-crimp yarns can improve fabrics, and produce new fabrics with added *cover, fullness, softness, drape, moisture absorption, tear strength, and surface interest.*

WARP YARN

In the preceding section we have discussed one type of fabric only —fine denier, low twist, thermoplastic warps filled with stretch yarns. Textured filling yarns improve and change the appearance, hand, drape, etc., of all types of fabrics; and samples have been made weaving stretch filling in many different types of warps, most of them woven in existing warps rather than in warps especially designed for torque-crimp filling.

Polyester and cotton blends are improved by adding the softness and drape of torque crimp, especially torque crimp post-treated, without loss of any of the very desirable properties inherent in the cotton-polyester blend. Superior results can be produced by reeding slightly wider to provide room for the filling to shrink while permitting crimp to develop.

The extra suppleness of regenerated cellulose and cellulose derivative yarns when wet makes it possible to use these yarns with much less torque-crimp yarn than is necessary when harder yarns are used. It is necessary for the designer to always bear in mind that, cross-linked viscose excepted, these yarns swell laterally much more than other yarns when wet, thus requiring room for this swelling that must be provided by design. Cuprammonium yarns swell even more, creating a design problem; but because of finer diameter filaments they provide the maximum in softness and drape when design and wet processing operations are correct.

Actually there is no limit to the type of warp yarns that can be advantageously married to torque-crimp filling by designers who take into account the rigidity of the yarns, wet and dry, and the swelling while wet, providing in their designing for these properties.

WARP SIZING

Use of improper warp sizes or wrong sizing techniques can result in the creation of so much warp resistance that fabrics otherwise excellent in design can be ruined. A good example of this is the use of emulsified polyethylene warp size in the slashing of polyester warps. Although removable at high temperatures, this material is unaffected by scouring agents at low temperatures. For this reason the bulk of the torque-crimp latent energy in stretch-type filling yarns becomes dissipated from pushing uselessly against the rod-like yarns resemble monofilament yarns rather than the softer multifilament yarns, which they become after the crimping energy has been lost and the size is removed at or near the boil.

Nylon and polyester warp yarns will react properly when slashed with polyacrylic acid sizes. Spun yarns should be sized with materials quickly softened and readily removed at low temperatures such as CMC, polyvinyl alcohol, starch ethers, and protein-based sizes. When the protein-based sizes are used the slashing temperature should be maintained lower than usual.

FILLING YARN

All types of thermoplastic yarns are suitable for use as torque-crimp filling yarns, the only limitation being the memory of the specific yarn used; the lower the memory the more yarn must be used either in the form of more picks, weaving two as one, or weaving heavier yarns. A few samples have been made by processing ply yarns consisting of torque-crimp and non-torque-crimp yarns through torque-crimp spindles. When this is done the non-torque-crimp yarns are pulled into crimped positions by the torque-crimp yarns during relaxing and boil-off, and contribute to the softness and drape of the finished fabric even though they do not possess torque-crimp memory. When the companion yarn is a viscose process yarn its presence eliminates static from the finished fabric and assures much greater moisture retention, often a very desirable property. There is every reason to anticipate that an astute designer will use this combination of torque-crimped thermoplastic yarn and continuous filament, viscose process rayon, high strength, cross-linked, to produce medium-weight economical dress fabrics that are static free, moisture absorbent, dimensionally stable, and possessing the maximum possible amount of drape, softness, and fullness of hand, yet are wrinkle-free.

RELAXING

Many well-designed and manufactured woven fabric samples based on utilizing the torque-crimp power of thermoplastic yarns to produce desired special effects have been ruined by improper relaxing in the dyehouse, resulting in abandonment of this line of endeavor by designers and mills that should have continued to be active in the field. Regardless of information given by the mill to the sales representatives of the dyer, samples must eventually reach the dyehouse where they are promptly considered nuisances by all called upon to participate in their processing because a sample piece is always much harder to process than production lots, and costs the dyehouse money rather than earning it. For years this unfavorable situation has adversely affected sampling. In torque-crimp fabrics the problem is considerably magnified by lack of experience of many dyers with the fabrics, often resulting in the first step in their processing being wrong; this in turn causes the dyer to state, honestly in his opinion but erroneously in fact, that the samples constitute unprocessable merchandise.

Fabrics depending on the proper release of the latent energy in torque-crimp yarns for their appearance, drape, hand, etc., must be so processed that the torque-crimp energy is released slowly and gently, preferably at a much slower rate than that used to remove the warp size. This warp size removal is, of course, partly a function of the size itself and partly of the technique used in removal. Fortunately many fabrics, particularly those utilizing floats, can be relaxed properly by running the greige goods directly into the beck, running at approximately room temperature for 20 to 30 minutes, then slowly raising to the boil, in a bath containing proper desizing and cleansing agents.

There are exceptions, these being fabrics that tend to crack and crease. Such fabrics must be given a preliminary treatment in flat form through a Henniken or similar full-width boil-off machine. To get the best out of the fabric, the temperature should be adjusted for the fabric; although at today's dye prices it is practically impossible to find a dyer willing to lose through-put on his machine for sufficient length of time to make this possible. Some difficult-to-process fabrics have been relaxed very successfully by running them continuously or intermittently through two Henniken units that are set at different temperatures, the lower temperature used first. In rare instances the fabrics can be advantageously tumbled, although this is to be avoided when possible and can be avoided by proper design modification before proceeding with production.

Many of the problems that arise in relaxing can be eliminated or controlled by proper prerelaxing heat treatments.

These treatments consist of application of heat and/or pressure, or both, in such a manner that the Fluflon® or Superloft® type of torque-crimp yarn is partially converted to post-treated type yarn in fabric form; this decreases the speed with which the fabric will respond to relaxing operations, and modifies the type of crimp in individual filaments, yarns, and the fabric, in the direction of finer crimps and wider boiled-off fabrics much smoother in appearance. These treatments consist of passing the fabric through an embossing machine or through a heat-setting unit at temperatures well below heat-setting, or passing the fabric through a calender in the greige. All effect the nature of the surface of the finished fabric and the softness and flexibility.

Instances have been encountered where fabrics were designed and woven so out of balance that the normal boil-off procedure would permit or cause such fabrics to shrink to as narrow as 11 inches, such fabrics of course being completely non-commercial at this point. By proper prerelaxing treatments, the final dyed and dried width can be controlled within very narrow limits; it is absolutely necessary of course that the dyed and dried fabric should be 29 to 30 inches wide to permit easy framing and other handling. A designer not familiar with the possibilities inherent in prerelaxing treatments and relaxing could very easily abandon a line of endeavor when confronted with a ruined sample and the dyer's statement that the fabric is unprocessable. This has happened many times in the rapid development of stretch and textured fabrics made from torque-crimp yarns because of the difficulty of achieving proper communications in our complex textile industries.

BOIL-OFF AND DYEING

Once the fabric has been properly pretreated if necessary, and properly relaxed, boil-off and dyeing become routine and need not be discussed in detail here.

EXTRACTING

As with boil-off and dyeing, fabrics properly designed and woven, pretreated, and properly relaxed present no difficulties in extracting. They can be extracted in regular rotary extractors. It is wise, however, to avoid excessive extracting; otherwise portions of the fabric may become actually dried in the extractor, which is an undesirable condition.

DRYING

Drying is critical. The fabrics should be slack dried at a moderately high temperature, permitting a re-run through the dryer at a higher temperature after straightening on a steam frame if the maximum in width shrinkage is desired. When possible, a net dryer should be used and the speed of the nets should be controlled to permit proper warp shrinkage to take place.

FINISHING

The fabrics are finished by applying cationic or nonionic softeners on the quetch, slack drying, steam framing, heat setting in some instances and not in others, calendering, or decatizing, depending on the hand desired.

CONCLUSION

We have confined this chapter to a discussion of the designing of fabrics depending on the latent crimping power of torque-crimp thermoplastic yarns because these are the only textured yarns proven uniform enough to be useful in a full range of colors and effects. As stated elsewhere it is probable that improved equipment will make possible the production of crimped yarns by other processes sufficiently uniform to be used broadly in weaving. This should lead to the design, promotion, and maufacture of such fabrics along lines parallel to, although narrower in scope than, the fabrics based on the torque-crimp thermoplastic yarns presented herein.

13

Producer Textured
Thermoplastic Yarns

Producers of thermoplastic yarns are moving into the texturing field with all possible speed. The surprisingly large number of patents issuing to producers in this field indicates that this move has been preceded by a very considerable amount of research and development. Activity is known to be currently continuing at an ever-accelerating pace.

Producer textured thermoplastic yarns sold in the United States in 1963 include:

DENIER	FILAMENT	FIBER	DENIER	FILAMENT	FIBER
3700	204	Nylon	1200	68	Nylon
3690	204	Nylon	1040	68	Nylon
2460	136	Nylon	520	34	Nylon
2080	136	Nylon	45	7	Nylon
1300	68	Nylon	15	1	Nylon
1230	68	Nylon			

Producers sell acrylic tow that can be stretched, heat-set, and broken into varying lengths for spinning in a single step; relaxed by exposure to steam, blended with unrelaxed stretched, heat-set, and broken tow; and spun into yarns that texture when steamed or relaxed in hot water. The texturing is due to shrinkage of the unrelaxed fibers. The yarns gain in bulk and produce very soft, lightweight fabrics, especially desirable in knitted garments.

In a similar manner yarns spun from Sayelle®, a bicomponent acrylic fiber sold by E. I. du Pont de Nemours and Company, Inc., consisting of double filaments, each component having a different shrinkage characteristic, produces textured yarns and fabrics when the variable shrinking effects are permitted or caused to exert their proper influence.

The du Pont company marketed confined and limited quantities of their Spandex yarn (Lycra®) blended with their acrylic fiber (Orlon®) in blends ranging from 4 to 15 per cent Lycra® and 85 to 96 per cent Orlon® in 1962. Though a spun-type blend, these yarns texture when relaxed and are directly competitive with plys of spun acrylic and torque-crimp textured nylon. Very rapid developments and expansion are anticipated in this field.

The throwing industry has been told that du Pont, in an orderly way, will market polyester stuffer box type, polyester torque-crimp type, nylon stuffer box type, and nylon torque-crimp type, all in fine deniers, in the very near future. Du Pont initiated the merchandising of the first of these yarns, type-H nylon, in 1963. Type H was made available in limited quantities in 15-denier monofil and 45-denier, 7-filament nylon.

Exact poundage figures for producer textured yarns sold in 1963 are not available, but sources considered reliable believe the total was in excess of 90 million pounds. Throwster output of textured thermoplastic yarns during 1962 is estimated to be in excess of 75 million pounds.

Understandably, throwsters are concerned. The economics favor the producers. Producer production of textured yarns eliminates freight one way, carton and shipping costs, and one inspection. Research, overhead, and sales costs, allocated in producer organizations, cannot help but be lower than in throwster plants. And producer merchandising and promotion can create a strong demand for branded or trademarked producer textured yarns that in turn can create a demand for garments made from them. In addition, texturing while producing can eliminate one more step in the process, and large-scale production of a lesser number of yarns effects further economies.

Investment and research and development expenditures by throwsters and suppliers of throwsters, synthetic yarn producers excepted, were sharply curtailed in 1962 and are expected to continue at a very low level in the foreseeable future. Many in the industry believe that the extension of producer activities into what has heretofore been the throwsters' main field must be followed by a continuing decline in the total number of firms operating in this field.

Any attempt to predict the direction of the expansion in producer textured yarn would be meaningless in view of the extensive continuing research activities.   All that can be safely surmised is that producer texturing will grow rapidly and that producer merchandising of garments and other fabric items made from producer textured yarns will expand the market to a volume many times that of the current market.

14

Spandex

Spandex is a generic term approved by the Federal Trade Commission that describes manufactured fibers in which the fiber-forming substance is a long-chain synthetic polymer comprised of at least 85 per cent of a segmented polyurethane.

Spandex fibers are elastic in nature. Like strands of elastic-type rubber they stretch up to several hundred per cent when strained and return substantially to their unstretched condition upon release. While similar to elastic-type rubber in their response to and release from strain, they differ from fine strands of elastic-type rubber, cut and extruded, in appearance, hand, chemical resistance, and other properties. Spandex fibers are far superior to elastic-type rubber strands, cut and extruded, in many properties. The more important will be discussed below.

SHELF LIFE

Fine strands of elastic-type rubber have a relatively short shelf life, particularly when stored in a partially stretched condition in areas where ozone is present. Some stretch is inevitable when textiles containing rubber strands are folded and stored in fabric or garment form.

Ozone attacks elastic-type rubber causing minute cracks that grow rapidly into actual breaks. This tendency of fine strands of elastic rubber to crack and break is greatly increased when the strands are stretched, even slightly, and held in a stretched condition.

Ozone exists in minute quantities in the atmosphere and is manufactured by many electric motors. The shelf life of fine strands of elastic-type rubber, poor at best, diminishes rapidly as the ozone content of the air in contact with the rubber increases.

The shelf life of polyurethane yarn is excellent.

222

HAND

Fabrics manufactured from fine strands of elastic-type rubber have a hand similar to that which we associate with rubber bands. For this reason most elastic-type fabrics utilize covered rubber yarns to eliminate the typical "rubber" feel. Covering is expensive and requires the use of very fine diameter yarns when medium to light-weight fabrics are required. These fine diameter yarns, in themselves expensive, increase the covering cost by requiring additional turns of twist.

Spandex yarns have the hand nominally associated with textile yarns. They may be used uncovered, and are so used, reducing the cost and weight of fabric of any given stretch and recovery power. They may be, and are, used in blends in which their presence cannot be detected by hand or visual examination, except under extreme magnification.

COLOR

Spandex fibers are white when undyed, and remain white, in the absence of bleaching quantities of chlorine, to the same extent that other synthetic textile fibers remain white. Fine strands of elastic-type rubber yarns are yellow, to tan, to gray in color, when freshly made, and are deepened and modified in color by many conditions encountered during processing, storage, and use.

DYEABILITY

Spandex fibers are dyeable. When proper techniques and precautions are used Spandex fibers can be dyed in fabric form, to match the desired shade, and to match many other fibers when used in combinations. Spandex has an affinity for most classes of dyestuff. Although in many instances the light and wash fastness must be classified as fair to poor, it is possible, by judicious choice of dyestuffs and dyeing methods, to produce dyeings having very acceptable wash and light fastness. Several million yards of bathing suit fabrics containing continuous filament Spandex and textured yarns have been manufactured, sold, and found satisfactory in use, even in sea water in semi-tropical areas. To be commercially satisfactory under such conditions the dyed Spandex must be quite fast to light and sea water, and reasonably comparable in fastness to the fastness of the continuous filament textured nylon with which it is plied.

This does not mean that fabrics containing Spandex can be dyed under all conditions and in all types of equipment. Many precautions must be taken in scouring, dyeing, bleaching, drying, and finishing. It is especially important that the equipment and techniques used are such that tension is maintained at the minimum possible level.

The scouring agents used must include dispersed solvents capable of dissolving the finish to provide a clean base for dyeing. These can constitute a problem as the solvents used are toxic and some are readily inflammable. Odorless petroleum solvents and chlorinated solvents emulsified with ethoxylated dispersing agent and mild polyphosphate type alkalies have been found satisfactory. Toxic fumes can be kept to a safe level by use of suction-type vents over the operating machines when completely enclosed scouring units are unavailable.

Bleaching, when necessary, mostly for other fibers present in combination, is best done in a unique manner. A reducing bleach, using hydrosulfite normally used in reducing vat dyes and in stripping many colors for redyeing, is used, followed, after rinsing, by a full peroxide bleach. Optical bleaching agents are used for other fibers present but not for Spandex.

Dyeing follows normal procedures. Boiling temperatures, dispersing agents, mild alkalies and acids, and even oxidizing agents, dichromates, may be used when necessary (the dichromates to produce fastness properties obtainable by after-chroming certain types of dyestuffs).

As stated earlier extreme care is exercised to maintain tension at a minimum throughout all wet processing operations, and good starting formulations are used to reduce actual dyeing time to a minimum.

Drying is critical. Drying temperature should be maintained below 230°F.

Most finishing agents, except thermosetting resins and other materials requiring high curing temperatures, may be used to modify the hand and improve dimensional stability. (Improved dimensional stability is desirable for aid in cutting and garment manufacture.)

In contrast to the flexibility of Spandex with respect to boil-off, bleaching, dyeing, and finishing procedures, the extreme difficulty of processing fabrics containing fine strands of cut or extruded rubber is too well known to require any elaboration herein.

STABILITY TO OILS

Many oils used in processing textiles through manufacturing operations, and encountered during the normal wearing of garments, have severe deleterious action on rubber. Spandex is stable to most oils and oil-based preparations such as suntan lotions, although some will cause a slight yellowing and others a very slight deterioration.

STABILITY TO DRY CLEANING

Fabrics made of and containing Spandex yarns may be dry-cleaned. Immersion of the yarns in each of the commonly used solvents has no ascertainable effect on Spandex. A series of commercial dry cleanings, thirty or more individual trips through a dry-cleaning plant, will develop a slight discoloration and slight modification of the yarn, much less than that due to usage sufficient to cause a garment to require thirty or more dry cleanings.

Fabrics containing fine rubber strands cannot be dry-cleaned.

STABILITY TO SEA WATER

Exposure to sea water produces no effect on Spandex yarns. Fine strands of rubber are slowly degraded on exposure to sea water and sun.

STABILITY TO SUNLIGHT AND ULTRAVIOLET

Fad-o-meter exposure indicates that Spandex is unaffected by exposure to the maximum amount of sunlight anticipated during the normal life of elastic-type garments, such as bathing suits, whereas rubber is obviously affected by similar exposure.

STABILITY TO CHLORINE BLEACH

Spandex is severely and rapidly degraded and yellowed by chlorine bleach solutions (sodium hypochlorite) and should never be exposed to the action of chlorine-type bleach. Even the concentrations used to sanitize swimming pools can be slightly harmful, although the concentration of available chlorine falls rapidly when compounds such as calcium hypochlorite are added to pools; such additions are usually made when the pools are not in use.

Garments containing Spandex may be home-laundered in the absence of chlorine-type bleach under conditions usually suggested for synthetic and wash and wear loads—100°F washing temperature and 140° to 160°F drying temperature—without adverse effects on the Spandex. Cut and extruded rubber yarns gradually lose their elasticity even when washed under these mild conditions.

The excellent stretch and recovery properties of Spandex, and its superiority over rubber in so many properties, shelf life, resistance to laundering, resistance to dry cleaning, resistance to light, oils, sea water, and many other materials, chlorine-type bleaches excepted, plus its outstandingly superior color and softness (due in part to its availability in multifilament form) assure Spandex of an immediate and large (multi-million pounds per year) market in all segments of the textile industry currently using fine rubber yarns.

In this book we are not concerned with stretch fabric of the type heretofore manufactured, with rubber as the material providing stretch and recovery. Rather, we are concerned with the production of stretch and textured fabrics utilizing much finer filaments and having properties of hand and appearance totally different from those normally associated with rubber and rubber covered yarns.

Spandex as a Staple Fiber

E. I. du Pont de Nemours and Company, Inc., recognizing the tremendous expansion possible in the use of elastic-type yarns in textiles, applied for a patent in April 1957 covering blends of staple elastomeric fibers intermingled with fibers that they define as "hard inelastic staple fibers." Issued in November 1961, as U.S. Patent 3,007,227, it appears to cover, very tightly, all blends of "inelastic fibers" and elastomeric synthetic staple fibers having a breaking elongation above 100 per cent and a staple fiber denier of less than 30.

The patent shows the methods of drawing the blend of elastic and inelastic fibers in such a manner that the finished yarn is elastic as desired. Various fibers characterized as inelastic fibers are named in the body of the patent, and there is indication that the preferred percentage of elastic fiber lies between 5 and 30 per cent in most instances. However, the claims are not limited to these percentages.

The patent claims cover the blend of the fibers, a fabric made from the blend, a non-woven fabric made from the blend, a woven fabric made from the blend, a high stretch woven fabric made from the blend, a yarn made from the blend, and other claims more specifically limited than the first group of broad claims. Whether or not this patent can stand litigation is yet to be determined.

In the event that the patent is as strong as it appears to be it is still probable that du Pont will not attempt to use it as a monopoly because of the objections clearly expressed by the Department of Justice to any firm using any patent as a means of creating an absolute monopoly in industry. It is to be anticipated that by payment of royalties it will be possible for other manufacturers of Spandex fibers to sell into this new field and for textile manufacturers to buy Spandex fibers other than those manufactured by du Pont.

A surprisingly large group of other manufacturers are currently manufacturing such fibers and preparing to do so. Some of these are rather large and well-known firms, and it is unlikely that they would have embarked on this sort of venture without seeking proper patent counsel and guidance with respect to patents pertaining to the use of the fibers in textiles.

Whereas, at this point any prognostication of the extent of the eventual usage of elastomeric-type fibers in blends must be a guess, the properties of finished garments made from these yarns indicate that the future of elastic blends of this type will be many times the present market for rubber yarns and covered rubber yarns.

The divisions of the textile industry familiar with the new yarns have been very pleasantly surprised at the extent of recovery possible, the resistance to decay of elastomeric properties, and the amazingly small percentages of the elastomeric fibers required to do the work.

The first blend to be merchandised in any quantity contained 15 per cent elastomeric fiber and was offered to the men's stocking industry where it was found unsatisfactory because it had too much recovery and hugged the foot too tightly. It was found advisable and advantageous to reduce the amount of elastomeric fiber to 4 per cent. This very low percentage provides the maximum amount of stretch and recovery required in men's stretch stockings.

The industry eagerly awaits the availability of the millions of pounds of Spandex cut staple blends that will be required to fill the demand for the new and improved fabrics possible with these blends. Figure 66, comparing certain of the more important physical properties of Spandex with the properties of more conventional synthetic

	Spandex	Nylon Polyester Polypropylene
Break elongation per cent	500–800	10–40
Break tenacity, g.p.d.	0.6–0.8	4.0–8.0
Power at 50% elongation	0.03–0.04	—
Power at 200% elongation	0.10–0.12	—
Moisture regain at 70°F, 65% R.H.	1.3%	0.2–5.0
Specific gravity	1.0%	0.92–1.38
Color	White	White
Luster	Dull	Bright and dull
Melting point	482°F	338°F–482°F

Fig. 66. Comparison of physical properties, nylon versus Spandex.

yarns, makes it rapidly apparent that the only important difference between the conventional synthetic fibers and Spandex are the factors of tenacity and elongation. From the processing viewpoint, the increased elongation is eliminated as a problem by the teachings of U.S. Patent 3,007,227, and the low tenacity is eliminated as a problem in blends by the higher tenacity of the "hard" fibers that provide protection when the yarn is stretched to the limit permitted by construction.

Black market prices paid over the past year indicate that the only deterrent to the widespread use of the product at this time is the lack of available fiber. As production increases, consumption will increase in the markets in which it has already been offered, and its use will rapidly extend to many other types of fabrics.

Currently the list prices quoted are low enough to seriously concern the throwing industry. If Spandex were available in quantity, and indications are that it soon will be, "stretch" could be produced much cheaper with Spandex than by texturing thermoplastic yarns, as per the following figures.

Fiber cost, nylon stretch vs. cotton Spandex stretch

Nylon		$1.71
Cotton and Spandex		
Cotton	0.9 × $0.35 = $0.315	
Spandex	0.1 × $6.00 = $0.60	
	———	
	$0.915	$0.915

Possible prices finished stretch yarns, nylon stretch vs. cotton, Spandex stretch

Nylon
　Fiber $1.71
　Processing $0.50
                                             ——————
                                             $2.21 $2.21

Cotton and Spandex
　Cotton   0.9 × $0.35 = $0.315
　Cotton Processing   0.9 × $0.53 = $0.477
　　(1 lb combed cotton sells @ $0.88)
　Spandex   0.1 × $6.00 = $0.60
　Extra processing cost due to
　　Spandex $0.25
                                             ——————
                                             $1.642 $1.642

The $0.25 "extra processing cost due to Spandex" provides for the actual cost and much more profit than the cotton spinning industry normally makes.

The figure $1.64, based on today's quoted price for Spandex, will be much lower when Spandex prices are lowered by competition. Consideration of raw material costs, in comparison to the raw material costs of synthetic fibers such as nylon and polyester, indicates that very great price reductions are possible once production reaches multi-millions of pounds annually and after development costs are liquidated.

The future market for Spandex blended with other fibers appears almost unlimited even though it cannot currently be sold as a component of fabrics that must be bleached when washed, as are men's shirts and many other garments and textile items. Spandex blends are expected to replace part of the market now using torque-crimp thermoplastic yarns, part of the market using thermoplastic yarns textured by other processes, and part of the rapidly growing market for "thermal" fabrics. In addition it is anticipated that Spandex will move into many markets not currently utilizing stretch and textured yarns.

Spandex as a Core Yarn

E. I. du Pont de Nemours and Company, Inc., applied for a patent in December 1958 covering the use of high-bulk elastic yarns as core yarns. Issued in June 1962 as U.S. Patent 3,038,295 it appears to cover elastic yarns used as core yarns when the elastic core constitutes less than 40 per cent of the total weight of the yarn, and when the non-elastic sheath is staple fiber roving.

Such yarns appear ideally adapted for the production of stretch fabrics, especially stretch fabrics having a high degree of stretch and recovery.

The nature of core yarns, designed especially for woven stretch fabrics, combining an elastic fiber and staple roving, is such that the yarn contains a built-in safety factor practically guaranteeing uniformity of stretch and recovery. Even though the core itself could be stretched several hundred per cent, if not controlled by the sheath, the core *yarn* can be stretched only to the full length of the inelastic sheath. Thus the per cent of stretch of the fabric can be controlled by the design of the yarn.

The recovery is fully controlled by design of the fabric. The stretch yarn, used as warp or filling, can contract until the non-stretch warp or filling is held firmly against itself, and no further. Thus the fabric is fully controlled in respect to stretch and recovery.

It is unlikely that the yarns used in making woven stretch fabrics intended for use as garments will contain high percentages of Spandex. Samples shown to date have contained relatively low percentages of Spandex (5 to 15 per cent), yet they stretch and recover better than most commercially available stretch fabrics based on false-twisted stretch yarns.

It is believed that as Spandex core yarns become more readily available this new family of stretch fabrics will be used whenever maximum stretch and recovery properties are desired.

15

Merchandising and Promotion

The promotion and merchandising of garments by manufacturers of synthetic yarns have become a way of life in the textile business. It started back in the 1920's, shortly after rayon and acetate yarns were successfully manufactured in appreciable quantities in the United States. Manufacturers of rayon and acetate yarns found it necessary to learn how to process these yarns into cloth in cotton and silk mills, how to dye and finish the fabrics, how to cut and sew the garments, and then how to merchandise the garments to department store buyers and eventually to the retail market. Fortunately for them, introductory yarn prices were high enough to provide for these very expensive operations.

Very early in the growth of the rayon and acetate yarn manufacturing industries, manufacturers perceived that their strength lay in promoting and merchandising their own tradenames and in maintaining all possible control over the quality of the garments that reached the public.

This fact was brought home to them, forcibly and expensively in reverse fashion. Manufacturers of circular knit rayon and acetate fabrics started manufacturing and selling garments at a very fast rate possibly because fewer technical difficulties were involved than in the weaving industry. It did not take long for knitters to discover that their fabrics could be weighted, softened, delustered, and stretched, thus producing many more yards of much better looking and feeling fabric than when these weighting, softening, and stretching operations were eliminated. To a lesser extent finishers of woven cloth did the same thing, adding an extra step, calendering, that still further improved the hand and opacity of the fabric. Usage of these diluting and cheapening operations proceeded so rapidly and were carried to such extremes that the public revolted against the purchase of garments that looked and felt like silk until the first wash, whereupon they more closely resembled cheesecloth. When the manufacturers of rayons and acetates found it impossible to reason with their customers to persuade them to stop, or at least curtail the practices that were rapidly ruining the industry for all, each manufacturer found it expedient to purchase one large knitting manufacturer and then manufacture and sell good undiluted and unstretched garments. This soon eliminated from the scene those manufacturers who persisted to the end in delivering inferior merchandise.

The effects of the tidal wave of inferior merchandise produced primarily by the knitters, and to a lesser extent by certain weavers, are still being felt today. To the public, rayon is a "dirty word" signifying the lowest type of, and the cheapest, merchandise made. Yet, in the 30 years that have elapsed since these first almost worthless rayon fabrics were foisted on the public, tremendous strides have been made in rayon and acetate manufacture and hundreds of fabrics made from these improved yarns have been designed, tested, and found excellent in every way. For the most part these new and improved rayons and these new and improved and most excellent quality rayon fabrics are not being manufactured and sold because it is much more profitable for yarn manufacturers to promote and sell the newer types of synthetics. It is these that are receiving the lion's share of the promotional funds that continuously increase the public acceptance of synthetic fabrics. The greater proportion of the rayon used today is spun rayon, which is used as a diluent with other fibers that are promoted, including cotton. The stronger, superior rayon fabrics that could be made have never reached the public and presumably never will because of lack of promotional funds, this in turn due to the low price of ordinary rayons that precludes promotion, and to the federal trade ruling that all man-made fibers that are cellulose must be called rayon regardless of their properties. This ruling, intended to protect the public, effectively prevents the public from purchasing superior garments made from superior "rayon" fibers.

Having learned the dangers of unrestricted and uncontrolled distribution and sale of new and valuable fibers to the textile industry from the costly rayon fiasco in the twenties, manufacturers of the many new synthetic fibers have very carefully controlled the quantity and quality of their newer fibers, and of the fabrics and garments made therefrom. This is done by detailed research, development, and testing programs, and by working with carefully chosen outlets in fields best adopted to accentuate the better properties of each, minimizing any less desirable properties. New synthetic fibers are introduced to the public in the form of well-designed garments, usually by "name" designers and well-established garment manufacturers.

Well-planned, carefully executed, and very expensive merchandising and promotional programs, utilizing all media found to be effective, have assured initial success for each fiber launched. Continued quantity, quality, and merchandising controls have maintained production, quality, and demand at levels that have assured full production and very high profits for fiber manufacturers, and good profits and production schedules for those chosen as partners in each fiber launching program.

The inventor, developer, and licensor of the first texturing process for thermoplastic yarns, the multistep torque-crimp process, appear to have recognized the value of the "formula" for successfully merchandising new fibers developed by domestic producers of synthetic fibers. This company, Heberlein and Company AG of Wattwil, Switzerland, invented, developed, patented, and trademarked their process; and developed, tested, and proved the merit of garments manufactured from thermoplastic yarns textured by their process.

The Heberlein Patent Corporation of New York City promoted, licensed, and controlled the manufacture and sale of thermoplastic yarns torque-crimped by their process in a very orderly manner benefiting all concerned. From the beginning Heberlein restricted availability of their Helanca® textured nylon by controlling and limiting licenses to make yarn by their patented and trademarked process, issuing licenses and trademarks only as fast as market demand increased, and only to firms agreeing to maintain the high standards set by them. They assured steady increase in market demand by spending large proportions of their income from patents and trademarks on merchandising and promotional programs.

As a result Helanca® yarns were very carefully manufactured by Heberlein licensees in accordance with that company's teachings, and garment manufacturers, mostly half-hose manufacturers at the outset, did their part to produce the finest possible merchandise for sale to the public.

This happy situation continued, with benefit to all, especially the purchasing public, until the false-twist process of producing a similar appearing, but less well-set, yarn appeared on the scene.

This yarn, Fluflon®, produced on low cost converted uptwisters, operating at higher speeds than heretofore found possible, used a single process replacing five processes and was sold at lower prices with no restrictions to all who wished to purchase. When Fluflon®

first appeared on the market, 70-denier, 34-filament, 2-ply nylon, Helanca®, sold at $5.00 per pound and Fluflon® at $4.90 per pound.

Step-by-step prices dropped until today Fluflon® sells as low as $2.10 per pound, far below the cost of producing Helanca® by the conventional multistep process.

It is conceded by all concerned that Helanca® torque-crimp nylon half-hose, consisting of multi-ply yarns, using sufficient number of courses and properly dyed and finished, constitutes excellent merchandise. Because of the minute interstices between crimps they retain moisture well. Because of the resilience of the nylon itself and that which is added by the torque-crimp process that increases resilience and makes it effective in all directions in the finished half-hose, and because of the bulk created by the torque-crimp process, these half-hose have an excellent hand and are very soft to walk upon. Because of the elasticity created by torque crimp the fit is excellent and the feel of the half-hose on the foot and leg is excellent throughout the life of the half-hose, which has proved to be several years in many instances.

Immediately after the introduction of false-twist torque-crimp yarns in uncontrolled quantities, the price of torque-crimp nylon dropped and the price of unbranded half-hose knit from false-twist torque-crimped nylon dropped faster. In the absence of quantity and quality controls, and a centrally guided promotional program, unbranded manufacturers produced and sold hundreds of thousands of dozens of underconstructed and poorly finished half-hose at lower and lower prices. The inevitable result was slow rejection by purchasers, a gradual slowing down of the rate of growth of stretch half-hose followed by a leveling-off period, and, eventually, a decline in sales due to customer dissatisfaction with underconstructed and poorly finished merchandise. Meanwhile sales of branded lines of stretch half-hose, properly constructed and dyed and finished, rose to a pleasingly high peak, leveled off, and remained constant.

Meanwhile machine manufacturers improved the equipment used in texturing, and texturers improved the processing of false-twist torque-crimp yarns to such an extent that in 1955 the Heberlein Corporation permitted their valuable trademark, Helanca®, to be used in conjunction with fabrics knitted from torque-crimp yarns produced on false-twist machines, provided that the proper licenses were obtained, and provided that the yarn and fabrics passed their quality control standards.

Had the timing been different, and the Helanca® name and promotion been made available sooner to manufacturers knitting false-twist stretch half-hose, it is possible that a substantial part of the rapid growth would have been in Helanca® rather than in stretch, and the resultant high-quality merchandise would have assured continuous growth and a leveling-off at a much higher plateau. This is not intended to imply a criticism of the Helanca® program. The Heberlein Patent Corporation owed it to its licensees to be very sure of quality and is well justified in having withheld the trademark Helanca® from false-twist items until certain that the development of high and sustained quality justified their use of their trademark with the new product.

Meanwhile Joseph Bancroft & Sons Company initiated a promotional and quality control program in Ban-Lon® half-hose based on their Textralized® yarn. The success of this program that has brought about a steady growth of Ban-Lon® half-hose during the slow decline of unbranded false-twist half-hose is an excellent example of the need for promotion and quality control to assure a sustained market in the synthetic branch of the textile industry. Textralized® yarn is an excellent yarn. Ban-Lon® half-hose knit from Textralized® yarn have a fine soft hand, and, when the half-hose are properly designed with heavy enough yarns and a sufficient number of courses, and the half-hose are finished properly, the merchandise is of excellent quality, soft in hand and comfortable on the foot because of its resilience and high moisture absorption properties. It has some stretch and recovery properties, but not nearly the stretch and recovery and close fit of properly designed and finished false-twist half-hose. In spite of this, good promotion and careful quality control has created a continuous growing market with profit to all: Bancroft, throwsters, knitters, retailers, and consumers. Consumers have benefited most from having good merchandise that looks, feels, and wears well.

To a degree the above is an oversimplification of the benefits of quality control of branded items in the synthetic branch of the textile industry in that it does not take into account the importance of control of the quantity produced. Heberlein issued licenses to produce stretch nylon by the multistep process at such a rate that, until false-twist yarns were available, supply and demand were in good balance. Joseph Bancroft & Sons Company, proceeded in the same manner, issuing licenses at the rate of increase of demand for the yarn. This control of the rate of production assured a good market for all Helanca® and Textralized® yarn produced. Also, it prevented cutthroat competition until the advent of unlimited quantities of false-twist torque-crimp yarns permitted the quality of unbranded half-hose made from good false-twist yarns to drop rapidly because of low construction and poor finishing. As stated previously, this caused a substantial proportion of the purchasing public, actually the larger proportion (the group that must, or chooses to, buy low-priced merchandise), to decline to purchase unsatisfactory merchandise—poor quality half-hose manufactured from good torque-crimp yarns.

The uncontrolled manufacture and sale of false-twist yarns, and the absence of a controlled, guided merchandising and promotion program resulted in the eventual loss of business and profits by all concerned, and in a reduction in the use of the best-fitting and wearing half-hose ever produced. It is to be regretted that the lack of guidance and control by the licensor of the process caused this situation to eventuate.

The rapid rise and fall of the market for stretch leotards knitted first from Helanca®, and later from stretch yarns, further illustrates the need for control of the quantity of yarn available for quality controlled merchandising and promotional programs. Unless the quantity is controlled, manufacturers seeking quick "hit and run profits" can produce sleazy merchandise priced just below the market, make a big profit in a short time, and leave behind them the ruination of well-planned and expensive quality control merchandising and promotional programs that would otherwise have benefited all.

The market for leotards was developed by the Heberlein Patent Corporation. Leotards made from a properly constructed non-run knitted fabric gave excellent service and, together with the fine promotion of Heberlein, created a very large market in a very short time. Soon sleazy, knitted fabrics, simple circular knit fabrics, appeared in leotards priced at slightly reduced levels, and were sold as stretch rather than as Helanca®. These fabrics, owing in part to their low construction and in part to the use of simple circular knit fabric that runs readily, gave extremely poor customer satisfaction and quickly killed this item that otherwise should have remained a staple, particularly for children's play garments. Leotards continue to be used to some extent, particularly in the colder areas, and in some places for children. Control of quality would have assured a higher peak market and a much higher leveling off to a staple item.

The development and merchandising of textured, continuous filament, thermoplastic carpet yarns also illustrate the need of promotion and quality control to create and maintain a market for new good quality textile merchandise.

The inventors of the false-twist process of producing durable torque-crimped thermoplastic yarns, the Permatwist Company of Coatesville, Pennsylvania, recognized the value of their process to the carpet industry and the need of a low cost, bulked, continuous filament carpet yarn early in their work.   Their licensing agreement with throwsters specifically excepted carpet yarns to make it possible to handle them on a specialized basis.

Very early in the development the Permatwist Company produced good carpet yarns, and good carpets from these yarns, the cost being below that of carpets of lesser value produced from spun nylon yarns. The lower cost of these yarns and carpets is due to the use of a one-step continuous process in place of batch process requiring multiple steps.

Durably crimped textured carpet yarns made by the torque-crimp process, and the carpets made from these yarns, were shown to the carpet industry and offered for sale without the benefit of controlled production, quality or merchandising, and without a promotional program, long before producer textured, continuous filament carpet yarns were available.   As should have been anticipated, the industry declined to use these yarns in spite of the improved quality and lower costs of the finished merchandise.   The product, without merchandising and control, had no appeal for the industry.

Much later the manufacturers of nylon produced continuous filament, textured carpet yarns, carpets from these yarns, *a market for the carpets,* backed up with quantity and quality controls and excellent merchandising and promotional programs.   The industry rushed to purchase the yarns and to exploit carpets made from them.   These yarns and carpets, first sold in 1959, have grown steadily in sales and public acceptance, to such an extent that it is estimated that the sales in 1963 will be in excess of 80,000,000 pounds.   And the growth continues.

The most startling feature of the development is the fact that carpet yarns textured by the false-twist process are outstandingly superior to the textured carpet yarns currently produced and sold by the producers.   Both produce beautiful carpets at very low costs.   The superiority of the false-twist yarns lies in the spring-like effect imparted to every minute fraction of an inch of every filament, producing millions of springs in each square yard of carpet, in the permanence of the crimp (producer textured yarns, as currently manufactured, can be reduced to "flat" yarn by applying strain), and in the versatility of the torque-crimp process that permits a wide variety of effects to be produced, making possible a much wider styling range than is currently possible with producer textured yarns.   Very wisely the tufting industry has turned its back on these advantages, offered without benefit of controls or merchandising and promotional programs.

Taslan® yarns, textured by the air-bulking process by licensees of du Pont, controlled with respect to quality of yarn but uncontrolled with respect to quantity produced, and uncontrolled with respect to quality of garments and other items made therefrom, constitute a good example of the result of incomplete control, promotion, and merchandising programs. Although these yarns, made by the most versatile of all texturing processes, applicable to all types of yarns (continuous filament and spun, thermoplastic and non-thermoplastic) have achieved a degree of success, particularly in the drapery field where fabrics woven from continuous filament glass yarns, air-bulked into Taslan® yarns, have become a recognized staple. They have grown in volume considerably more slowly than the processes that have been more completely merchandised and promoted.

Agilon® yarns, edge-crimped, outstandingly successful in the ladies' hosiery field where royalties are high and where the yarns are used in top quality merchandise, lag badly in the intermediate field. The quality of Agilon® yarns in the intermediate denier field is excellent; they possess high bulk, outstanding softness, high moisture absorption, and are very uniform in dyeing properties. The process is the most economical of all in the multi-ply low twist field. Yet growth is slow. Presumably this is for lack of a quality control program at the garment level and lack of a merchandising and promotional program based on quality controlled garments. Many anticipate that this situation will be corrected in the near future, possibly by use of a new trademark for quality controlled items made from Agilon® yarns.

The need and value of control of production, quality, merchandising, and promotion are very well illustrated by the success of the Tycora® mark. Tycora® yarns, manufactured and sold by the Textured Yarn Company, Inc., of Philadelphia, Pennsylvania, are textured continuous filament thermoplastic yarns, each designed to produce specific results. Some are nylon, some polyester and other fibers. Various texturing processes are used. These textured yarns have been controlled in quantity and quality since their inception. The quantity and quality of garments made from these yarns have been carefully guarded. The retail outlets have been well chosen and widely separated. As a result Tycora® promotion has been most effective. Tycora® garments have given excellent customer satisfaction, and all involved have earned and presumably will continue to earn normal and necessary business profits based on the manufacture and sale of these yarns and garments.

Since the rise and fall of the half-hose and leotard markets for torque-crimp thermoplastic yarns, as a result of price cutting on similar appearing but less serviceable merchandise than the good merchandise sold under the Helanca® trademark, the Heberlein Patent Corporation has confined the bulk of its promotional activities to higher quality garments, such as stretch bathing suits and sportswear, and to quality markets dominated in the top brackets by branded lines appreciative of the need and value of sustained quality and sound merchandising and promotion.

Heberlein's promotion of Helanca® consists of well-planned advertisements of specific items, all excellent garments, manufactured and sold by top quality "name" manufacturers. These advertisements have been placed in good "name" fashion magazines, and, to a lesser extent, advertised in trade papers that serve the industry. Promotional money spent in this manner has resulted in specific advertisements in newspapers and in other media reaching the purchasing public directly, amounting to many times the amount of money spent by Heberlein, extensive as that is, and in a surprisingly large amount of editorial mention, the latter possibly being as valuable as the many advertisements paid for directly by retailers.

Heberlein's other services, development of specific items, testing the items for their consumer value, policing of their mark by observation of the manufacture of yarns, fabrics, and garments made from these fabrics, and detailed and continual testing of merchandise purchased on the open market, assists and protects manufacturers indirectly paying for the use of the mark through the royalty payments made as part of the cost of purchasing Helanca® yarns.

Joseph Bancroft and Sons Company are in a more fortunate position than the Heberlein Patent Corporation in that its patents control the manufacture of stuffer box crimped thermoplastic yarns and as yet no one has come up with another means of making a similar yarn at a lower per pound cost. Thus, by judicious licensing, Bancroft has been able to control the quantity of yarn produced by its patented methods. This simplifies the problem of making sure that all merchandise reaching the public with the Ban-Lon® trademark is of outstandingly good quality, assuring steady growth of a sustained market.

This same company has developed fabrics, designed garments, tested the garments extensively, policed this market assiduously and continuously, and promoted and protected its mark so well that Ban-Lon® has become a household name, very valuable to the ethical manufacturers licensed to use it. All involved have profited by their participation in the program, and its smooth operation has benefited the purchasing public by providing a never-ending stream of well-styled, up-to-the-minute serviceable merchandise.

In the weaving field literally hundreds of samples of new and different stretch and textured woven fabrics have been produced and shown by recognized, reputable weavers. Although millions of yards of these fabrics have been woven and sold, mostly those in the low price bracket as converters jockeyed for price rather than quality advantage, these new and beautiful fabrics offered without control of quantity or quality have, for the most part, been passed by while inferior merchandise backed by controlled quantity and quality programs and merchandising and promotional programs have forged ahead.

Now that cotton stretch (cotton cloth woven from cotton yarns resin-treated, false-twisted, heat-set, and untwisted) has become commercially practical, the false-twist group has a golden opportunity to start anew in a field that should become many times larger than all of the current markets for textured thermoplastic yarns combined (see Chapter 16). It is to be hoped that the owners and licensors of this process will follow the route to continual growth and sustained volume clearly mapped by synthetic yarn producers, other texturers as described earlier in this chapter, and the finishing branch of the cotton industry who have so well benefited the public through controlled promotions of the caliber of Sanforized®, Everglaze®, Millium®, and Belfast®.

16

Cotton Stretch, Bulked, and
Stabilized Fabrics Caustic-Treated,
Cross-Linked, and Resin-Treated

Excellent all-cotton stretch yarns have been produced and presented to the textile industry by the Southern Regional Research Laboratory of New Orleans, Louisiana.[1] This excellent work, performed by dedicated workers and paid for by the taxpayers, has been given the same treatment that many other equally good developments of this same group have been given. It has been ignored. Just as flameproofed cotton, also developed by the Southern Regional Research Laboratory, that should currently be used throughout our armed services (uniforms, sheets, towels, etc., especially in ships and ground installations at air bases) has been ignored by the cotton industry.

Presumably this is because the textile industry has been "spoiled" by the producers of synthetic yarns, who develop yarns, assist mills to design, weave, dye, and finish the fabrics from these yarns, develop garments, and finally develop a market for the garments by extensive promotion and development programs.

Southern Regional Research Laboratory does not have available funds for moving their excellent developments past the manufacturing mills, through the dyeing and finishing operations, through the cutters and department store buyers to the general public. (Bureaucrats please ignore—my taxes are high enough now.)

Southern Regional Research Laboratory has produced good stretch and bulked cotton yarns and fabrics, and has warned the cotton in-

---

[1] One of the laboratories of the Southern Utilization Research Branch, Agricultural Research Service, U.S. Department of Agriculture.

241

dustry what to expect in terms of business lost to synthetics if the industry does not take advantage of the new and improved properties of these yarns. The laboratory has outlined a number of obvious markets for fabrics made from the stretch and bulked cotton yarns they have produced. More than this they cannot do with the funds available to them.

Southern Regional Research Laboratory produced woven cotton stretch cloth in 1942—stretch bandages used to some extent during World War II, to a much greater extent during the Korean Police Action, and finally made available to the public in 1952 by Johnson & Johnson, Medical Fabrics Company, and Bauer and Black. This excellent job, master-minded by Charles F. Goldthwait of the Laboratory, involving slack shrinking of loosely woven bandage fabric, has improved the comfort and utility of bandages by providing the needed "give" and recovery—stretch bandages without undue increase in cost. Details of this development will be found further on in this chapter.

More recently Southern Regional Research Laboratory produced woven stretch cotton fabric for garments and other end uses by imparting stretch properties to cotton yarns through utilization of cross-linking and thermo-setting resins that impart to cotton yarns memory of their set while in a highly twisted condition. This process, very expensive in a multiple of steps, is very cheap when a high-speed false-twist machine does the entire job in a single pass at speeds higher than those of normal cotton spinning.

Market for Cotton Stretch

The potential market for cotton stretch is the current market for thermoplastic stretch yarns plus many times this market, as will be outlined in the following paragraphs. C. H. Fisher of Southern Regional Research Laboratory, in his presentation to the Cotton Chemical Finishing Conference, Washington, D.C., November 8–9, 1961,[2] estimated that the market for stretch materials alone will grow to 1 billion, 600 million (1,600,000,000) pounds annually, and that the market for cotton in fabrics where increased warmth is a factor (bulked cotton) should increase by 375 million (375,000,000) pounds per year. He mentions twenty-four uses for stretch cotton alone.

These figures, undoubtedly backed by an impressive amount of evidence, make today's production of stretch and bulked thermoplastic

[2] All cotton stretch and bulked yarns and fabrics by C. F. Fisher, Southern Regional Research Laboratory.

yarns look relatively small and unimportant in the over-all picture. Nevertheless, three firms are collecting royalties ranging from 4½ to 25 cents per pound, six firms are manufacturing and selling machinery into this market, and fifty firms are manufacturing and selling the thermoplastic bulked and stretched yarns.

Manufacturing firms in the cotton industry, notoriously slow to adopt new ideas, and notoriously slow to spend money in research to develop new ideas, have, to all intents and purposes, with one exception, ignored the development of stretch and bulked cotton. Regrettably, this one exception marketed fabrics as stretch which had too little stretch and much too little recovery. This ill-advised venture, based on too little research and development, was doomed to failure. Its failure has delayed the development of all cotton stretch fabrics suitable for marketing by others. An item as good, as potentially profitable, and as economically sound as cotton stretch cannot lie dormant indefinitely. Some progressive cotton mill will inevitably spend the necessary funds to produce good cheap cotton stretch and bulk yarns, and reap an impressive share of the harvest. Others will hasten to follow on a "me too" basis.

In the following paragraphs we outline four of the many potential markets for stretch and bulked cotton yarns.

MEN'S AND CHILDREN'S HOSIERY

Knitters of men's and children's stockings reluctantly process 18 million pounds per year of nylon into 25 million dozen pair of stretch and bulked men's and children's hose. The industry does this reluctantly, in response to market demand, because shortly after the introduction of stretch nylon into the men's and children's hosiery market the gross volume of the market dropped because of the long life of stretch stockings compared with the anticipated life of cotton and other stockings. The normal course of business, price competition followed by lower quality–lower twists, reduced courses, utilization of substantially cheaper more fugitive dyestuffs, has restrained the growth of stretch stockings, particularly in the unbranded lines, to such an extent that the market for strictly stretch stockings is a diminishing one. The market for textured hosiery (Textralized® nylon knitted into Ban-Lon® hose) has grown more rapidly than the market for stretch hose has dropped off, because of the quality control and promotional program that has prevented inferior Ban-Lon® hosiery from reaching the market. Primarily as a result of Joseph Bancroft and Sons Company's quality control and promotion program, the gross market for stretch and bulked thermoplastic yarns in the stocking industry continues to show a steady annual growth.

Cotton is still *King* in the hosiery industry. The introduction of cotton stretch and bulked knitting yarns for hosiery should create an immediate demand in this field alone for more cotton stretch and bulked yarns than can be produced during the first year, since production is limited by the capacity of available equipment. Properly manufactured, stretch and bulked cotton stockings will have all the desirable properties of nylon stretch stockings and nylon Textralized® stockings except long life; thus the adoption of cotton stretch and bulked stockings will not reduce the gross market for stockings but rather will increase this market because cotton stretch and bulked stockings, though superior to non-stretch and non-bulked stockings with respect to stretch and recovery, softness, bulk, hand, appearance, and moisture absorptive properties, will be inferior in useful life. The fact that it will wear out quickly should prove to be the important one to knitters and merchandisers of hosiery and should spark an immediate and rapid growth of business for cotton stretch and bulked hosiery.

KNITTED OUTERWEAR

The knitted outerwear field can consume much more stretch and bulked cotton than the hosiery industry. Some imagination is required to visualize this market, particularly for those not thoroughly familiar with the development of the growing market for stretch and bulked thermoplastic yarns in this field, and the reasons for this growth. The use of stretch and bulked thermoplastic yarns expanded rapidly and continues to expand because bulking changes harsh, wiry, thermoplastic yarns to very soft, flexible yarns that can be processed to produce a hand or feel softer than the softest silk or more resilient than the finest wool. It has made hydrophobic yarns moisture absorptive in fabric form and has created new and very profitable markets. These and other advantages in stretch and bulked yarns were not evident in the very first samples. It required the expenditure of hundreds of thousands of dollars by the inventors, machine manufacturers, and licensees to refine the process to such an extent that the specific properties now built into thermoplastic yarns could be introduced to the public in the form of well-engineered yarns and well-designed fabrics. On second thought the figure above, hundreds of thousands of dollars, is ridiculously low. Actually several million dollars have been and are to be spent in the development of stretch and bulked thermoplastic yarns, fabrics, and garments. For the most part this money represents reinvestment of a small proportion of the earnings of stretch yarns and fabrics.

Cotton stretch and bulk yarns, starting with good, relatively long-staple, combed cotton, resin-treated and made into bulked yarns in a single pass through false-twist spindles, can vary from cotton yarns produced heretofore fully as much as stretch and bulked thermoplastic yarns vary from producer twist thermoplastic yarns.

This means cotton yarns can be economically produced having:

1. Several times the bulk of conventional cotton yarns.
2. An illusion of lightness due to bulk.
3. An increase in warmth of such a magnitude that cotton fabrics made from these yarns will be much warmer than wool.
4. Softness and drape far beyond expectations.
5. Wrinkle resistance exceeding the best produced to date by resin-treating fabrics.
6. Firmness and body when desired *with* softness and drape.
7. Many other properties as desired and required in specific fabrics.

All of the above, and more, can be built into stretch and bulked cotton yarns at costs far below the costs of wool and bulked thermoplastic yarns.

At this point it should be easy to understand why stretch and bulked cotton yarns have a big future in the knitted outerwear field. They (the yarns) will possess all the properties necessary and desirable to make the production of sweaters, double knit jackets, suits, dresses, and other knitted items having all of the very desirable properties now associated only with garments knitted from wool, stretch, and bulked thermoplastic yarns, at costs that will permit the garments to sell at popular prices, thus broadening the base of the rapidly growing knitted outerwear industry, and benefiting the manufacturers, knitters, and the purchasing public.

WOVEN OUTERWEAR

Woven stretch fabrics, ski fabrics, and good quality ladies' slack fabrics, well designed, containing a sufficient quantity of torque-crimp stretch nylon to assure good recovery throughout a long and useful life of the garments made therefrom, using good quality wool as the companion fiber, have been manufactured and sold in sufficient quantities to have won a permanent place in the textile industry for good quality stretch fabrics.

It is fortunate that the first woven stretch fabrics were well designed, and were manufactured and sold in quantity before the market was flooded with underdesigned, very poor quality stretch fabrics containing too little expensive stretch nylon and too much low-grade companion fibers. Most of these poor quality fabrics resulted from attempts to capitalize on the word stretch. Many of them were cotton warp, stretch filled fabrics designed by price-conscious fabric sales people based on yarn costs rather than on yarn properties. Many started with coarse cotton yarns which were much too rigid to react properly, especially when filled with too few picks and too low-count stretch nylon yarns. These fabrics did stretch to a degree but lacked the necessary recovery properties resulting in the production of thousands of unsatisfactory garments and in sharp curtailment in manufacturing, thus giving stretch cotton an undeserved bad name.

When good quality, cross-linked, torque-crimp stretch cotton yarns become available in quantity it will be possible to make good, all-cotton stretch fabrics at popular price levels, possessing good stretch and recovery properties, good resilience, a full, soft hand and heat-retaining properties equal to or better than wool. Immediate acceptance should be anticipated, and a new market for cotton will be created.

DRESSES AND BLOUSES

The new cotton yarns, stretch and bulk, made by continuously durably crimping and cross-linking cotton yarns, will make possible the production of entirely new and different cotton fabrics that are soft in hand, outstandingly more resilient, and wrinkle free. These fabrics can be soft or firm as desired, as resilient as the finest wool, stretch or bulky as required, and new and different in many other ways, all at popular prices. After being introduced in the blouse field they should quickly find a large and substantial market in the dress field, particularly in view of their low cost and amazing versatility.

OTHER MARKETS

From the foregoing outline of the markets for the new, durably torque-crimped cotton yarns in the hosiery, knitted outerwear, woven outerwear, and dress and blouse fields it should be evident that this new family of cotton yarns can be used to produce new and very desirable styles and effects in all markets currently utilizing cotton yarns and in some markets now not available to cotton. The latter are markets that require the resilience and stretch inherent in some and built into other yarns, now for the first time also readily attainable in cotton yarns.

Methods of Producing Stretch Cotton

Stretch cotton has been produced by four methods: slack mercerizing; slack mercerizing followed by cross-linking; twisting, cross-linking, and resin-setting, untwisting, multistep process; twisting, cross-linking, and resin-setting, untwisting, single-step continuous process.

In addition the literature describes the production of stretch cotton by twisting, heat-setting, and untwisting compounds of cellulose: cellulose ethers and esters; benzylcellulose, the cellulose derivative of phenyl isocyanate, etc. We consider these and other thermoplastic derivatives of cellulose, such as cellulose diacetate and cellulose triacetate, to be thermoplastic materials—not cotton. We have discussed the crimping of cellulose diacetate and triacetate in Chapter 7. Chapter 16 will be confined to stretch and bulked cotton, slack mercerized, cross-linked, and resin impregnated.

SLACK MERCERIZING

Cotton cloth was slack mercerized by John Mercer in 1844, and patented by Mercer in 1850 (British Patent 13,296).

Slack mercerizing shrinks fabrics as much as 70 per cent in area, accompanied by a corresponding increase in the diameter of the yarns. For these reasons, increase in yarn size and decrease in fabric area, the use of slack mercerizing has been limited to highly specialized uses such as women's knitted fine glove fabrics, and cotton plissé effects, the latter being accomplished by applying the caustic in stripes, the shrinking effect of the caustic causing an interesting pucker effect in the non-caustic treated areas.

Multi-millions of yards of cotton cloth and multi-millions of pounds of cotton yarn have been and continue to be treated with strong caustic to accomplish a number of valuable results such as an increase in luster, more level dyeing of ripe and unripe cotton fibers, a better base for dyeing, increased dyeing speed, increase in color value (fabrics appear to dye darker—actually more of the color is on the surface), modification of hand and drape, etc. With the two exceptions noted above—the deliberate shrinking of glove fabrics and the production of cotton plissé by caustic printing—cotton has not been caustic-shrunk for general commercial use, for economic reasons, loss of fabric area and increase in yarn diameter as noted previously.

Almost one hundred years after John Mercer noted the shrinking effect of strong caustic on cotton, Charles F. Goldthwait of Southern Regional Research Laboratory applied this knowledge to the processing of woven cotton cloth, taking advantage of an effect apparently unnoted by earlier workers. Goldthwait used the shrinking effect of cold caustic to produce a stretchable cotton cloth having an appreciable recovery under certain specific conditions. He caustic treated cotton gauze to produce new types of bandage fabrics that, when stretched sufficiently to remove unrecoverable stretch, exhibit sufficient stretch and recovery properties to warrant their use by the armed forces and later by industry for the benefit of the general public. These bandages "give" when strained and recover when strain is relaxed, providing better bandages and greater comfort for those who must be bandaged.

Effect of Caustic on Cotton Fibers. It has been recorded by Williams and Alexander and by Coward and Spencer that cotton fibers swollen to the maximum extent by strong caustic soda of approximately 20 per cent concentration swell 3.6 to 3.8 times their unswollen volume. This very great increase in volume is accompanied by a shortening of fiber length and a major change in the shape of the fiber. Figures 67 and 68 show the effect of caustic on cross sections and longitudinal sections of cotton fibers. Fibers swell, become almost round in cross section, and reduce the size of the hole in the center of the fiber. Also, fibers become more rod-like in shape, losing most of the convolutions visible in untreated fibers.

After complete removal of the caustic by washing and neutralizing, the fiber returns to approximately its original volume, even though its new shape remains intact. The fibers retain their strength and useful life, varying, from the textile viewpoint, from untreated fibers primarily in their modified shape, luster, and dye index.

Effect of Caustic on Cotton Yarns. Caustic soda at or about room temperature affects slack cotton yarns exactly as should be anticipated from the effects observed on the fibers. The shortening and the swelling of the fibers tighten the twist, swell and shorten the yarns, producing kinks in direct proportion to the twist factor employed in the production of the original untreated yarns. Actually it is difficult to treat cotton yarns slack and obtain the full effect

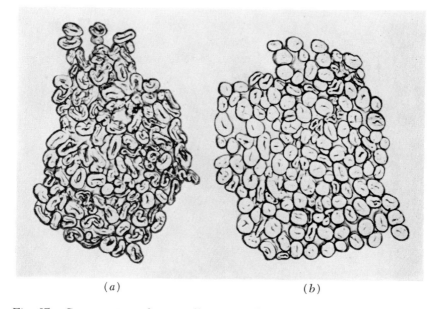

(a)   (b)

Fig. 67. Cross sections of cotton fibers magnified 500 times, courtesy Southern Regional Research Laboratories. (a) Untreated cotton fibers. (b) Stock mercerized cotton fibers.

of this shortening and kinking because the weight of the yarn, swollen with caustic, and the strain necessary to process the yarn through the machine when warps are treated are sufficient to partially overcome the shortening and kinking effect.

Effect of Caustic on Cotton Cloth. In cotton cloth treated with caustic, various opposing forces are at work. Caustic tends to shorten and kink the yarns. Warp threads are restrained by filling threads and vice versa; this restraining action reduces the degree of shrinking and kinking obtained. As the yarns swell, warp yarns bend filling yarns and filling threads bend warp yarns, imparting more or less regular crimps each to the other. This increases the apparent shrinkage of each if the fabric is loosely woven. Tightly woven fabrics cannot so respond, and when very tightly woven the total effect of the caustic is reduced because initial shrinking so tightens the goods that the caustic cannot penetrate completely.

Complete slack mercerizing of cotton cloth is very difficult to attain. The weight of the cloth, wet with caustic, constitutes a re-

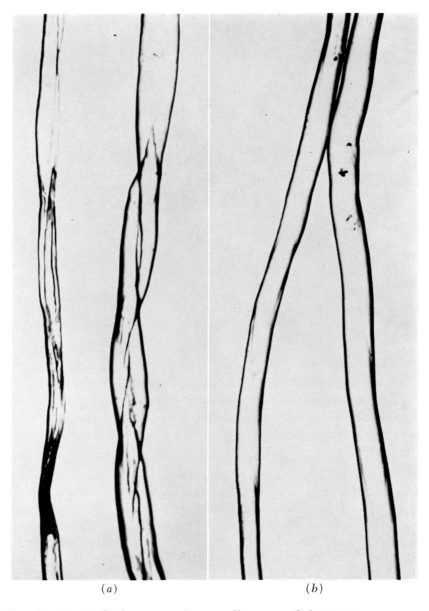

(a)   (b)

Fig. 68.   Longitudinal sections of cotton fibers magnified 500 times, courtesy Southern Regional Research Laboratories.   (a) Untreated cotton fibers.   (b) Stock mercerized cotton fibers.

straining force, and any strain on the warp necessary to move the fabric through the processing machine tends to stretch the cloth while the caustic shrinks it.

Actually the shrinking effect of a 20 per cent solution of cold caustic soda on cotton cloth is quite complex as outlined herein. Simultaneously:

1. The cotton fibers shrink approximately 15 per cent.

2. The fibers swell laterally up to almost four times their volume. This lateral swelling tightens the yarns, "crowding" the fibers to such an extent that the yarns kink if the weave is loose enough to permit kinking and if the twist employed is high enough to promote kinking.

3. The lateral swelling, plus fiber shortening and kinking, shortens the yarns and increases their bulk to such an extent that warp yarns bend filling yarns and filling yarns bend warp yarns, producing additional crimping and further reducing of fiber area.

The combined effect of the above can cause a cotton fabric to shrink in area when processed slack in caustic soda, as much as 70 per cent in extreme circumstances even though the individual fibers shrink only 15 per cent.

Figure 69 is a drawing graphically showing the effect of the slack mercerizing of a loosely woven fabric that shrank 30 per cent both warpwise and fillingwise. Note that the combined effect reduces fabric area by 51 per cent.

Figure 70 shows photomicrographs of two pieces of cotton gauze suitable for use in bandages. Sample (*a*) is the untreated fabric; sample (*b*) is the same fabric slack mercerized with caustic. These photomicrographs, made at the same magnification, show that the

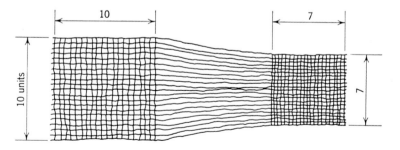

Fig. 69. Diagram, prepared by Southern Regional Research Laboratories, showing the effects of slack caustic mercerizing on the area of cloth. Note that the cloth shrank 30% in each direction resulting in an area loss of 51%.

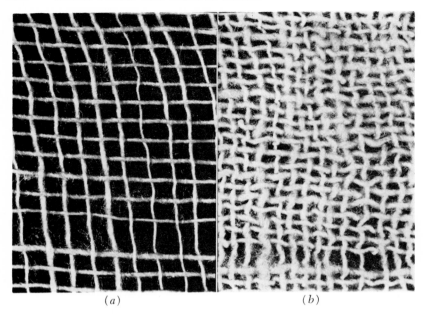

(a)   (b)

Fig. 70. Photomicrographs prepared by Southern Regional Research Laboratories showing the effects of slack caustic mercerizing on 28 x 24 cotton gauze. (a) Gauze before mercerizing. (b) Gauze after mercerizing. The gauze shrank 45% in one direction, 34% in the other, reducing the fabric area by 66%.

gauze shrank 45 per cent in one direction, 34 per cent in the other, the combined effect reducing fabric area by 66 per cent.

Stretch and Recovery Properties of Slack Mercerized Cotton Fabrics. Cotton fabrics vary so widely in weave, count, and twist of yarns used, picks and ends, etc., that many broad statements regarding the stretch and recovery properties of slack mercerized cotton could be successfully challenged. One such statement can be made without danger of contradiction. At best the stretch and recovery properties of slack mercerized cotton fabrics are inferior to the stretch and recovery properties of well-designed and well-dyed and finished fabrics built around torque-crimp stretch nylon.

The literature discusses stretch and recovery properties of slack mercerized fabrics in such a manner that it might be assumed that many of these fabrics possess good stretch and recovery characteristics. This is quite misleading. Slack mercerized cotton fabrics do have useful stretch and recovery properties in certain fields, as in stretch bandages. Slack mercerized bandage fabrics have recovery sufficiently good to warrant their manufacture and sale. They also have a very high degree of non-recoverable elongation. In use, these fabrics are stretched sufficiently during bandaging to remove the bulk of the non-recoverable elongation, thus permitting the much smaller percentage of elastic recovery to function efficiently after the bandage is in place.

To be useful in most fabrics that can be benefited by the addition of stretch and recovery properties, fabrics should have very little non-recoverable elongation and should recover close to 100 per cent after literally thousands of applications of strain and release, as in ski fabrics. Many slack mercerized cotton fabrics produced and offered for sale commercially do not have this degree of recovery or elasticity, even after removal of non-recoverable elongation. As greige goods are woven with more and more ends and picks, the percentage of non-recoverable elongation diminishes and the ratio of recovery to total stretch increases. When special weaves, such as waffle weaves, are employed this recovery can be very impressive even after several hundred strains and releases from strain. To date in most constructions slack mercerized commercially, the recovery, particularly after a number of applications of strain and release, diminishes to such an extent that garments made from these fabrics "grow," thus losing most of the benefit of the remaining recovery in the fabric. Garments that "grow" lose their well-tailored appearance.

It is possible to produce excellent stretch fabrics having very good recovery properties by the slack mercerizing process, and it is probable that this will be done. For the optimum results, long staple cotton, more highly twisted than usual, should be used, and the fabrics should be especially designed and finished. This can be accomplished by designing and redesigning after the processing of relatively large samples through commercial finishing in a cooperating finishing plant. A proper combination of long-staple cotton, highly twisted, properly designed to permit just the right amount of shrinking, development of special finishing techniques, carefully followed in practice, can produce excellent merchandise.

Costs must be high. Expensive cotton, higher than usual twists, very substantial loss of fabric area, and higher than usual finishing costs due to the need for special handling, all add up to high cost goods.

Properly promoted (see Chapter 15 about the need for control of quality and quantity and promotion of a protected tradename), garments made from such fabrics can find a ready market. *Unless* properly promoted, cheaper, less desirable merchandise, also sold as cotton stretch, may adversely affect the total market.

Method of Determining the Recovery Properties of Stretch Fabrics. The confusion in the literature regarding the degree of recovery of slack mercerized fabric is due to lack of recognized and accepted test methods. Test methods used originally for determining the utility of stretch bandages are not drastic enough to determine the utility of stretch ski fabrics, stretch slacks, etc. To date, good acceptance tests for determining the degree of stretch and recovery in stretch fabrics do not exist. Nor is there an accepted test method for determining the shrinking of stretch fabrics. Lack of such a test has permitted thousands of garments to be delivered, possessing adequate recovery *and too much shrink* for the delivered size; this causes fully as much trouble as lack of recovery, especially in slacks. It is to be hoped that test methods for determining the comparable stretch and recovery properties of stretch fabrics, acceptable to industry, will soon be developed.

SLACK MERCERIZING FOLLOWED BY CROSS-LINKING

Slack mercerized fabrics are improved in stretch and recovery properties by cross-linking, dry, at elevated temperatures.

Well-designed fabrics, slack mercerized, readily recover their "bounce," stretch, and recovery properties, etc., when washed and dried, even without the addition of cross-linking resins during finishing. The value of the resin application in relation to stretch and recovery is to maintain stretch and recovery during each wearing for a longer period of time and, by increased recovery, to provide *more* easy recovery without distortion. This is very important because, in use, garments are often subjected to considerable strain over a long period of time.

It is to be anticipated that in most instances fabrics used in promoted garments will be cross-linked after slack mercerizing.

TWISTING, CROSS-LINKING AND RESIN-SETTING, UNTWISTING MULTISTEP PROCESS

Southern Regional Research Laboratory has produced stretch and bulked cotton yarns by two multistep processes, stating that these processes produce excellent stretch and bulked cotton yarns.

It is at once obvious that both processes must be very expensive, and are subject to most if not all of the problems encountered in processing thermoplastic yarns by the conventional step-by-step method, plus additional problems due to unavoidable trash in the cotton, problems associated with resin-treating and cross-linking of cotton, and problems of uniformity of drying. We will discuss briefly each step of the two processes.

SOUTHERN REGIONAL RESEARCH LABORATORY COTTON STRETCH AND BULKING, PROCESS 1

Wind. Yarn is wound on a tube as for dyeing.

Scour. Cotton wax and other impurities are removed to assure rapid penetration of cross-linking agents. Depending on the intended end use of the fabric, it may also be necessary to destroy the bits of seed, leaf, etc., in the cotton; this process requires hot caustic to start the action and a bleaching treatment to complete it.

Since it is impractical to attempt to dye cotton cloth which has been cross-linked and resin-treated in yarn form, the yarn must be dyed after scouring, and after trash destruction should color be required in the finished fabric.

Extract. It is important that the tubes of yarn be extracted uniformly to assure necessary uniform drying; otherwise subsequent pickup of cross-linking agents may vary.

Dry. Equipment utilized should be so constructed that drying from unit to unit will be as uniform as possible.

Continuously Resin Impregnate and Ply Twist, Twist on Twist (Cable Twist). The singles comprising the ply are treated with resin solution, the concentration of resin, and other necessary ingredients, and the quantity applied being so adjusted that the add on of weight after drying, curing, washing, and redrying is $3\frac{1}{2}$ to 4 per cent.

The resin used is dimethyol ethylene urea (DMEU). Others have been found effective.

Plying is done on a downtwister operating at 5500 to 6500 rpm. When two 20/1 yarns are plied 20 turns per inch at 6500 rpm, the through-put per spindle is 9 yards per minute. This calculates to less than 12 pounds per spindle per 7-day week, assuming an efficiency of well over 90 per cent.

The turns of ply twist that can be used are limited to twist that will not cause a serious kinky condition when the yarn is subsequently skeined.

Skein. At best an expensive operation and a slow one, owing to the necessity of lacing the skeins.

Dry. It is difficult to dry skeins impregnated with water-soluble resins without encountering a serious wicking action that can cause a variation in resin content by drawing a resin to the surface of the skeins. The best method is to dry the skeins in an atmosphere of water vapor, laying the skeins on racks in a room heated by closed coil steam pipes, exhausted by fans. The fans draw out and expel the water vapor. Moist skeins in a warm or hot atmosphere consisting of water vapor only will not wick. This is a slow process requiring 24 to 48 hours to dry the skeins thoroughly. The skeins must be thoroughly and uniformly dried before curing to assure the possibility of obtaining a uniform cure.

Cure. The curing time and temperature should be uniform. This means the temperature at the center of the skeins must reach curing temperatures very quickly. The skeins in the center of a large lot, hanging or lying on racks, should reach maximum temperature as quickly as skeins on the outside of these racks or poles if batch curing is used—a condition obviously impossible to attain. It is, therefore, advisable that the skeins be cured in a continuous conveyor system.

Wind on Tubes, Wash, Centrifuge, Dry. These 4 time-consuming and moderately expensive operations are much less critical than the 8 preceding operations. Considerable latitude is possible in these four.

Back Twist Using a Greater Number of Turns Than Used in Ply Twisting. As commercial twisting machines, belt driven, vary somewhat from spindle to spindle with respect to turns of twist inserted (up to 2 turns per inch variation being common when high twist is involved), it is possible for the twist of two adjacent ends on a single machine to vary as much as 4 turns after untwisting. This would require a yarn accidentally undertwisted by 2 turns to be overtwisted by 2 turns. For this reason, variation in turns of individual spindles, some variation from spindle to spindle is unavoidable.

Conclusion. The process can produce good bulk and stretch yarns, limited in degree of stretch by twist limitations due to the necessity of skeining, and varying somewhat from spindle to spindle. The process has many danger spots and is very expensive.

SOUTHERN REGIONAL RESEARCH LABORATORY COTTON STRETCH AND BULKING, PROCESS 2

Wind, Scour, Extract, Dry. (See Process 1.)

Twist to a High Degree, Twist on Twist (Cable Twist). Process 2 eliminates the need of skeining. Higher turns of twist can be employed because the danger of kinking and snarling in skein form is eliminated. Good stretch and bulk can be produced. Through-put per spindle is reduced when more turns are employed.

Wind on Perforated Tube. Because retained liquor after centrifuging is related to package density it is important that the density be maintained very uniformly, and that hard ridges in the package be avoided.

Resin Impregnate in Package Dyeing Machine. To assure proper penetration within individual strands of yarn and throughout the yarn wound on perforated tubes, the resin impregnation mix must be so constituted that polymerization does not occur in the solution. This is not easy to accomplish.

Centrifuge. All lots should be uniform in weight. The time of centrifuging must be identical from lot to lot. Centrifuge must be maintained in very good mechanical condition to insure uniform time from start to full speed and from full speed to stop.

Dry. The drying problem is greater than in Process 1 where skeins must be dried. The resin impregnated yarn on perforated tubes should be dried in an atmosphere of hot water vapor—a room heated with closed steam coils, exhausted by a fan.

Cure with Dielectric Heat. In a properly engineered machine, uniformity should exceed the best that can be done with heated air.

Wash, Dry. Not especially critical operations.

Back Twist, Using a Greater Number of Turns Than Used in Ply Twisting. (See Process 1.)

Conclusion. Process 2 should produce better yarn than Process 1 because more twist can be used and the cure can be more uniform.

TWISTING, CROSS-LINKING AND RESIN-SETTING, UNTWISTING, SINGLE-STEP CONTINUOUS PROCESS

Cotton yarns, in experimental quantities only, have been continuously resin-treated, twisted, dried, cured, and untwisted on specially constructed machinery at rates of speed exceeding 50 yards per minute, the resultant yarn having fully as much stretch and recovery as the best false-twist nylon of comparable yarn count and denier. The stretch and recovery properties of these yarns far exceeded the expectations of the inventors (Seem and Stoddard, U.S. Patent 3,025,659) in that it was anticipated that the stretch and recovery of these yarns, while appreciable, would be much less than the stretch and recovery of comparable nylon yarns.

Other cotton yarns have been processed by variations of the above outlined technique, for example, resin impregnated and dried both continuously and batchwise prior to false twisting. Mercerizing, bleaching, dyeing, etc., one operation only, or a multiple, prior to processing through the false-twist spindle. Dyeing and resin treating is done in separate but continuous, and composite baths, and in many other variations of the basic continuous process that are readily obvious once the premise of the processing by the basic continuous steps is fully realized.

The economy of this process, as compared with slack mercerizing (evident once the unavoidable economic loss due to loss of fabric area and gain in yarn diameter and weight caused by the swelling and shortening in length of cotton fibers and cotton yarns burdening the slack mercerizing process are fully realized), makes this very attractive in terms of cost, in addition to the attractiveness due to the added merit of the fabric in terms of stretch and recovery. The increased bulk which provides softness of hand, added moisture absorption, apparent lightness of touch, etc., still further enhances the value and appeal of fabrics woven and knitted from these yarns.

It would be presumptuous, out of order, and very misleading to those not actually engaged in the manufacture of yarns and fabrics for the author to discuss costs of both processes on a step-by-step basis, particularly at this time when cotton yarns continuously processed by the twisting, cross-linking and resin-setting, untwisting, single-step continuous process are not yet in commercial production; and in view of the unavoidable great variations in cost from count to count of yarn and type to type of cloth. However, some cost comparisons are possible.

Throwsters or texturers process 70-denier nylon from producer twist yarn to plied false-twist yarn, delivering on cones for as little as 40 to 50 cents per pound, 70-denier starting basis. This price covers all costs, and, obviously there is enough profit to keep them in business.

It is readily obvious that throwsters and texturers can process two ends of 40/1 cotton, totaling 266 denier, at a cost well below the cost of processing 70-denier nylon.

The 40-to-50-cent mark-up for processing charged by throwsters must necessarily carry research, sales, financing (the cotton yarn itself), and a profit burden, all reduced or eliminated in integrated plants. It is further obvious that the rather expensive coning operation, the cone itself, and packing and shipping costs are all eliminated when the work is performed in integrated plants. Thus the true cost of processing 266-denier cotton in an integrated plant can be far below the visible cost of processing 70-denier nylon in texturer plants.

Even at 48 cents per pound, the increase in cost per yard of a fabric containing 2 ounces per yard of stretch cotton calculates to only 6 cents per yard.

Unavoidable shrinkage during slack mercerizing carries two cost burdens: actual yarn shrinkage of at least 15 per cent in length due to fiber shrinkage, causing a change in the count of the yarn that decreases its value in terms of market price; and fabric area shrinkage, usually in excess of 15 per cent even when the fabric is fully extended to the limit of its "easy" stretch. In fine count yarns these two costs due to shrinkage usually amount to more than the entire cost of 6 cents per yard calculated for false-twisting and resin-treating cotton, even if purchased from texturers and throwsters, at prices assuring them of greater mark-up than they currently enjoy when processing finer denier nylon.

In addition to the cost due to unavoidable shrinkage, there has to be some added cost in finishing plants actually doing the slack mercerizing. No matter how low the cost, it is still appreciable. To produce the full benefit of slack mercerizing added twist should be used and an extra step—resin treating—should be added to produce the full attainable bounce or stretch and recovery in slack mercerized goods. In the composite these costs calculate to considerably more per yard than when the yarns are processed and resin-set through false-twist equipment.

The slack mercerizing process, and the slack mercerizing followed by resin-treating process, can be used to produce a wide variety of effects, the primary variations being based on count and single-end twist of the cotton yarns, and on the fabric construction used in weaving.

The false-twist cross-linking process can be used to produce a much wider range of effects, including all those possible with slack mercerizing and resin treating. Additional possible effects are greatly increased softness, light weight due to the spring-like effect of fibers, twisted, cross-linked and untwisted, resiliency with softness in whatever degree desired, even far beyond that of wool, warmth exceeding the best that can be done with wool pound for pound because of the minute interstices between fibers. There are other beneficial effects; many are far too involved to be readily absorbed when presented in detail, in fact, they are beyond the scope of this book.

The wide range of beneficial results attainable in fabrics woven from false-twisted, cross-linked, long-staple cotton yarns can best be appreciated by considering the changes made in each individual fiber. Cross-linking in tightly twisted form changes each relatively limp cotton fiber into a minute spring. Untwisting (removing the false twist) produces fibers in which every minute fraction of an inch contains latent torque-crimp energy usable when yarn and fabric design and yarn and fabric processing are correct.

It is quite possible that the eventual utilization of the false-twist, cross-linked continuous process may eventually become much more important in the *thermal* field—the producing of extra lightweight, extra soft, extra warm fabrics—than in the stretch field. The desire for stretch may wax and wane. The desire for extra warmth, light weight, and softness will always be with us.

"Flash" Cross-Linking and Resin Curing

Much that is "known" about the reaction of cross-linking agents and the curing of resin in cloth form becomes "unknown" when single ends of cotton yarn are resin-treated and flash cured by passing through the center of a long tube, which is heated far above the temperatures customarily employed in resin curing. In cloth each individual yarn is insulated to a very great degree by the adjoining yarns parallel to it and by the crossovers of the opposing threads. This insulation effect produces uneven rates of curing even within short lengths of individual yarns, in cloth, and greatly increases the time that must be employed to produce a full cure. The added time causes or permits the percentage of side reactions (reactions that produce the unwanted compounds which cause trouble in resin) to be greatly increased. When one individual strand of yarn is passed through the center of a tube, the curing and cross-linking can be carried to completion in as short a period of time as 1 second; this quick reaction goes to a greater degree of completion than is possible when cloth is treated, with far less production of undesirable side effects.

The high percentage of desirable reactions, both cross-linking and resin-setting, that takes place in the flash curing of resin-treated highly twisted cotton yarns processed in single-end form is undoubtedly the primary reason for the unexpected excellence of the stretch and recovery observed in finished cotton fabrics manufactured from these yarns.

Twisting, Cross-Linking and Resin Setting, Untwisting, Single-Step Continuous Process (U.S. Patent 3,025,659)

The basic process, a single pass through the machine, is obviously very economical. Depending on the yarn, and the fabric to be produced, various preliminary steps may be necessary: to remove trash, to bleach, to dye, or to otherwise pretreat the yarn before false-twisting. These treatments are too well known to require any elaboration herein. We will discuss the process below, point by point.

Cotton yarn is continuously:

Drawn from Supply Package. As stated above the yarn may be raw yarn or may have received one or more treatments prior to being creeled for false-twisting. The yarn may be creeled as singles or as a ply. In any event it enters the process as a ply and is treated and false-twisted as a ply.

Saturated with Cross-Linking Agents, Resin, and Other Chemicals as Required. It is possible to apply the resin at an earlier step in the process, drying the yarn in any one of several ways. One way is to draw off the water vapor from a closed heated box or unit in which the moisture leaves the yarn in an atmosphere of water vapor; the water vapor being constantly evacuated from the unit by a fan or a vacuum pump. Another way is to continuously saturate and dry on a progressive reel as used in the most modern continuous filament rayon systems.

It is also possible to apply the resin just prior to leading the yarn into the first twist trap, thus going from dry yarn to dried cross-linked false-twisted yarn in one continuous step. Various other chemicals as desired, softeners, especially chosen dyestuffs, etc., may be applied simultaneously with the cross-linking agents and chemicals necessary to speed up the cross-linking operation.

Drawn Over a Guide to a Twist Trapper. This guide can also function as a wiping or squeezing agent when necessary, a means of removing excess liquor from the yarn before entering the twist trapper and heated tube.

Drawn or Impelled Through the Twist Trapper. The twist trapper can be a rolling one, this to more uniformly control the tension and, if sufficient surface or dual rolls as in a 10B are utilized, to eliminate any tension variations due to snagging, etc., prior to entering the twist trapper.

Twisted as It Comes Out of the Twist Trapper, by the Turning of the Twist Trapper Located in the False-Twist Spindle, and Drawn into Heated Tube. The yarn, being under considerable tension, can be twisted to a very high degree without kinking. In most instances the absolute maximum number of turns possible without causing the yarn to double upon itself are utilized in order to produce maximum stretch and recovery and maximum bulk in the finished yarn when bulk is desired.

Dried and Flash Cured. In the cloth finishing industry it is almost universally believed that drying and curing in a single step constitute a very bad practice, resulting in a sort of case hardening effect that produces a papery effect in the cloth, leaves the inside less well set than the surface, and creates other undesirable effects. In single-end yarn processing this has not been found to be true. It is possible to dry and cure in a single operation, producing, as stated previously, superior cross-linking and resin-set conditions.

Cooled and Drawn Through the Twist Trapper in the Spindle. A single strand of yarn cools below the temperature of cross-linking and curing in an amazingly short time. For this reason only a very short distance is required between the bottom of the heated tube and the spindle.

Untwisted as It Moves Out of the Spindle Twist Trapper. As the yarn leaves the twist trapper all of the false twist comes out, leaving the yarn containing the same number of turns that it contained when drawn from the creel.

Guided to the Take-up Package. Once the yarn is past the twist trapper the action is over and there remains only the problem of guiding the yarn to the take-up package and taking it up properly and uniformly; this constitutes no real problem with cotton yarns.

As this is written, cross-linked, false-twisted, cotton yarns having the properties described are not commercially available. Production machines capable of producing thousands of pounds of yarn per week do not exist. A few spindles exist, these being in effect a variation of the 553 machine manufactured by Leesona Corporation for false-twisting nylon. The only important variation is that an electrically heated tube replaces the heater block, making it possible to heat the yarn uniformly and effect the beneficial flash cure described earlier.

Normal commercial development should be expected to proceed approximately as follows:

1. A manufacturer of cotton yarns can be expected to purchase a full-scale production machine.

2. This one machine must be engineered, then built practically by hand, an expensive and time-consuming item.

3. A reasonable amount of research must go into getting the best possible results on a variety of yarns. These results are actually determinable only after the yarns are manufactured into cloth, cut and sewn into garments, and the garments tested for desirable properties, utility, and probable public acceptance. This obviously cannot be done quickly. At best it will require months of work and many thousands of dollars of expenditure of research funds.

4. Once acceptable garments exist, additional orders for equipment can be placed.

5. Detailed drawing board work and the setting up of a production line must follow.

6. Production of machines can start.

If commercial development follows normal procedure as outlined above quantity production of garments made from false-twist, cross-linked cotton is at least two years away.

Summary

Cotton fabrics produced by the slack mercerizing and cross-linking of fabrics made from long-staple cotton especially designed for cross-linking and carefully finished can produce excellent stretch fabrics and may become an important item in the stretch field. Whether or not this happens depends primarily on whether or not a far-sighted manufacture or merchandiser of cotton fabrics takes the trouble to set up a good promotional program built around top quality merchandise.

Fabrics possessing far better thermal properties than heretofore possible with cotton, and stretch and recovery properties exceeding the best that can be done in comparable constructions with slack mercerizing and cross-linking in fabric form, can be produced by utilizing equipment yet to be produced in quantity. Commercial production of this equipment, its utilization by the cotton manufacturing industry, and promotion of quality controlled garments and other items made therefrom can be of great benefit to all directly and indirectly concerned with the production, manufacture, and sale of cotton and fabrics manufactured from cotton.

Addendum: Slack Mercerizing—1964
Resilient Cotton, Deferred Cure

During 1963 many cotton fabric merchandising organizations offered all cotton "easy stretch" fabrics, averaging 15 per cent "easy stretch," with good recovery. These basic fabrics, reeded wider than heretofore, slack mercerized, and popularly priced, achieved an immediate success based on good merchandising, added comfort, and utility. It is anticipated that these "easy stretch" fabrics will become popular in 1964 and 1965.

Currently progressing intensive work on all slack mercerized cotton stretch warp fabrics and resilient, soft, drapey fabrics, based on false-twist resin-set yarns, combined with deferred cure durable finishes, will assure cotton a continuing dominant position in the family of fibers.

17

Patents

This chapter presents issued patents licensed for the texturing of thermoplastic yarns, including non-thermoplastic yarns in the air-bulking process.

We also list five issued patents not licensed as this is written. We recommend that those seriously interested in textured yarns and stretch and textured fabrics obtain copies of these five nonlicensed patents and read the body of each, as well as the claims. They may be a guide to certain probable future developments in the texturing field. They contain much more information than is indicated in the coverage by the Patent Office Gazette.

We contacted the various firms issuing licenses on the texturing processes used commercially in the United States: Joseph Bancroft and Sons Company—Textralized®, Deering Milliken Research Corporation—Edge-crimped and torque crimp, E. I. du Pont de Nemours and Company, Inc.—Air-bulked, Heberlein Patent Corporation—Torque crimp, Leesona Corporation—Torque crimp; and obtained the patent numbers of the patents that have been included in their license agreements. We obtained copies of the patents and checked the U.S. Patent Office Gazette as the best available source of unbiased information on the content of each. We present the patent numbers and the published data of the Patent Office Gazette on each patent.

Joseph Bancroft and Sons Company, Wilmington, Delaware, U.S.A.

Patents licensed to manufacturers of Textralized® thermoplastic yarns:

U.S. Patent Re. 23,824   PROCESS FOR TREATING PROTEINACEOUS FIBERS

Leo W. Rainard, Nyack, N.Y., assignor to Alexander Smith, Incorporated, a corporation of New York
Original No. 2,575,837, dated November 20, 1951
Serial No. 38,657, July 14, 1948.   Application for reissue November 19, 1952, Serial No. 321,535
Seven Claims (Cl. 19-66)

Claim 7. The method of imparting a permanent artificial crimp to textile fibers, which comprises gripping said fibers between closely spaced conveyor surfaces discharging into a substantially closed zone, and forcing the gripped fibers into said zone against the pressure of a mass of fibers held compacted under pressure in said zone, said pressure being adapted to cause the fibers to be progressively folded over and crimped as they are delivered from said conveyor surfaces, holding the mass of crimped fibers compacted under a substantially constant pressure throughout their travel in said zone to retain the crimp therein, and heating the mass while thus compacted in said zone to a temperature above that at which the natural resilience of the fibers resists deformation and below that at which degradation occurs to bring the fibers to the plastic condition necessary to set said crimp.

U.S. Patent 2,505,618   MEANS FOR TREATING WOOLEN SLIVERS AND THE LIKE

Alfred T. Hammerle, Boston, Mass.
Application July 15, 1948, Serial No. 38,798
Eight Claims (Cl. 19-66)

Claim 1. In a means for treating woolen sliver and the like, the combination of a pressure chamber having an inlet and an outlet, positively locked closure means for said outlet, means for forcibly feeding woolen sliver into said chamber through the inlet and tightly compressing and packing the same therein, and means for unlocking the closure means upon the attainment of a predetermined pressure in said chamber to discharge the compressed sliver.

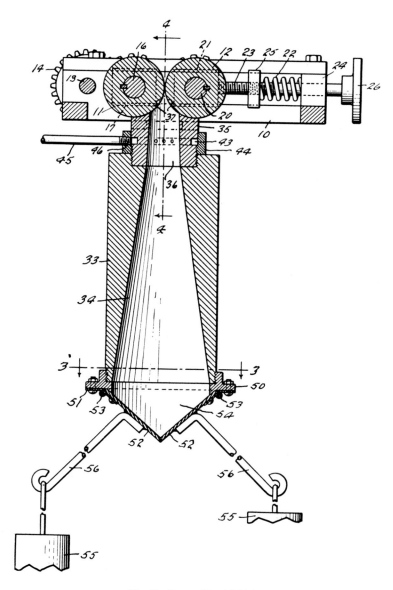

Fig. 2.   Patent Re. 23,824.

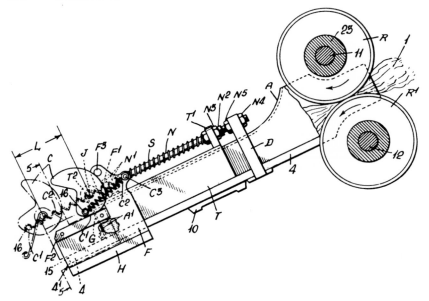

Fig. 1.   Patent 2,505,618.

U.S. Patent 2,514,557 CRIMPING APPARATUS

Julius H. Pfau, Yonkers, N.Y., assignor to Alexander Smith & Sons
   Carpet Company, Yonkers, N.Y., a corporation of New York
Application August 7, 1948, Serial No. 43,120
Thirteen Claims (Cl. 19-66)

Claim 1. An apparatus for crimping fibers, comprising a member
having a bore forming a chamber, a pair of feed rolls at one end of
said member and a movable closure at the other end of said member
forming end closures for said chamber, means driving said rolls to
feed said fibers there-between into said chamber, means causing said
movable closure to resist the discharge of the fibers so as to hold the
fibers in said chamber under a predetermined pressure, and injector
means disposed to inject a fluid into an intermediate part of said
chamber into contact with said fibers.

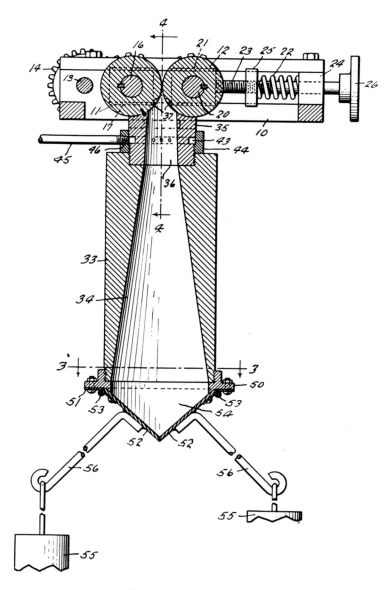

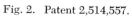

Fig. 2.   Patent 2,514,557.

U.S. Patent 2,575,781   METHOD OF CRIMPING TEXTILE FIBERS

Joseph L. Barach, Montclair, N.J., assignor to Alexander Smith, Incorporated, a corporation of New York
Application October 14, 1949, Serial No. 121,440
Four Claims (Cl. 19-66)

Claim 1. The method of imparting an artificial crimp to textile fibers, which comprises passing said fibers through a zone containing a heated fluid and moisture, maintaining the fibers in said zone for a time to presoften the fibers for crimping, gripping said fibers between closely spaced conveyor surfaces discharging into a substantially closed zone, and forcing the gripped fibers into said zone against the pressure of a mass of fibers held compacted under pressure in said zone, said pressure being adapted to cause the fibers to be progressively folded over and crimped as they are delivered from said conveyor surfaces, holding the mass of crimped fibers compacted under a substantially constant pressure to retain the crimp therein, introducing a setting agent under pressure into said zone, treating the mass while thus compacted with said setting agent under conditions to produce a permanent set of said crimp in said fibers, and withdrawing the crimped fibers from said zone.

U.S. Patent 2,575,833   METHOD FOR CRIMPING TEXTILE FIBERS

Julius H. Pfau, Yonkers, N.Y., and Leo W. Rainard, Nyack, N.Y., assignors to Alexander Smith, Incorporated, a corporation of New York
Application October 14, 1949, Serial No. 121,438
Three Claims (Cl. 19-66)

Claim 1. The method of imparting a permanent artificial crimp to textile fibers, which comprises gripping said fibers between closely spaced conveyor surfaces discharging into a substantially closed zone, and forcing the gripped fibers into said zone against the pressure of a mass of fibers held compacted under pressure in said zone, said pressure being adapted to cause the fibers to be progressively folded over and crimped as they are delivered from said conveyor surfaces, holding the mass of crimped fibers compacted under a substantially constant pressure to retain the crimp therein, introducing superheated water under pressure into said zone, treating the mass while thus compacted with said superheated water under conditions to produce a permanent set of said crimp in said fibers, and withdrawing the crimped fibers from said zone.

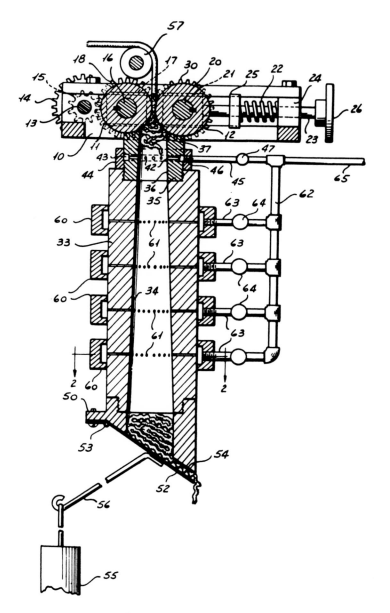

Fig. 1.   Patent 2,575,781.

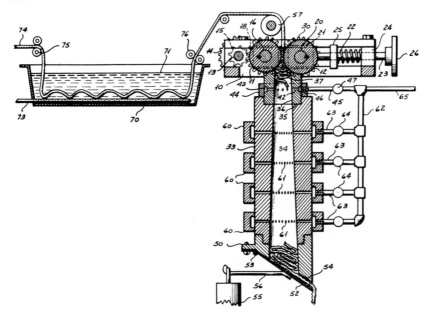

Fig. 1. Patent 2,575,833.

U.S. Patent 2,575,837   PROCESS FOR TREATING PROTEINACEOUS FIBERS

Leo W. Rainard, Nyack, N.Y., assignor to Alexander Smith, Incorporated, a corporation of New York
Application July 14, 1948, Serial No. 38,657
Six Claims (Cl. 19-66)

Claim 1. The method of imparting a permanent artificial crimp to textile fibers, which comprises gripping said fibers between closely spaced conveyor surfaces discharging into a substantially closed zone, and forcing the gripped fibers into said zone against the pressure of a mass of fibers held compacted under pressure in said zone, said pressure being adapted to cause the fibers to be progressively folded over and crimped as they are delivered from said conveyor surfaces, holding the mass of crimped fibers compacted under a substantially constant pressure to retain the crimp therein, introducing a setting agent under pressure into said zone, treating the mass while thus compacted with said setting agent under conditions to produce a permanent set of said crimp in said fibers, and withdrawing the crimped fibers from said zone.

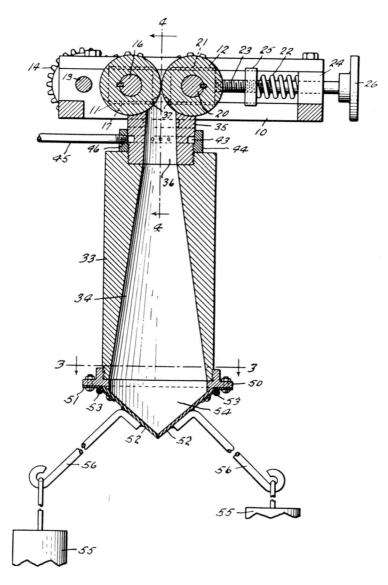

Fig. 2.   Patent 2,575,837.

U.S. Patent 2,575,838   METHOD OF CRIMPING PROTEINACEOUS FIBERS

Leo W. Rainard, Nyack, N.Y., assignor to Alexander Smith, Incorporated, a corporation of New York
Application November 30, 1948, Serial No. 62,727
Twelve Claims (Cl. 28-75)

Claim 1. The method of imparting an artificial crimp to proteinaceous fibers which comprises feeding said fibers into a crimping zone maintained full of a mass of said fibers and held under a pressure adapted to cause the fibers to be folded over and crimped as they are forced into said mass of fibers, holding the mass of crimped fibers under pressure in a setting zone, maintaining setting conditions of temperature and moisture content in said setting zone, discharging the crimped fibers from said setting zone, and passing the crimped fibers through a relaxing bath at a temperature and rate to at least partially relax the internal stress produced by crimping and to improve the spinning characteristics of said fibers.

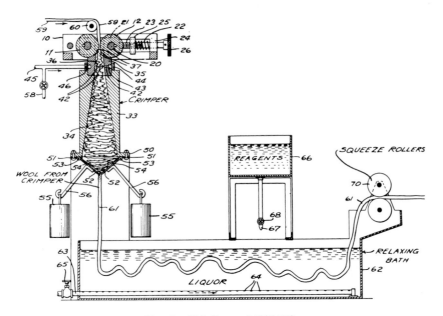

Fig. 1.   U.S. Patent 2,575,838.

U.S. Patent 2,575,839   PROCESS FOR CRIMPING UNCROSSLINKED FIBERS

Leo W. Rainard, Nyack, N.Y., assignor to Alexander Smith, Incorporated, a corporation of New York
Application December 15, 1948, Serial No. 65,440
Five Claims (Cl. 19-66)

Claim 1. The method of imparting a permanent artificial crimp to vegetable fibers and uncrosslinked thermoplastic synthetic fibers, which comprises gripping said fibers between closely spaced conveyor surfaces discharging into a substantially closed crimping zone, and forcing the gripped fibers into said zone against the pressure of a mass of fibers held compacted under pressure in said zone, said pressure being adapted to cause the fibers to be progressively folded over and crimped as they are delivered from said conveyor surfaces, holding the mass of crimped fibers compacted under a substantially constant pressure to retain the crimp therein, injecting a hot fluid into the mass of fibers in said zone to heat the fibers to a temperature to bring the fibers to a plastic condition in which permanent angular bends are formed at the folds therein, advancing said fibers while held under said pressure through a cooling zone, cooling the fibers in said cooling zone to a temperature below that at which they are in a plastic condition to set said crimps and discharging the crimped fibers from said cooling zone.

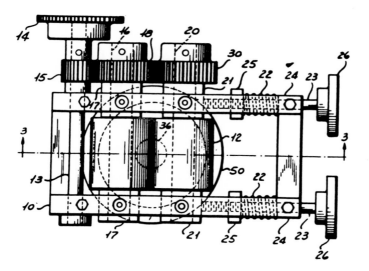

Fig. 2. Patent 2,575,839.

U.S. Patent 2,647,285   METHOD FOR CRIMPING TEXTILE FIBERS

Julius H. Pfau, Yonkers, N.Y., assignor to Alexander Smith, Incorporated, a corporation of New York
Application July 20, 1950, Serial No. 174,870
Five Claims (Cl. 19-66)

Claim 1. The method of imparting a permanent artificial crimp to textile fibers, which comprises gripping said fibers between closely spaced conveyor surfaces discharging into a substantially closed zone, and forcing the gripped fibers into said zone against the pressure of a mass of fibers held compacted under pressure in said zone, said pressure being adapted to cause the fibers to be progressively folded over and crimped as they are delivered from said conveyor surfaces, removing the crimped fibers from said zone and releasing the compacting pressure thereon, transferring the fibers while free from said compacting pressure to a second pressure zone, applying pressure in said last zone to compress said fibers into a compacted mass, and subjecting said mass while under said compacting pressure to a setting agent for a period of time to effect a permanent set of said crimp.

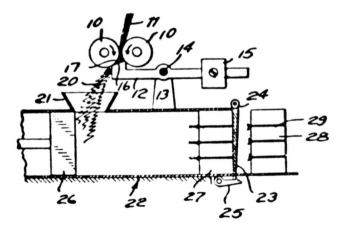

Fig. 1. Patent 2,647,285.

U.S. Patent 2,734,228   CRIMPING APPARATUS

William D. Hay, Peekskill, N.Y., assignor to Alexander Smith, Incorporated, White Plains, N.Y., a corporation of New York
Application October 28, 1952, Serial No. 317,238
Ten Claims (Cl. 19-66)

Claim 1. An apparatus for crimping tow or yarn, comprising a pair of feed rolls adapted to feed said tow or yarn therebetween, a member having a bore forming a crimping chamber, said member having at one end a saddle conforming to the bight of said rolls and having at the other end a tube having a bore tapering to a small opening at its discharge end.

U.S. Patent 2,734,229   CRIMPING APPARATUS

Ewart H. Shattuck, Wilmington, Del., assignor to Joseph Bancroft & Sons Company, Wilmington, Del., a corporation of Delaware
Application November 22, 1954, Serial No. 470,297
Six Claims (Cl. 19-66)

Claim 1. Apparatus for crimping yarn or the like comprising a member having a bore forming a crimping chamber, a pair of feed rolls to feed said yarn into one end of said chamber for crimping, take-up means to withdraw crimped yarn from the other end of said chamber, a member bearing against the mass of crimped yarn at said other end of said chamber and movable in accordance with changes in the quantity of said yarn therein, and feed control means responsive to movement of said member to vary the pressure of said feed rolls on said yarn to control the yarn slippage in a sense to maintain a constant quantity of yarn in said chamber.

U.S. Patent 2,734,251   CRIMPING APPARATUS

Leo W. Rainard and Ewart H. Shattuck, Wilmington, Del., assignors to Joseph Bancroft & Sons Company, Wilmington, Del., a corporation of Delaware
Application October 8, 1954, Serial No. 461,134
Seven Claims (Cl. 28-1)

Claim 1. Apparatus for crimping yarn or the like, comprising a member having a bore forming a crimping chamber, a pair of feed rollers to feed said yarn into one end of said chamber for crimping, take-up means to withdraw crimped yarn from the other end of said

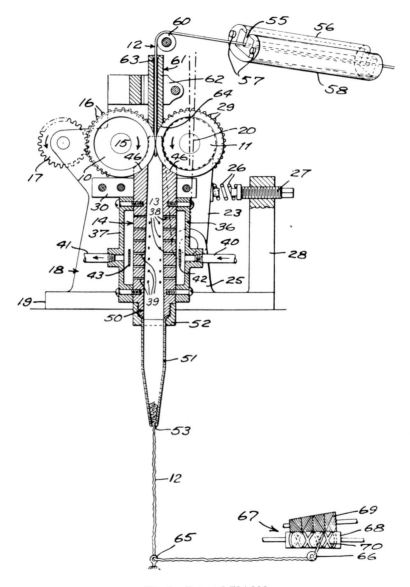

Fig. 1.   Patent 2,734,228.

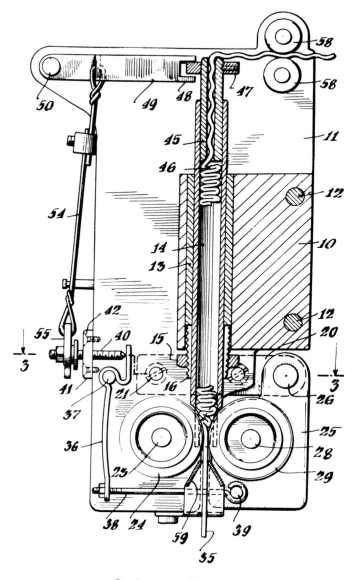

Fig. 2.   Patent 2,734,229.

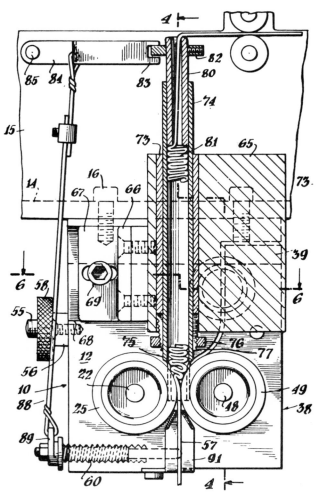

Fig. 3.   Patent 2,734,251.

chamber, a member bearing against the mass of crimped yarn at said other end of said chamber and movable in accordance with changes in the quantity of said yarn therein, and feed control means responsive to movement of said member to vary the spacing between said feed rollers to control the yarn slippage in a sense to maintain a constant quantity of yarn in said chamber.

U.S. Patent 2,734,252   CRIMPING APPARATUS

Ewart H. Shattuck, Wilmington, Del., assignor to Joseph Bancroft &
  Sons Company, Wilmington, Del., a corporation of Delaware
Application February 11, 1955, Serial No. 487,589
Eight Claims (Cl. 28-1)

Claim 1. Apparatus for crimping yarn or the like comprising a
member having a bore forming a crimping chamber, a pair of feed
rolls to feed said yarn into one end of said chamber for crimping, a
pair of take-up rolls to withdraw crimped yarn under tension from
the other end of said chamber, a member bearing against the mass

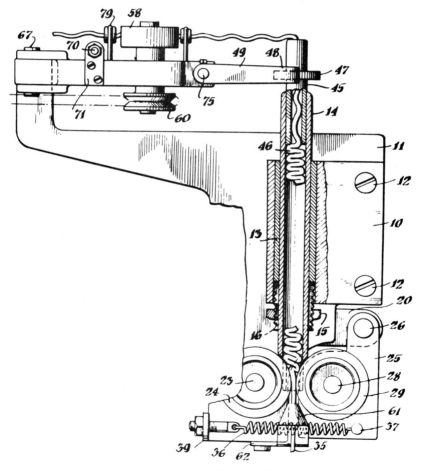

Fig. 2.   Patent 2,734,252.

Woven Stretch and Textured Fabrics

rimped yarn at said other end of said chamber and movable in
.cordance with changes in the quantity of said yarn therein, and
control means responsive to movement of said member and acting on
said take-up rolls to vary the yarn slippage in a sense to maintain a
constant quantity of yarn in said chamber.

U.S. Patent 2,740,992 CRIMPING AND WINDING APPARATUS

Ewart H. Shattuck, Wilmington, Del., assignor to Joseph Bancroft &
    Sons Company, Wilmington, Del., a corporation of Delaware
Application March 1, 1955, Serial No. 491,464
Eight Claims (Cl. 19-66)

Claim 1. Apparatus for crimping yarn or the like comprising a
member having a bore forming a crimping chamber, a pair of feed

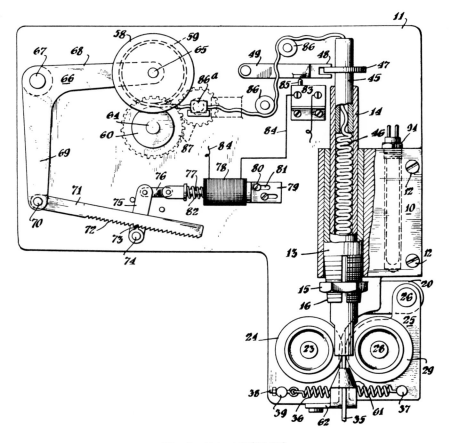

Fig. 1. Patent 2,740,992.

rolls to feed said yarn into one end of said chamber for crimping, a member bearing against the mass of crimped yarn at the other end of said chamber and movable in accordance with changes in the quantity of said yarn therein, a constant speed winder to withdraw crimped yarn under tension from said other end of said chamber, and control means responsive to movement of said member and acting on said winder to vary the yarn slippage in a sense to maintain a constant quantity of yarn in said chamber.

U.S. Patent 2,758,357 APPARATUS FOR TREATING CONTINUOUS STRIP MATERIAL

William Goodhue, North Kingstown, R.I., assignor to Alexander Smith, Incorporated, White Plains, N.Y., a corporation of New York
Application October 15, 1953, Serial No. 386,155
Eight Claims (Cl. 28-1)

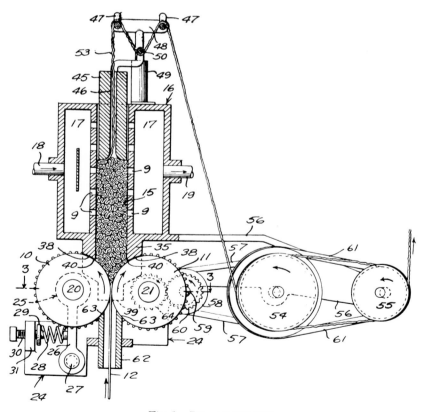

Fig. 1.   Patent 2,758,357.

m 1. An apparatus of the class described comprising a cham-
means feeding yarn or the like into said chamber, a delivery
d withdrawing the yarn from said chamber, and means controlling
the rate of withdrawal of said yarn by said delivery roll comprising a
variable tension device between said chamber and said delivery roll
adapted to exert a variable drag on the yarn fed to said delivery roll,
and means responsive to variations in the quantity of yarn in said
chamber to adjust said device to vary the drag exerted thereby on
said yarn.

U.S. Patent 2,758,358   FILAMENT CRIMPING APPARATUS

Ewart H. Shattuck, Ardsley, N.Y., assignor to Alexander Smith, In-
corporated, White Plains, N.Y., a corporation of New York
Application March 1, 1954, Serial No. 413,205
Nine Claims (Cl. 28-1)

Claim 1. An apparatus of the class described, comprising a chamber, means feeding yarn or the like into said chamber, a tapered
control roll withdrawing said yarn from said chamber after passing
therethrough, a member movable longitudinally of said chamber in
accordance with the quantity of yarn therein, and means responsive
to longitudinal movement of said member to shift the yarn laterally
on said tapered roll in a direction to vary the rate of withdrawal so
as to maintain a substantially uniform quantity of yarn in said chamber.

Claim 7. Apparatus for crimping filaments or the like, comprising
a housing, a tubular sleeve disposed in said housing with a portion
projecting therefrom, feed rolls to feed filaments into said sleeve for
crimping and to feed the crimped filament along said sleeve to said
projecting portion, means heating said housing to transfer heat to
the portion of said sleeve therein, and cooling means to cool said
projecting portion of said sleeve.

U.S. Patent 2,760,252   FILAMENT CRIMPING APPARATUS

Ewart H. Shattuck, Ardsley, N.Y., assignor to Alexander Smith, In-
corporated, New York, N.Y., a corporation of New York
Application August 6, 1953, Serial No. 372,692
Twenty-one claims (Cl. 28-1)

Claim 21. An apparatus for crimping yarn, comprising a member
having a crimping chamber, a pair of feed rolls below said member

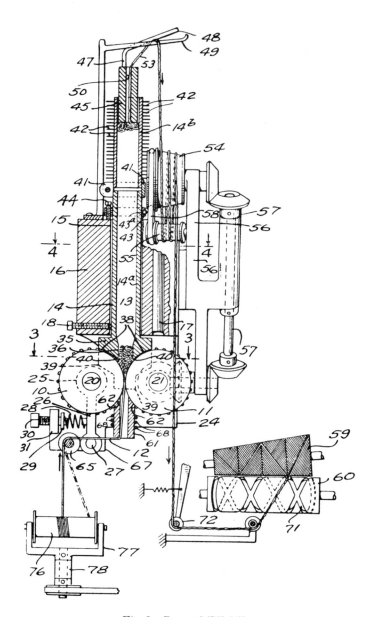

Fig. 1.   Patent 2,758,358.

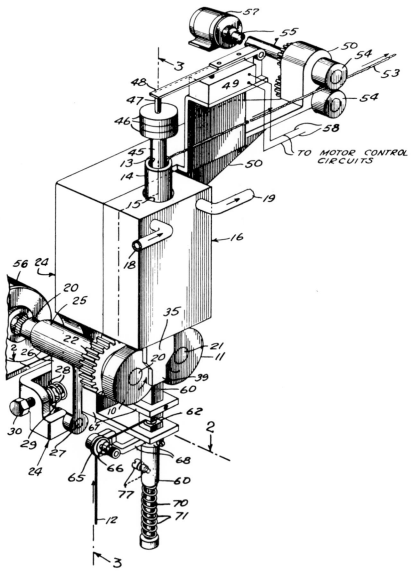

Fig. 1.   Patent 2,760,252.

positioned to feed yarn upwardly into the lower end of said chamber, a plunger loosely mounted in the upper end of said chamber to rest by gravity upon the yarn therein and to exert pressure upon the yarn in said chamber and means for withdrawing the crimped yarn from said upper end of said chamber.

U.S. Patent 2,854,701 CRIMPING METHOD AND APPARATUS

Leo W. Rainard, Wilmington, Del., assignor to Joseph Bancroft &
Sons Co., Wilmington, Del., a corporation of Delaware
Application March 7, 1956, Serial No. 570,145
Eight Claims (Cl. 19-66)

Claim 1. The method of imparting a permanently set crimp to
cellulosic textile fibers, which comprises feeding said fibers continuously in the form of a tow or yarn into a closed crimping zone
against a mass of crimped fibers held compacted in said zone to
cause the fibers to fold and form zig-zag crimps as they contact said
mass of crimp fibers, advancing the crimped fibers along said zone
to a discharge point, applying to the fibers at a point in advance of
their discharge point a resinous impregnant capable of setting the
crimp in said fibers under the action of heat, applying heat to said
crimped fibers, as said crimped fibers pass through said zone, at a
plurality of sequential heating areas and feeding a catalyst for said
resinous material into said zone in advance of at least one of said
heating areas, whereby permanent setting of the crimp in said fibers
is effected prior to the removal of said crimp fibers from said discharge point.

U.S. Patent 2,854,728 CRIMPING APPARATUS

Leo W. Rainard and Ewart H. Shattuck, Wilmington, Del., assignors
to Joseph Bancroft & Sons Company, Wilmington, Del., a corporation of Delaware
Application March 18, 1955, Serial No. 495,128
Four Claims (Cl. 28-1)

Claim 4. Apparatus for crimping yarn comprising a member having a bore extending therethrough, a tube disposed in said bore, a
pair of feed rolls disposed to feed said yarn into one end of said
tube, said tube having a saddle disposed at the bite of said feed
rolls to form a confined crimping chamber in which said yarn is
crimped as it is fed by said rolls against a mass of yarn held compacted in said tube, said tube having an enlarged inner bore beginning at a point adjacent to the crimping chamber and extending to
the other end of said tube, a sleeve disposed in said enlarged bore
and having an inner passage forming a continuation of said crimping chamber, and means securing said sleeve for axial adjustment
with respect to said tube.

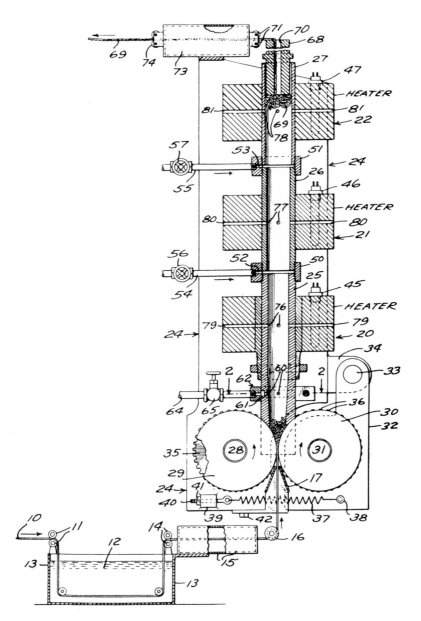

Fig. 1.   Patent 2,854,701.

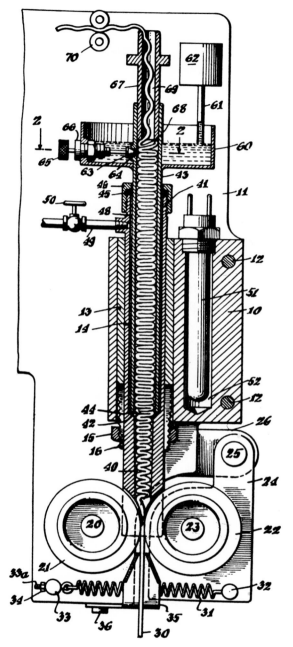

Fig. 1.   Patent 2,854,728.

U.S. Patent 2,854,729   CRIMPING APPARATUS

Carl J. Russo, Claymont, Del., and Henry A. Sinski, Aldan, Pa., assignors to Joseph Bancroft & Sons Company, Wilmington, Del., a
corporation of Delaware
Application April 21, 1955, Serial No. 502,828
Two Claims (Cl. 28-1)

Claim 1. Apparatus for crimping yarn comprising a housing having a passage extending therethrough to form a crimping chamber, a
pair of feed rolls disposed to feed said yarn into one end of said
passage against the mass of crimped yarn held compacted therein, a
plurality of longitudinal members extending upwardly above said
housing and peripherally spaced to provide openings therebetween
and thereby to define a cooling passage which is a continuation of
said first passage, said longitudinal members being spaced to expose
the yarn in said cooling passage to the atmosphere, and take-up
means to withdraw the crimped yarn from said cooling passage after
said yarn has passed along said crimping chamber and through said
cooling passage.

U.S. Patent 2,960,729   APPARATUS FOR TREATING TEXTILE FIBERS

Carl J. Russo, Newark, and Alexander L. Trifunovic, Wilmington, Del.,
and Henry A. Sinski, Alden, Clifton Heights, Pa., assignors to Joseph
Bancroft & Sons Co., Wilmington, Del., a corporation of Delaware
Filed February 4, 1957, Serial No. 638,027
Nine Claims (Cl. 19-66)

Claim 1. Apparatus for treating textile fibers or the like, comprising a stuffer crimper having a bore forming an elongated crimping chamber with an entrance end and a discharge end, a pair of
feed rolls positioned to feed fibers for crimping into the entrance
end of said chamber against the pressure of a mass of crimped fibers
in said chamber and to exert pressure to advance said mass of fibers
to the discharge end of said chamber, said discharge end having an
opening substantially coextensive with said bore adapted to discharge
said mass of crimped fibers in the form of a continuous ribbon having a cross section conforming substantially to that of said bore, a
flexible support tape positioned to receive said ribbon as discharged
from said discharge opening, means advancing said tape with said
ribbon, and means wrapping said ribbon in successive convolutions

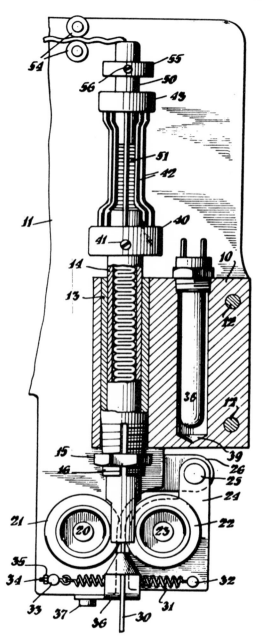

Fig. 1.   Patent 2,854,729.

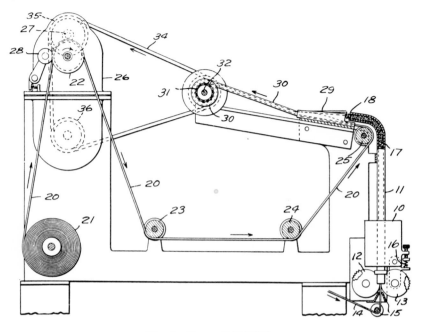

Fig. 1.   Patent 2,960,729.

in the form of a helical winding with said tape interposed between adjacent convolutions of said ribbon to maintain separation therebetween.

U.S. Patent 2,960,730   CRIMPING APPARATUS

Ewart H. Shattuck, Wilmington, Del., assignor to Joseph Bancroft & Sons Co., Wilmington, Del., a corporation of Delaware
Filed June 13, 1957, Serial No. 665,518
Six Claims (Cl. 19-66)

Claim 1. Apparatus for imparting an artificial crimp to textile filaments, comprising a crimping and setting chamber adapted to contain a mass of crimped filaments, means including a feed roll disposed to feed the filaments into one end of said chamber against the mass of crimped filaments therein and to exert pressure to cause the mass to advance along said chamber, closure means closing the other end of said chamber against the discharge of said mass, take-up means for withdrawing the crimped filament under tension in filament form from said other end of said chamber, drive means for said feed

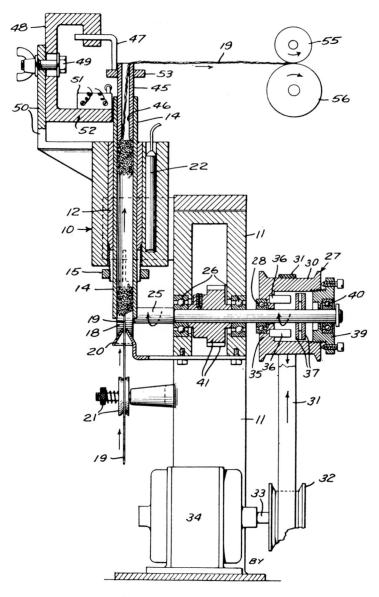

Fig. 1.   Patent 2,960,730.

roll and a constant torque member interconnecting said drive means and said feed roll whereby the pressure on said mass is limited by the torque characteristics of said member.

U.S. Patent 2,997,747   CRIMPING APPARATUS FOR TREATING FIBERS

Carl J. Russo, Newark, Alexander L. Trifunovic, Wilmington, Del., and Henry A. Sinski, Alden, Pa., assignors to Joseph Bancroft & Sons Co., Wilmington, Del., a corporation of Delaware
Filed December 21, 1959, Serial No. 861,001
Eleven Claims (Cl. 19-66)

Claim 1. Apparatus for crimping and packaging textile fibers comprising a bored tube forming a crimping chamber having inlet and discharge ends, a pair of feed rolls positioned to feed said fibers into inlet end of said tube against a mass of previously crimped fibers held compacted therein and to exert pressure for advancing said mass of fibers along said tube to the discharge end thereof, said discharge end having a cross section substantially coextensive with the bore of said tube for discharging the mass of crimped fibers as a continuous core corresponding in section to the bore of said tube, a package winder comprising a rotatable spindle, carrying a package support, a tape supply, means feeding said tape from said supply to said support for winding thereon in successive convolutions in superimposed layers, the discharge end of said tube being disposed substantially within the bite of said tape with said package at the point of winding whereby the core is wound with said tape in successive convolutions and is held confined and compacted by said tape with successive convolutions of said core separated by said tape.

U.S. Patent 3,000,059   METHOD OF TREATING CRIMPED TEXTILE FIBERS

Carl J. Russo, Newark, Alexander L. Trifunovic, Wilmington, and Henry A. Sinski, Aldan, Del., assignors to Joseph Bancroft & Sons Co., Wilmington, Del., a corporation of Delaware.
Original application February 4, 1957, Serial No. 638,027, now Patent No. 2,960,729, dated November 22, 1960.   Divided and this application March 9, 1960, Serial No. 13,926
Six Claims (Cl. 19-66)

Claim 1. The method of treating textile fibers which comprises feeding said fibers against a compacted mass of previously crimped

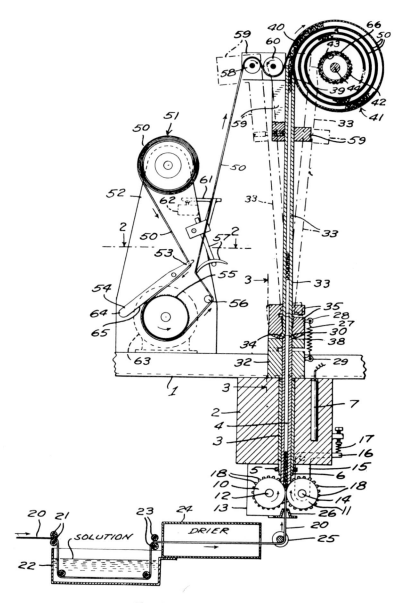

Fig. 1.   Patent 2,997,747.

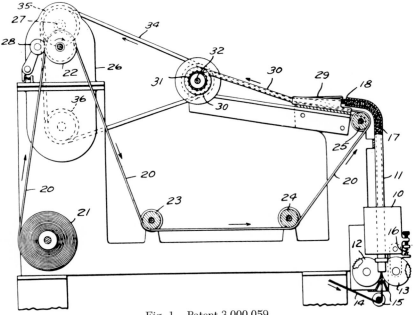

Fig. 1. Patent 3,000,059.

fibers in an elongated crimping zone in a stuffer crimper to cause the fibers to be folded over and crimped, advancing said compacted mass of crimped fibers along said zone while held compacted in said crimper to a discharge point, discharging the mass fibers from said crimper in the form of a compact core having a cross section corresponding to that of said zone, confining said core in a tape, reeling said tape with said core to form a package, treating said package for processing the fibers therein, unreeling said tape and core and withdrawing the treated fibers under tension from said core.

U.S. Patent 3,000,060   CRIMPING APPARATUS

Ewart H. Shattuck and Andrew A. Benedek, Wilmington, Del., assignors to Joseph Bancroft & Sons Co., Wilmington, Del., a corporation of Delaware
Filed January 8, 1959, Serial No. 785,619
Fourteen Claims (Cl. 19-66)

Claim 1. A stuffer crimper comprising a member forming an elongated crimping chamber, feed rolls disposed to feed yarn or the like into one end of said chamber against the pressure of a mass of

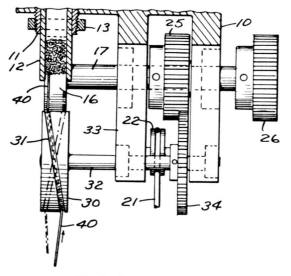

Fig. 2.   Patent 3,000,060.

crimped yarn held compacted therein whereby said yarn is folded over and crimped as it enters said chamber, guide means positioned to guide said yarn in its passage to said feed rolls, said guide means including means to reciprocate said yarn axially of said feed rolls for causing said yarn to be distributed uniformly within said crimping chamber.

U.S. Patent 3,016,677   APPARATUS FOR PLYING CRIMPED YARN

Paul W. Langway, Claymont, Del., assignor to Joseph Bancroft & Sons Co., Wilmington, Del., a corporation of Delaware
Filed March 30, 1960, Serial No. 18,739
Five Claims (Cl. 57-34)

Claim 1.   Apparatus for plying a plurality of ends of crimped continuous filaments directly from core packages in which said ends are in the form of a compacted mass of crimped filaments held confined by a tape and wound with said tape in the form of helical windings with adjacent convolutions of the core separated by said tape, which comprises means supporting a plurality of said core packages for unwinding, a tape reel mounted to receive the tape from each of said packages, means driving each of said reels to unwind the tape from the corresponding package and to expose said core at a discharge

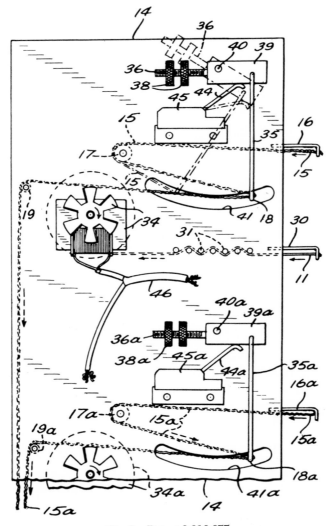

Fig. 2. Patent 3,016,677.

point, a driven feed roll and a twister, means feeding the ends from each of said cores to said feel roll, individual tension control means disposed to engage and be actuated by each of said ends in advance of said feed roll, means controlled by each of said tension control means to actuate the respective tape reels in a sense to withdraw tape from said packages at a rate to maintain a substantially constant tension on said ends as they are fed to said feed rolls, means feeding the combined ends from said feed roll to said twister for plying said ends into a yarn, said twister having means winding said plied yarn onto a package.

U.S. Patent 3,027,108 APPARATUS FOR WITHDRAWING YARN FROM A CORE PACKAGE

Carl J. Russo, Brookside Park, Alexander L. Trifunovic, Wilmington, and Henry A. Sinski, Aldan, Del., assignors to Joseph Bancroft & Sons Co., Wilmington, Del., a corporation of Delaware

Original application February 4, 1957, Serial No. 638,027, now Patent No. 2,960,729, dated November 22, 1960. Divided and this application March 9, 1960, Serial No. 13,924

Four Claims (Cl. 242-54)

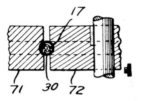

Fig. 8.   Patent 3,027,108.

Claim 1. Apparatus for extracting a yarn from a package containing a continuous core composed of a mass of crimped yarn and a confining tape wound in successive convolutions in a plurality of layers of helical windings with the core in adjacent convolutions separated by the intervening tape which comprises an unwinding spindle for said package, tape winding means connected to withdraw said tape from said package and thereby progressively advance said core to a discharge point, constant speed delivery means withdrawing said yarn from said core at said discharge point, and control means connected to control the withdrawal of said tape for maintaining said core exposed at said discharge point.

Deering Milliken Research Corporation, Spartanburg, S.C., U.S.A.

Patents licensed to manufacturers of false-twist torque-crimped thermoplastic yarns:

U.S. Patent 2,741,893   METHOD AND APPARATUS FOR PRODUCING CRINKLED YARN

Louis Vandamme and Louis Rouyer, Saulce, France, assignors to
    Moulinage et Retorderie de Chavanoz, Paris, France, a corporation
    of France
Application January 14, 1953, Serial No. 331,158
Claims priority, application France January 23, 1952
Three Claims (Cl. 57-34)

Claim 1. The method of producing a crinkled yarn from a bundle of substantially parallel, synthetic thermoplastic filaments, which

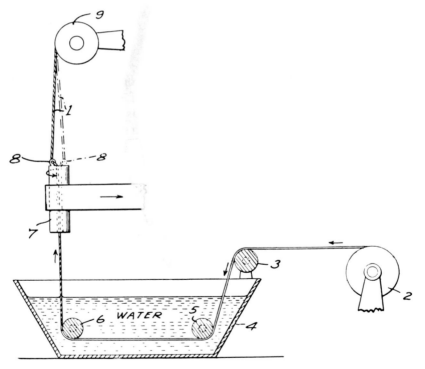

Fig. Patent 2,741,893.

comprises passing said bundle through a heating medium, applying a false twist to the bundle in a twisting zone after emerging from said heating medium and while unconfined between said heating medium and said twisting zone to cause the twist to feed along the bundle backwardly into said heating medium, and confining the bundle to arrest the twist at a point within said heating medium to prevent the twist from feeding to the bundle in said medium in advance of the confining point, whereby the crinkle becomes set between the confining point and the false twisting zone and the twist disappears again after the bundle passes the twisting zone.

U.S. Patent 2,761,272   APPARATUS FOR PRODUCING CURLED YARN

Louis Vandamme and Louis Rouyer, Saulce, France, assignors to Moulinage et Retorderie de Chavanoz, Chavanoz, France, a corporation of France
Application June 11, 1954, Serial No. 436,077
Claims priority, application France June 19, 1953
One claim (Cl. 57-34)

Claim. An apparatus for producing a curled yarn from a bundle of synthetic thermoplastic filaments comprising a false twister, feed rolls for feeding yarn to said false twister, a bobbin on which the yarn is wound after passing through said false twister, means driving said feed rolls and said bobbin at a predetermined speed ratio for maintaining a constant predetermined shrinkage in said bundle, and a curved hollow fixed plate disposed between said feed rolls and said false twister in a position such that the bundle passes thereover and means circulating hot liquid through said hollow plate for heating the same and thereby applying dry heat to the bundle suited to heat the bundle to a temperature to set the curl therein.

U.S. Patent 2,780,047   APPARATUS FOR PRODUCING CURLED YARN

Louis Vandamme and Louis Rouyer, Saulce, France, assignors to Moulinage et Retorderie de Chavanoz, Chavanoz, France, a corporation of France
Application September 19, 1955, Serial No. 534,945
Claims priority, application France September 22, 1954
Three Claims (Cl. 57-34)

Claim 1. Apparatus for setting a false twist in thermoplastic filaments comprising a heater composed of a metal strip having electri-

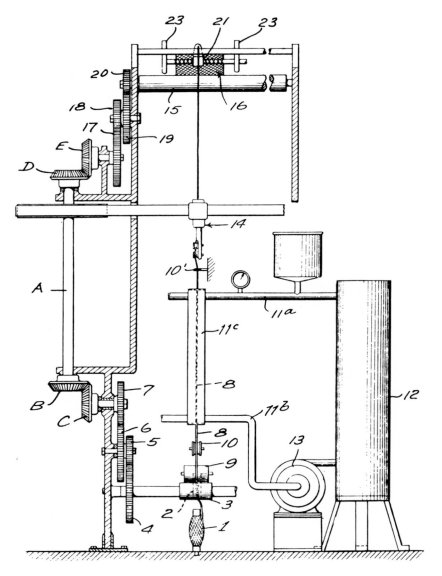

Fig. 1.   Patent 2,761,272.

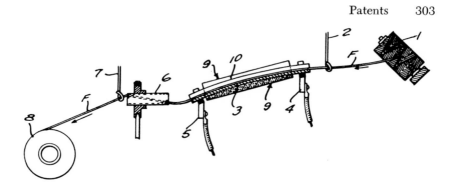

Fig. 1.   Patent 2,780,047.

cal resistance characteristics, said strip being of U-shaped section providing a longitudinal groove to receive the filaments, said strip being arcuate in form to provide a convex surface on which the filaments rest as they advance along said groove, means passing an electric current through said strip for heating said strip due to its resistance, means feeding the filaments through said groove for heating therein, and a false twisting device disposed to impart a false twist to the filaments emerging from said heater whereby the twist feeds along said filaments into the heater and is set therein, and is later removed as the filaments pass the false twisting device.

U.S. Patent 2,788,634   TWIST ARRESTORS FOR YARN TWISTERS

Henri Crouzet, Roanne, France, assignor to Ateliers Ronnais de Constructions Textiles, Roanne, France, a limited liability company of France
Application May 14, 1956, Serial No. 584,503
Claims priority, application France June 6, 1955
Six Claims (Cl. 57-106)

Claim 1.   A twist arrestor for yarn twisters having twisting means to impart a twist to a bundle of filaments, comprising an idler roller around which said bundle passes in advance of the twisting means, said roller being polygonal in cross section with a plurality of flat sides intersecting in angular edges, said edges being in contact with said bundle and being adapted to arrest the twist without introducing complementary tension to said bundle.

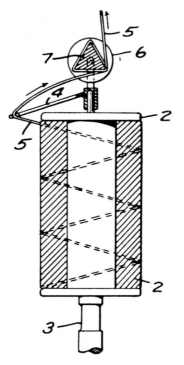

Fig. 1.   Patent 2,788,634.

U.S. Patent 2,823,513   APPARATUS FOR PRODUCING CURLED YARN

Louis Vandamme and Louis Rouyer, Saulce, France, assignors to
    Moulinage et Retorderie de Chavanoz, Chavanoz, France, a cor-
    poration of France
Original application June 11, 1954, Serial No. 436,077, now Patent
    No. 2,761,272, dated September 4, 1956.   Divided and this appli-
    cation July 11, 1956, Serial No. 597,302
Claims priority, application France June 19, 1953
One Claim (Cl. 57-34)

Claim. An apparatus for producing a curled yarn from a bundle of
synthetic thermoplastic filaments comprising a false twister, feed
rolls for feeding yarn to said false twister, a bobbin on which the
yarn is wound after passing through said false twister, means driving
said feed rolls and said bobbin at a predetermined speed ratio for
maintaining a constant predetermined shrinkage in said bundle, a
pair of electrodes disposed between said feed rolls and said false
twister on opposite sides of the bundle path and means supplying

high frequency current to said electrodes to produce an alternating field therebetween for thereby applying dry heat to the bundle suited to heat the bundle to a temperature to set the curl therein.

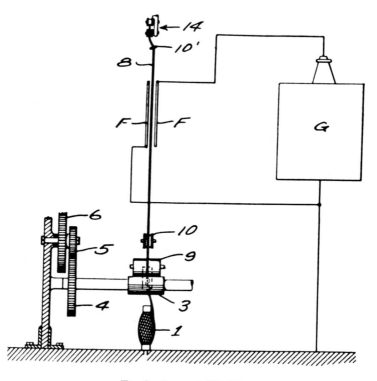

Fig. 3.   Patent 2,823,513.

U.S. Patent 2,823,514   APPARATUS FOR PRODUCING CURLED YARN

Louis Vandamme and Louis Rouyer, Saulce, France, assignors to Moulinage et Retorderie de Chavanoz, Chavanoz, France, a corporation of France
Original application June 11, 1954, Serial No. 436,077, now Patent No. 2,761,272, dated September 4, 1956. Divided and this application July 11, 1956, Serial No. 597,303
Claims priority, application France June 19, 1953
One Claim (Cl. 57-34)

Claim. An apparatus for producing a curled yarn from a bundle of synthetic thermoplastic filaments comprising a false twister, feed rolls for feeding yarn to said false twister, a bobbin on which the yarn is wound after passing through said false twister, means driving

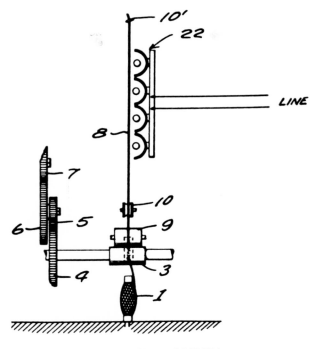

Fig. 4.   Patent 2,823,514.

said feed rolls and said bobbin at a predetermined speed ratio for maintaining a constant predetermined shrinkage in said bundle, and a source of infra red radiations disposed along the path of the bundle between said feed rolls and said false twister to apply dry heat to the bundle suited to heat the bundle to a temperature to set the curl therein.

U.S. Patent 2,891,375   APPARATUS FOR THE PRODUCTION OF HIGH-BULK YARN

Louis Vandamme and Louis Rouyer, Saulce, France, assignors to Moulinage et Retorderie de Chavanoz, Chavanoz (Isere), France, a corporation of France
Application January 2, 1957, Serial No. 632,141
Claims priority, application France January 6, 1956
Three Claims (Cl. 57-34)

Claim 1. Apparatus for setting a false twist in synthetic thermo-plastic filaments comprising a heater tube composed of a peripheral

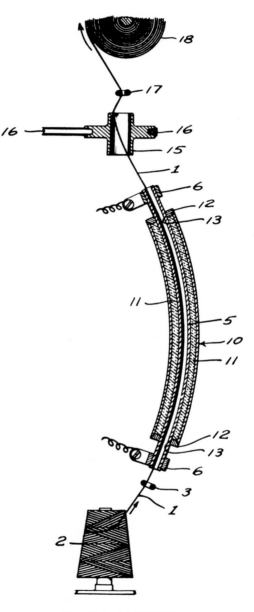

Fig.   Patent 2,891,375.

wall completely surrounding a heating zone and made from metal having electrical resistance characteristics, said tube being curved axially into arcuate shape, means passing an electric current through said heater tube for heating said tube due to its resistance, means feeding said filaments through said tube in contact with the inner arcuate surface thereof, and a false twisting device disposed to impart a false twist to the filaments emerging from said tube, whereby the twist feeds along said filaments into the tube and is set therein and is removed after the filaments pass the false twisting device.

U.S. Patent 2,944,319   HEATING DEVICE FOR FILAMENTS

Henri Crouzet, Roanne, France, assignor to Moulinage et Retorderie de Chavanoz, Chavanoz (Isere), France, a corporation of France
Filed April 7, 1959, Serial No. 804,764
Claims priority, application France April 8, 1958
One Claim (Cl. 28-62)

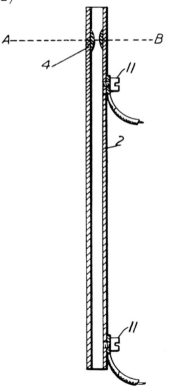

Fig. 1.   Patent 2,944,319.

Claim. Apparatus for the treatment of textile filaments comprising a fixed tube having a substantially vertical axis, means heating said tube to a temperature suited for the treatment of said filaments, a sleeve disposed at the upper end of said tube and a second tube removably mounted in said sleeve in axial alignment with said first tube, said sleeve having heat-insulating means to retard the transfer of heat from said first tube to said second tube whereby condensation of vapors rising from said first tube may take place on the walls of said second tube, and means feeding a textile filament for treatment upwardly through said tubes.

U.S. Patent 3,012,397   METHOD OF MAKING HIGH-BULK YARNS

Henri Servage, Cremieu, Isere, France, assignor to Moulinage et Retorderie de Chavanoz, Chavanoz (Isere), France, a company incorporated of France
No Drawing.   Filed November 30, 1959, Serial No. 856,014
Fourteen Claims (Cl. 57-157)

Claim 1. The method of producing high-curl polyacrylonitrile, acrylonitrile co-polymer, and polyester yarns of the "high-bulk" type, comprising twisting in a first direction a first yarn of material selected from the group consisting of polyacrylonitriles, acrylonitrile co-polymers, and polyesters, setting of said first directional twist and untwisting of said yarn, twisting in the opposite direction to said first direction, a second yarn selected from said group, setting of said twist in said second yarn and untwisting of said second yarn, permitting filament heat shrinkage of each of said yarns during said first mentioned twisting thereof, overfeeding and mechanically spatially shrinking said yarns between approximately 5 to 12% subsequent to said first mentioned filament heat shrinkage, combining said yarns to form a combined yarn, and then subjecting said combined yarn to a subsequent heat treatment while under substantially no appreciable tension.

Deering Milliken Research Corporation, Spartanburg, S.C., U.S.A.

Patents licensed to manufacturers of edge-crimped thermoplastic yarns:

U.S. Patent 2,790,611   YARN TENSION REGULATOR

John M. Massey, Greenville, S.C., assignor, by mesne assignments, to Deering Milliken Research Corporation, near Pendleton, S.C., a corporation of Delaware
Application November 17, 1954, Serial No. 469,430
Eight Claims (Cl. 242-154)

Claim 1. In a yarn tensioning device, a support plate, a plurality of rigid pin members carried by said plate and extending from one surface thereof, an elongated arm carried by said plate and pivotally movable about an axis intermediate the two ends thereof, said arm carrying a yarn engaging eye on one end thereof and a plurality of yarn engaging elements on the opposite end adapted to extend between said pin members and intermesh therewith, a rotatable member extending from said plate, and a resiliency extensible member acting upon said arm to urge said arm to pivot so as to remove said yarn engaging elements from intermeshing relationship with said pin members, said extensible member having a readily flexible end portion secured to said rotatable member, whereby the force acting to pivot said arm can be varied by rotational movement of said rotatable member.

U.S. Patent 2,919,534   IMPROVED TEXTILE MATERIALS AND METHODS AND APPARATUS FOR PREPARING THE SAME

Edgar Dare Bolinger, Clemson, S.C., and Norman E. Klein, Pendleton, S.C., assignors to Deering Milliken Research Corporation, near Pendleton, S.C., a corporation of Delaware
Application November 2, 1955, Serial No. 544,521
Twenty-nine Claims (Cl. 57-34)

Claim 1. Yarn crimping apparatus comprising, in combination, a source of yarn supply, a blade having a sharp edge, yarn take-up means spaced from said blade, guide means to guide an end of yarn, passing from said source of supply to said take-up means, in an

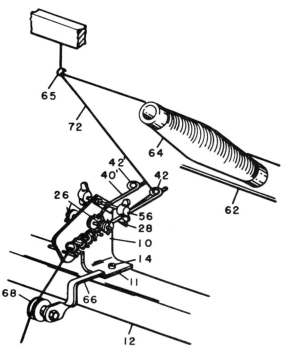

Fig. 1.   Patent 2,790,611.

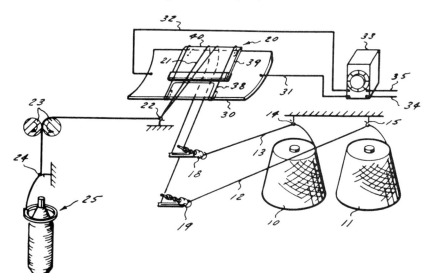

Fig. 1.   Patent 2,919,534.

angular path about said blade with said edge positioned at the apex
of the angle in the yarn path, tensioning means to place the yarn
under tension as it passes about said edge, and heating means to heat
the yarn so that it is at an elevated temperature during at least a
portion of the time it is in contact with said edge.

U.S. Patent 2,921,358   APPARATUS FOR PRODUCING ELASTICIZED THERMO-
PLASTIC YARNS

Fred W. Cox, Pendleton, S.C., and Cyril G. Evans, Clemson, S.C.,
    assignors to Deeering Milliken Research Corporation, Pendleton,
    S.C., a corporation of Delaware
Application January 26, 1956, Serial No. 561,563
Twenty-four Claims (Cl. 28-1)

Claim 2.   In an apparatus for processing a running length of yarn
and including a yarn supply means and a yarn takeup means; a driven
roll having a yarn engaging peripheral surface, means to heat at least

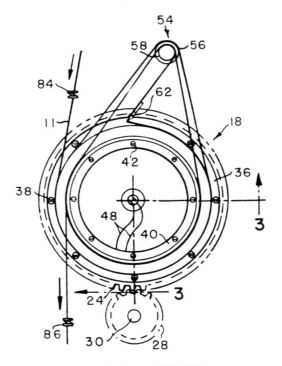

Fig. 2.   Patent 2,921,358.

a portion of said surface, blade means providing a yarn engaging edge adjacent said portion of said peripheral surface so that an end of yarn passing between the periphery of said roll and said edge can be withdrawn from the surface of said roll and passed, while at an elevated temperature, about said edge in a sharply angular manner.

U.S. Patent 2,925,641   METHOD FOR PROCESSING CELLULOSE ESTER YARNS

Cyril G. Evans, Clemson, S.C., assignor to Deering Milliken Research
    Corporation, Pendleton, S.C., a corporation of Delaware
Application February 9, 1956, Serial No. 564,509
Twelve Claims (Cl. 28-72)

Claim 1. A process for elasticizing continuous filament cellulose ester yarns which comprises treating the yarn, for a time sufficient to increase its elongation to break but insufficient to severely reduce the strength of the yarn, with an aqueous solution of a compound selected from the group consisting of non-oxidizing inorganic acids, salts thereof with polyvalent metals and mixtures of said salts and said acids, washing the yarn until it is substantially free of solution,

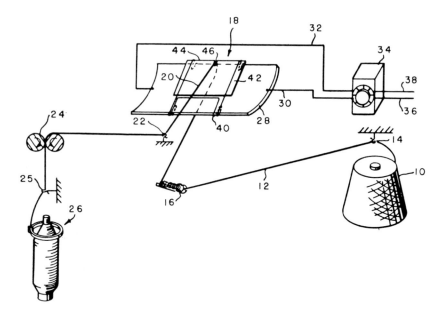

Fig. 1. Patent 2,925,641.

heating the yarn to a temperature of at least about 200°F but not above its sticking temperature, and passing the heated yarn, while under tension of at least about 0.05 grams per denier but insufficient to result in the yarn being severed, about the sharp edge of a blade member in an angular path with said edge disposed at the apex of the angle in the yarn path.

U.S. Patent 2,931,089   METHODS AND APPARATUS FOR PRODUCING YARN

Cyril G. Evans, Clemson, S.C., assignor to Deering Milliken Research
    Corporation, Pendleton, S.C., a corporation of Delaware
Application May 2, 1956, Serial No. 582,274
Ten Claims (Cl. 28-1)

Claim 1. Apparatus for elasticizing a thermoplastic filamentary yarn comprising in combination a yarn supply means, a yarn takeup means, means for withdrawing an end of yarn from said supply means and for advancing the same under tension over a linear path to said take-up means, and a blade member positioned adjacent the yarn path, said blade member having an edge about which the yarn is drawn to cause it to follow an acutely angular course, said edge having a radius of curvature not greater than about four times the diameter of the yarn to be elasticized and said blade member being formed primarily of unfused aluminum oxide particles sintered together and forming a coherent mass, said aluminum oxide particles having an average maximum diameter of not more than about 50 microns.

Claim 8. In a method for elasticizing thermoplastic yarns wherein an end of the yarn is passed under tension through a linear path and about the edge of a blade member to cause the yarn to undergo an acute change of direction, the improvement which comprises employing a ceramic blade formed of a material having a reduced, as compared to steel, coefficient of friction relative to said yarn, whereby the cross-sectional deformation of the yarn is appreciably less than is obtained with a steel blade.

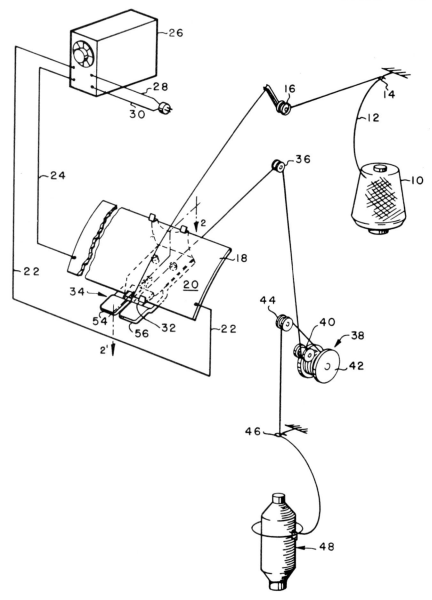

Fig. 1.   U.S. Patent 2,931,089.

U.S. Patent 2,973,161   CONE ADAPTER

Albert D. Harmon, Pendleton, S.C., assignor to Deering Milliken Research Corporation, near Pendleton, Oconee County, S.C., a corporation of Delaware
Filed March 9, 1956, Serial No. 570,489
Four Claims (Cl. 242-130)

Claim 1. In combination a spindle having a rotatable whorl and blade assembly, a frusto-conical base adapter removably secured to said assembly adjacent said whorl, a tube having a bore therein substantially complementary to said blade, a disc flange on said tube, a hollow cone having a tapered hollow interior the larger end being adapted to fit in wedging relation over the frusto-conical base adapter

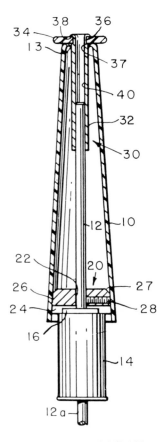

Fig. 1. Patent 2,973,161.

and the smaller end having a radially inwardly extending lip defining an axial opening and being adapted to fit in substantially snug complementary relation with the periphery of said tube, said tube being adapted to be freely slidably removably mounted on the end of said blade, said disc flange being engagable in abutting relation with the tapered end of said cone, whereby said tube and disc flange assembly and said cone are adapted to be removably secured on said blade and whorl assembly in axially and radially secured relation, said cone being in seated position on said base adapter longer than the effective length of said blade from said base adapter to its end, and said lip being removably disposed outwardly beyond the end of said blade.

U.S. Patent 2,977,661   YARN ELASTICIZING APPARATUS

Cyril G. Evans, Clemson, S.C., and Albert D. Harmon and Norman
    E. Klein, Pendleton, S.C., assignors to Deering Milliken Research
    Corporation, Pendleton, S.C., a corporation of Delaware
Filed November 18, 1955, Serial No. 547,682
Seven Claims (Cl. 28-1)

Claim 1. In a yarn processing apparatus including an elongated heater strip having a yarn engaging surface, a blade member having a yarn engaging edge positioned in close proximity to one edge of said yarn engaging surface and yarn transporting means for continually drawing an end of yarn under tension into effective relationship with said heater strip and thereafter about said yarn engaging edge, improved blade holding means comprising heat dissipating means formed of a material with a high specific thermal conductivity and having a mass which is large as compared to the mass of said blade, said heat dissipating means having an indentation to receive said blade and said heat dissipating means having at least one member extending from the immediate proximity of said heater strip to thereby remove heat from said blade, clip means carried by said heat dissipating means for engaging opposite sides of said heater strip and to thereby retain said heat dissipating means in fixed positional relationship with respect to said heater strip, at least one portion of said clip means acting to urge said blade against said heat dissipating means and to retain the same fixedly positioned in said indentation.

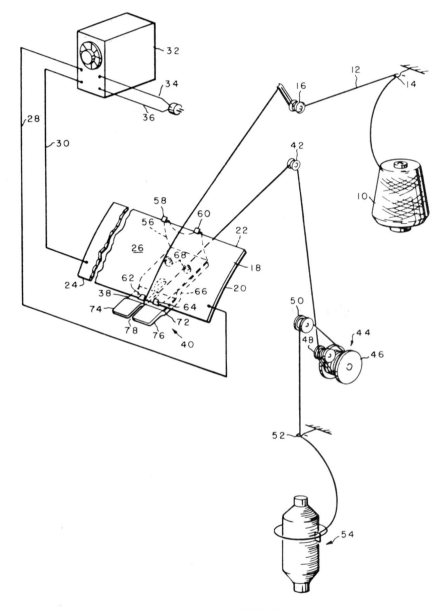

Fig. 1. Patent 2,977,661.

U.S. Patent 2,977,746 APPARATUS FOR PROCESSING THERMOPLASTIC YARNS

Norman E. Klein, Pendleton, S.C., and Cyril G. Evans, Clemson, S.C., assignors to Deering Milliken Research Corporation, Pendleton, S.C., a corporation of Delaware
Filed June 9, 1958, Serial No. 740,637
Twenty-four Claims (Cl. 57-34)

Claim 1. Apparatus for processing a running length of yarn comprising, in combination, a yarn supply means, a yarn heater means, a blade means having a sharp edge positioned adjacent said heater means, guide means to guide an end of yarn into contact with said heater means and thereafter about said blade means in an acutely angular path with said edge positioned at the apex of the angle, yarn advancing means to withdraw the yarn from said blade means and advance the same at a selected linear rate, guide means to again guide said yarn into contact with said heater means, and a second yarn advancing means to thereafter withdraw said yarn from said yarn heater means at a selected linear rate less than said first mentioned linear rate.

U.S. Patent 2,977,663 YARN PROCESSING APPARATUS

Cyril G. Evans, Clemson, S.C., assignor to Deering Milliken Research Corporation, Pendleton, S.C., a corporation of Delaware
Filed September 2, 1958, Serial No. 758,440
Sixteen Claims (Cl. 28-62)

Claim 1. Apparatus for processing a running length of yarn comprising, in combination, means for operatively transporting an end of yarn, disengaging means to render said transporting means inoperative, an electrical yarn heater to heat a segment of said running length of yarn, and means operatively connected to and actuated in response to the actuation of said disengaging means to compensatively decrease to a lower level the electrical energy supplied to said heater when said transporting means is inoperative.

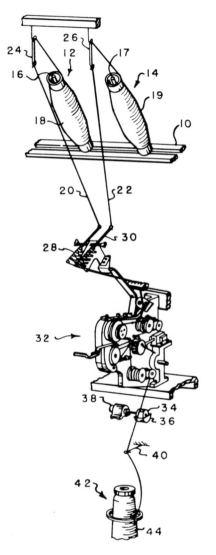

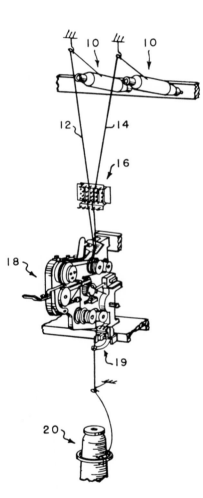

Fig. 1.   Patent 2,977,746.

Fig. 1.   Patent 2,977,663.

U.S. Patent 3,017,684 TEXTILE MATERIALS AND METHOD OF MAKING THE SAME

Edgar Henry Pittman, Clemson, S.C., assignor to Deering Milliken Research Corporation, Spartanburg, S.C., a corporation of Delaware
Filed January 24, 1956, Serial No. 560,963
Four Claims (Cl. 28-72)

Claim 1. The method which comprises placing, while at an elevated temperature, a plurality of continuous thermoplastic textile filaments in a tensioned and substantially straightened condition but not under a tension of more than about 1 gram per denier, said filaments in each instance having a pronounced tendency to assume a crimped configuration, cooling said filaments while in said straightened and tensioned condition to thereby result in said filaments being partially heat-set in said condition, chopping said filaments into staple fibers, and thereafter heating said staple fibers while in a positionally relaxed condition to at least partially eliminate the effect of said heat-setting and to cause said fibers to develop a more pronounced crimp.

U.S. Patent 3,021,588 KNITTED TEXTILE PRODUCTS AND METHODS FOR THEIR PREPARATION

Edgar Dare Bolinger, Clemson, S.C., assignor to Deering Milliken Research Corporation, Pendleton, S.C., a corporation of Delaware
No Drawing. Filed April 3, 1958, Serial No. 726,294
Seventeen Claims (Cl. 28-76)

Claim 1. A method for finishing textile products knitted from elasticized non-torque yarns containing heat setable internal latent stresses in the fibers which cause the yarn to assume a convoluted linear configuration when heated in a relaxed state which comprises wetting said textile products in an aqueous bath having a temperature of not more than about 100°F and thereafter heating the wetted textile products to a minimum temperature of about 140°F while continually agitating the same.

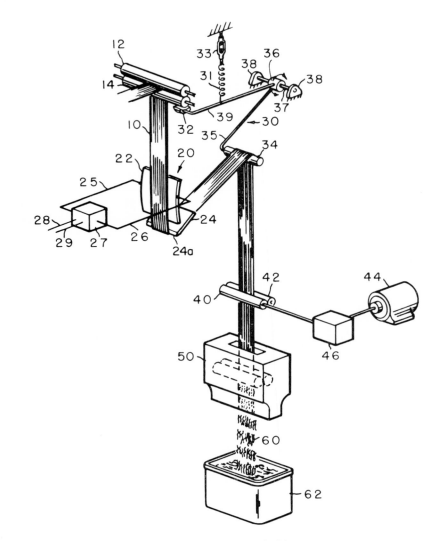

Fig. 1.   Patent 3,017,684.

U.S. Patent 3,025,584 APPARATUS FOR ELASTICIZING THERMOPLASTIC
MONOFILAMENT YARN

Cyril G. Evans, Clemson, S.C., assignor to Deering Milliken Research
    Corporation, Pendleton, S.C., a corporation of Delaware
Filed December 30, 1955, Serial No. 556,554
Thirteen Claims (Cl. 28-1)

Claim 1. Apparatus for elasticizing an end of monofilament yarn
which comprises in combination a yarn supply means, a yarn take-up
means for withdrawing an end of yarn from said supply means and
transporting the same under tension over a linear path, a blade member positioned in the yarn path and about which the yarn is drawn
to cause it to follow an acutely angular course, said blade member
having an opening therein to receive the yarn with one boundary
surface of said opening providing a yarn engaging surface, arcuate
in a plurality of planes, positioned at the apex of the angle in the
yarn path, said yarn engaging surface being concavely arcuate in
planes parallel to the plane of said blade member such that when a
monofilament, having a cross-sectional radius selected to approxi-

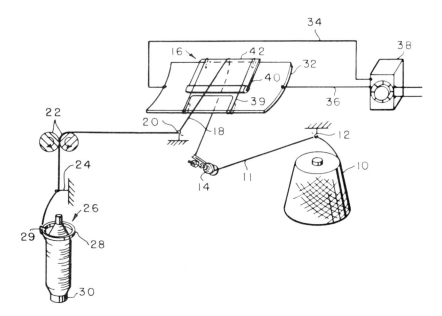

Fig. 1. U.S. Patent 3,025,584.

mately correspond to the minimum radius of concave curvature of said yarn engaging surface, is passed in an angular manner about said yarn engaging surface, said monofilament while in contact with said yarn engaging surface is laterally restrained to prevent cross-sectional deformation, and said yarn engaging surface being convexly arcuate in planes perpendicular to the plane of said blade member, the mean radius of convex curvature in a plane bisecting said yarn engaging surface being not greater than 150 microns.

U.S. Patent 3,028,653 IMPROVED METHODS AND APPARATUS FOR PRE-PARING ELASTICIZED THERMOPLASTIC YARNS

Cyril G. Evans, Clemson, S.C., assignor to Deering Milliken Research Corporation, Pendleton, S.C., a corporation of Delaware
Filed December 24, 1956, Serial No. 630,325
Thirty-three Claims (Cl. 28-1)

Claim 1. Apparatus for processing a running length of yarn comprising a yarn supply means, a first yarn advancing means to positively advance an end of yarn from said supply means along a linear path at a first selected linear rate, a second yarn advancing means to thereafter positively advance said end of yarn along said path at a second linear rate which is in excess of said first linear rate so that said yarn is stretched, heater means to heat said yarn in a portion of the yarn path between said first yarn advancing means and a point in the yarn path where the yarn is positively advanced by said second yarn advancing means so that the stretching of said yarn occurs in a heated segment thereof, a blade means, means including contact heater means proximate to but spatially separate from said blade means to heat said yarn in a portion of the yarn path immediately preceding said blade means to guide said yarn about an edge of said blade means in an angular path with said edge positioned at the apex of the angle in the yarn path, a yarn advancing means to receive said yarn following its contact with said edge and to positively advance the same along the yarn path at a third selected linear rate, and means to thereafter collect said yarn.

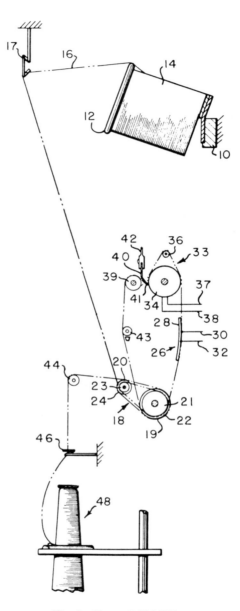

Fig. 1.   Patent 3,028,653.

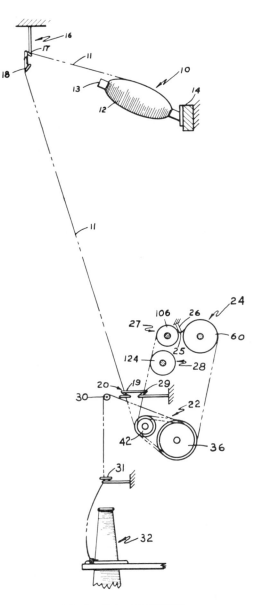

Fig. 1.   Patent 3,028,654.

U.S. Patent 3,028,654 APPARATUS FOR PROCESSING YARN

Cyril G. Evans, Clemson, S.C., assignor to Deering Milliken Research
    Corporation, Pendleton, S.C., a corporation of Delaware
Filed April 11, 1957, Serial No. 652,153
Eight Claims (Cl. 28-1)

Claim 1. Apparatus for processing a running length of yarn comprising a first yarn unheated advancing means to positively advance
an end of yarn at a first selected linear rate, a second unheated yarn
advancing means to thereafter positively advance said end of yarn
at a second linear rate which is less than the linear rate which said
yarn is advanced by said first yarn advancing means, a roll member
positioned in the yarn path between said first and second yarn advancing means, means to heat at least a portion of the surface of
said roll member so that the temperature of said yarn in contact
therewith is elevated, a blade member, positioned between said roll
member and said second yarn advancing means, having a sharp
edge positioned immediately adjacent the peripheral surface of said
roll member, guide means to guide said end of yarn a partial warp
only around the periphery of said roll member for sliding frictional
contact therewith and immediately thereafter about said sharp edge
in an acutely angular manner with said edge positioned at the apex
of the angle in the yarn path, means to rotate said roll member such
that it has a surface speed in excess of the linear rate at which the
yarn is operatively advanced by said first yarn advancing means.

U.S. Patent 3,035,328 METHOD OF PREPARING CRIMPED YARNS

Edgar Dare Bolinger, Clemson, S.C., assignor to Deering Milliken
    Research Corporation, near Pendleton, S.C., a corporation of
    Delaware
Original application November 2, 1955, Serial No. 544,521, now Pat-
    ent No. 2,919,534, dated January 5, 1960. Divided and this appli-
    cation March 2, 1959, Serial No. 796,423
Seven Claims (Cl. 28-72)

Claim 2. A method of crimping continuous filament thermoplastic yarn which comprises continuously passing said yarn through a
heating zone maintained at a temperature sufficient to plasticize but
insufficient to melt the yarn, immediately thereafter passing the heated
yarn in an angular path over the sharp edge of a blade while under
tension, said edge being disposed at the apex of the acute angle

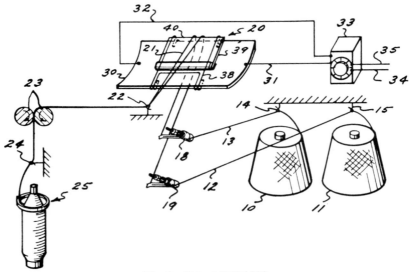

Fig. 1. Patent 3,035,328.

formed between the path of delivery to, and the path of withdrawal of the yarn from said edge and thereafter heating the yarn before the yarn is formed into fabric to a temperature of at least 120°F while it is under insufficient tension to prevent the same from contracting in length.

U.S. Patent 3,047,932 APPARATUS FOR INTERMITTENTLY EDGE-CRIMPING YARN

Edgar Henry Pittman and Edgar Dare Bolinger, Spartanburg, S.C., assignors to Deering Milliken Research Corporation, Spartanburg, S.C., a corporation of Delaware
Filed August 18, 1959, Serial No. 834,517
Thirteen Claims (Cl. 28-1)

Claim 1. Intermittent yarn-crimping means and means for advancing yarns through said intermittent yarn-crimping means, said intermittent yarn-crimping means comprising an edge-crimping element having a crimping edge engagable by yarn passing thereby and means for intermittently rendering said element ineffective on yarn passing thereby including a member other than said edge-crimping element and movably engagable with yarn passing by said edge-crimping element, said member being movable along a path intersecting transversely the path of yarn passing by said element.

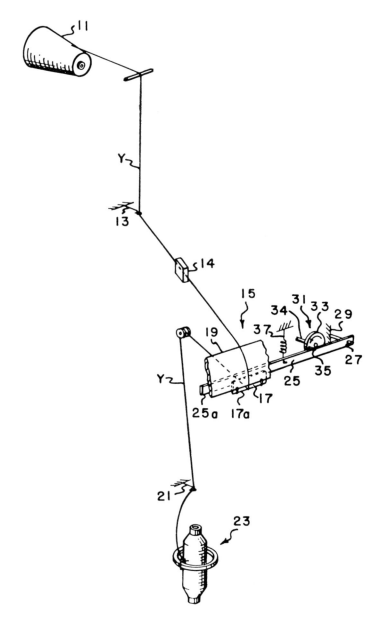

Fig. 1.   Patent 3,047,932.

E. I. du Pont de Nemours and Company, Wilmington, Delaware, U.S.A.

Patents licensed to manufacturers of air-bulked yarns:

U.S. Patent 2,783,609   BULKY CONTINUOUS FILAMENT YARN

Alvin L. Breen, West Chester, Pa., assignor to E. I. du Pont de Nemours and Company, Wilmington, Del., a corporation of Delaware

Application December 14, 1951, Serial No. 261,635

Fifteen Claims (Cl. 57-140)

Claim 1.   A bulky yarn comprising a plurality of substantially continuous filaments which are individually convoluted into coils, loops, and whorls at random intervals along their lengths, and characterized by the presence of a multitude of ring-like loops irregularly spaced along the yarn surface.

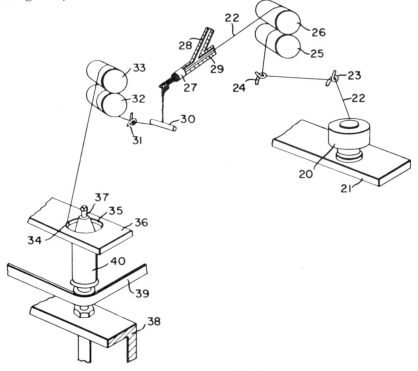

Fig. 1.   Patent 2,783,609.

U.S. Patent 2,852,906 METHOD AND APPARATUS FOR PRODUCING BULKY
CONTINUOUS FILAMENT YARN

Alvin L. Breen, West Chester, Pa., assignor to E. I. du Pont de
  Nemours and Company, Wilmington, Del., a corporation of Dela-
  ware
Application August 20, 1953, Serial No. 375,372
Eleven Claims (Cl. 57-34)

Claim 1. A process for making bulky continuous filament yarn
from a bundle of substantially straight continuous filaments which
comprises passing the filament bundle through a fluid jet, jetting the
fluid with sufficient force to separate the filaments and form the
filaments individually into convolutions, and removing the filaments
from the jetted fluid and combining the convoluted filaments into a
yarn while avoiding tension sufficient to remove the convolutions.

Claim 4. Apparatus for making bulky continuous filament yarn
which comprises a fluid nozzle adapted to create a turbulent zone,

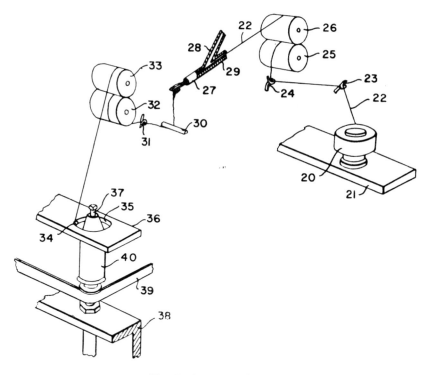

Fig. 1. Patent 2,852,906.

means for feeding yarn continuously through the turbulent zone, means for supplying fluid to said nozzle under a pressure which will provide sufficient turbulence to separate the yarn filaments and form them into convolutions, and means for withdrawing the separated filaments from the turbulent zone and reforming them into yarn.

U.S. Patent 2,869,967   BULKY YARN

Alvin L. Breen, West Chester, Pa., assignor to E. I. du Pont de Nemours and Company, Wilmington, Del., a corporation of Delaware
Application August 23, 1957, Serial No. 679,891
Eight Claims (Cl. 57-140)

Claim 1. A bulky yarn comprising a plurality of discontinuous fibers twisted together, the fibers being convoluted into coils, loops, and whorls at random intervals along their lengths, and the yarn surface exhibiting a multitude of ring-like loops and protruding fiber ends irregularly spaced along the yarn surface.

Fig. 7.   Patent 2,869,967.

U.S. Patent 2,958,112   YARN-TREATING APPARATUS

John N. Hall, Newark, Del., assignor to E. I. du Pont de Nemours and Company, Wilmington, Del., a corporation of Delaware
Filed August 16, 1956, Serial No. 604,564
Six Claims (Cl. 28-1)

Claim 1. Yarn-treating apparatus comprising fluid-conducting means having a substantially straight bore for flow of fluid therethrough, yarn-introducing means terminating therein in the downstream direction at an appreciable acute angle therewith, and turbulence-generating means joined to the upstream edge of the yarn-introducing means and extending across the bore of the fluid-conducting means so as to bifurcate flow of fluid therethrough.

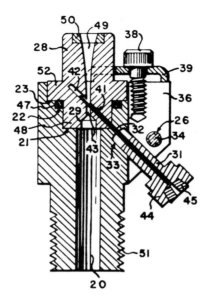

Fig. 4.   Patent 2,958,112.

U.S. Patent 2,994,938   YARN-TREATING APPARATUS

Chester L. Loveland, Dalton, and Pacific J. Thomas, Wyoming, Pa.,
    assignors, by mesne assignments, to E. I. du Pont de Nemours and
    Company, Wilmington, Del., a corporation of Delaware
Filed June 30, 1959, Serial No. 824,024
Four Claims (Cl. 28-1)

Claim 1.   A yarn-treating apparatus comprising a housing perforated by a cylindrical channel, a yarn needle of circular cross section
having an axial yarn passageway for introducing yarn into the apparatus, said needle being positioned in and concentric with the
cylindrical housing channel and closely fitted into one end of the
housing channel and comprising a cylindrical body portion and an
inner tapered tip portion, both within the housing channel, the body
portion being substantially smaller in cross section than the housing
channel to provide an annular plenum chamber, the tip portion extending from the body portion to a flat inner end of the yarn needle
and diminishing in cross section toward the inner end in at least one
graduated step in the form of a cylindrical section separated from
the flat inner end and the body portion of the yarn needle, respec-
tively, by shoulders, each in the form of a right conical section hav-

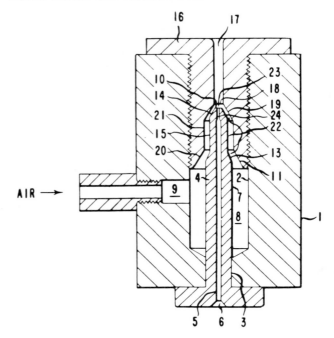

Fig. Patent 2,994,938.

ing a vertex angle between about 30° and about 120°, the vertex angle of the shoulder adjacent the inner end being at least 75% of the vertex angle of the shoulder adjacent the needle body; a cylindrical orifice block closely fitted into the opposite end of the housing channel from the yarn needle and longitudinally adjustable within said channel, said orifice block being perforated by an axial yarn outlet spaced from and in-line with the yarn passageway, said outlet being circular in cross section throughout and tubular at its outer end, but widened at its inner end to form a mouth-section surrounding the tip portion of the yarn needle and having a geometry complementary to that of the tip of the yarn needle but of substantially larger cross-sectional area, thereby forming the outer walls of an annular chamber about said tip, which annular chamber diminishes in diameter in the direction of the tip of the needle in the same step-wise manner as the diameter of the needle tip diminishes in size; an air conduit for introducing air into the annular chamber surrounding the body of the needle.

U.S. Patent 3,013,379   PROCESS FOR MAKING ELASTIC BULKY COMPOSITE
YARN

Alvin Leonard Breen, Kennett Square, Pa., assignor to E. I. du Pont
de Nemours and Company, Wilmington, Del., a corporation of
Delaware
Filed July 5, 1960, Serial No. 40,819
Four Claims (Cl. 57-157)

Claim 1. A process for producing a composite strand which comprises passing a hard fiber synthetic organic continuous filament
strand and an elastomeric fiber synthetic organic continuous strand
simultaneously through a turbulent zone formed by a jet of com-
pressible fluid moving at at least ½ sonic velocity, followed by
winding up the resulting composite strand at a tension sufficient to
elongate the elastomeric component between about 100% and about
600% based upon its length under zero tension, said hard fiber strand
being fed to the turbulent zone at an overfeed between about 5%

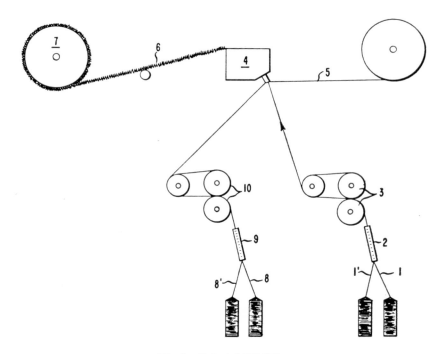

Fig. 1. Patent 3,013,379.

and about 1000%, the temperature of the fluid in the turbulent zone being between about room temperature and the lowest temperature at which any of the fibers becomes tacky.

U.S. Patent 3,017,737   METHOD AND APPARATUS FOR PRODUCING BULKY CONTINUOUS FILAMENT YARN

Alvin L. Breen, West Chester, Pa., assignor to E. I. du Pont de Nemours and Company, Wilmington, Del., a corporation of Delaware
Filed June 25, 1958, Serial No. 744,592
Six Claims (Cl. 57-34)

Claim 1. Apparatus for making novelty yarns, which comprises a zone for separating and whipping about the filaments of a bundle of filaments supplied thereto to form convolutions in said filaments, means for supplying said bundle of filaments in the form of yarn to

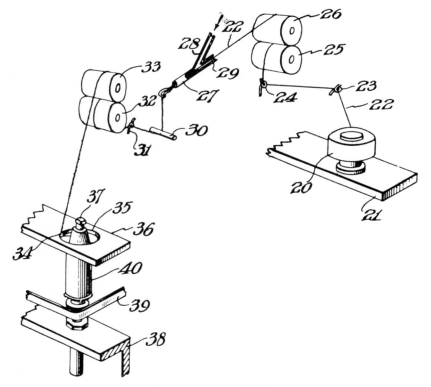

Fig. 1.   Patent 3,017,737.

said zone, means for withdrawing said filaments from said zone and for reforming them into yarn under a tension sufficiently low to prevent said convolutions from straightening out whereby to form a bulky yarn, and means for intermittently increasing the tension on the filaments passing through said zone to produce a yarn the bulkiness of which varies intermittently along its length.

U.S. Patent 3,043,088   PROCESS FOR MAKING BULKY YARN

Alvin L. Breen, West Chester, Pa., assignor to E. I. du Pont de Nemours and Company, Wilmington, Del., a corporation of Delaware
Filed November 26, 1958, Serial No. 776,566
Seventeen Claims (Cl. 57-157)

Claim 1.   A process for making a bulky yarn having a covering of projecting filament ends which comprises feeding a twisted yarn to a high velocity fluid jet and restraining the yarn from losing any substantial amount of its twist until the jet is reached, applying a false untwist to the yarn by means of the jet, jetting the fluid at a near sonic velocity to convolute yarn filaments and provide a multitude of projecting filament ends, withdrawing the yarn from the jet after travel through the jet of less than the shortest filament length, and retwisting the yarn adjacent to the jet to hold the filament convolutions and filament ends in place.

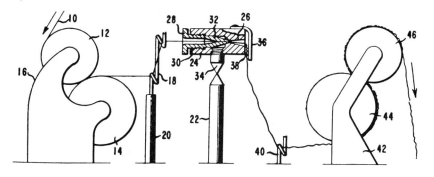

Fig. 1.   Patent 3,043,088.

Heberlein Patent Corporation, New York, New York, U.S.A.

Patents licensed to manufacturers of torque-crimp thermoplastic yarns:

SCHEDULE "A"

U.S. Patent 2,463,619   PROCESS AND APPARATUS FOR PRODUCING CURLY EFFECTS ON YARN

August Kunzle, Wattwil, Switzerland, assignor to Heberlein Patent Corporation, New York, N.Y., a corporation of New York
Application March 25, 1946, Serial No. 656,865
In Switzerland March 29, 1945
Four Claims (Cl. 57-58.5)

Claim 1. A process for producing curly effects on yarn which comprises, passing the yarn along the longitudinal axis of a rotating twisting head, rotating at a speed of the order of fifty thousand R.P.M., the yarn being of the order of 450 denier and being passed at the rate of the order of about one meter per second, maintaining the yarn aligned with the longitudinal axis of the head as it approaches and leaves same and crimping the yarn.

U.S. Patent 2,463,620   APPARATUS AND PROCESS FOR CRIMPING

Georg Heberlein, Wattwil, Switzerland, assignor to Heberlein Patent Corporation, New York, N.Y., a corporation of New York
Application January 21, 1947, Serial No. 723,249
In Switzerland January 21, 1946
Six Claims (Cl. 57-58.5)

Claim 1. An apparatus for crimping yarns comprising, in combination, a supply of endless yarn, means for moving said yarn along a path including supporting devices for said yarn at the entrance and exit of said path, a false-twisting head on said path for continuously highly twisting said yarn passing therealong and for releasing the twist in said yarn after it has passed the head, thus providing a crimp therein, said twisting head being located at a distance from said exit sufficiently short to prevent removal of any substantial amount of the crimp produced by such false-twisting, a reeling device and means to take up the crimped yarn thereon while exerting substantially no tension on said yarn between said exit and said reeling device.

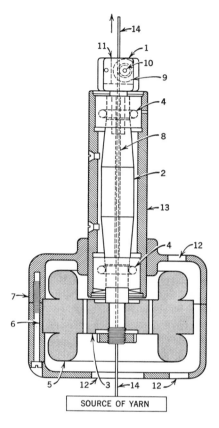

Fig. 1.   Patent 2,463,619.

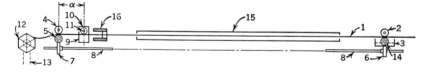

Fig. 1.   Patent 2,463,620.

U.S. Patent 2,655,781   APPARATUS FOR IMPARTING FALSE TWIST TO YARN

Georges Heberlein, deceased, late of Wattwil, Switzerland, by Georg
    Heberlein, heir and administrator, Wattwil, Switzerland, George
    Heberlein, Ernst Weiss, and Karl Risch, Wattwil, Switzerland, and
    Theodor Odinga, deceased, late of Wattwil, Switzerland, by Hein-
    rich Odinga, heir and administrator, Zurich, Switzerland, assignors
    to Heberlein Patent Corporation, New York, N.Y., a corporation of
    New York
Original application September 12, 1944, Serial No. 553,694, now
    Patent No. 2,463,618, dated March 8, 1949. Divided and this ap-
    plication February 19, 1948, Serial No. 9,484. In Switzerland
    October 18, 1943
Five Claims (Cl. 57-77.3)

Claim 1. An apparatus for imparting a false twist to textile yarn
which comprises, in combination, a source of supply of twisted textile yarn, a rapidly rotatable tube having its axis corresponding to
the path of straight line travel of the yarn passing therethrough between two fixed points outside of said tube, and guide roller means
mounted in said tube, said roller means rotating on an axis perpendicular to that of said tube and eccentric with respect to said line of
travel, and said roller means being disposed so that the yarn leaves
it at a point substantially along the path of said axis of said tube,
and means to rotate said tube rapidly to high twist the textile yarn
to at least 500 turns per meter and thereafter detwist the highly
twisted yarn.

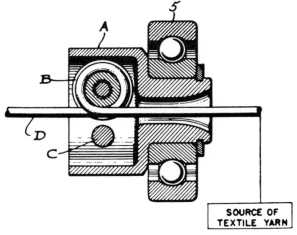

Fig. 2.   Patent 2,655,781.

U.S. Patent 2,904,952   PROCESS FOR PRODUCING CRIMPED YARNS

Ernst Weiss and Karl Risch, Wattwil, Switzerland, assignors to Heber-
lein Patent Corporation, New York, N.Y., a corporation of New
York
Application October 22, 1952, Serial No. 316,140
Three Claims (Cl. 57-157)

Claim 1. A process for producing a voluminous, permanently and
uniformly crimped synthetic organic textile yarn having a high total
elongation and a low fiber elongation, which consists of the steps of
twisting in a single operation a yarn of a denier of 20 to 450 in accordance with the following equation:

$$T = \frac{275,000}{D + 60} + 800$$

where T is the number of turns per meter twist and D is the denier
of the yarn, setting the yarn, then untwisting the same to a normal
twist, and plying said yarn with another similarly but oppositely
twisted, set and untwisted yarn, the extent of twisting, setting and
untwisting being such as to produce a plied yarn having a total
elongation between 150 and 400% and a fiber elongation between
about 5 and 20%.

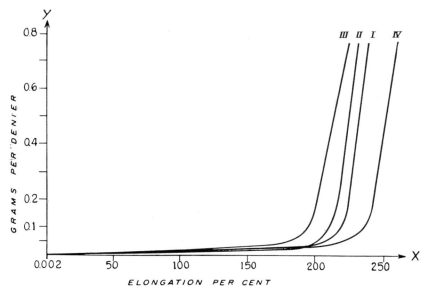

Fig. 1.   Patent 2,904,952.

SCHEDULE "B"

U.S. Patent 2,157,116   STOCKING AND METHOD FOR PRODUCING SAME

Wallace H. Carothers, Wilmington, Del., assignor to E. I. du Pont de Nemours and Company, Wilmington, Del., a corporation of Delaware
Application February 15, 1937, Serial No. 125,886
Fourteen Claims (Cl. 66-202)

Claim 1.   A stocking knitted from synthetic polyamide fibers.

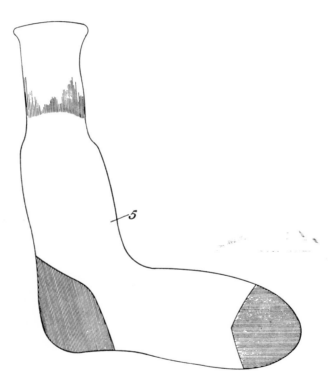

Fig. 1.   Patent 2,157,116.

U.S. Patent 2,157,117   STEAM TREATMENT OF POLYAMIDES

John B. Miles, Jr., Wilmington, Del., assignor to E. I. du Pont de
  Nemours and Company, Wilmington, Del., a corporation of Dela-
  ware
Application February 15, 1937, Serial No. 125,941
Fifteen Claims (Cl. 18-54)

Claim 1. In a process for manufacturing improved shaped articles
from fiber-forming synthetic polyamides, the step which comprises
treating the article formed from said polyamides with steam.

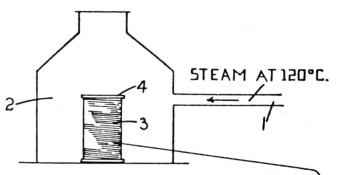

Fig. 1.   Patent 2,157,117.

U.S. Patent 2,157,118   SYNTHETIC FIBERS

Winfield W. Heckert, Ardentown, Del., assignor to E. I. du Pont
  de Nemours and Company, Wilmington, Del., a corporation of
  Delaware
No Drawing.   Application June 28, 1938, Serial No. 216,408
Eight Claims (Cl. 28-1)

Claim 1. A method for improving the properties of synthetic linear
condensation polyamides in the form of filaments, fibers, bristles,
films, fabrics and the like which comprises treating said polyamides
in such form with a setting agent in the presence of a water-soluble
sulfite.

U.S. Patent 2,157,119   METHOD OF MAKING FABRIC

John Blanchard Miles, Jr., Wilmington, Del., assignor to E. I. du
    Pont de Nemours and Company, Wilmington, Del., a corporation
    of Delaware
No Drawing. Application June 28, 1938, Serial No. 216,409. In Ger-
    many February 10, 1938
Six Claims (Cl. 28-1)

Claim 1. The process of fabricating knitted goods containing synthetic linear condensation polyamide fibers which comprises knitting
yarns comprising said fibers, pre-boarding the knitted goods, thereafter subjecting the goods to a hot liquid treatment, then re-boarding
the goods whereby to impart to the goods a smooth, wrinkle free
appearance.

U.S. Patent 2,197,896   ARTIFICIAL WOOL

John B. Miles, Jr., Wilmington, Del., assignor to E. I. du Pont de
    Nemours and Company, Wilmington, Del., a corporation of Dela-
    ware
No Drawing. Application February 15, 1937, Serial No. 125,940
Nine Claims (Cl. 28-1)

Claim 1. An artificial wool-like product comprising crimped fibers
of synthetic linear polymer having a crimp retentivity of at least
40%, said fibers exhibiting by characteristic X-ray patterns orientation along the fiber axis.

U.S. Patent 2,564,245   METHOD FOR TREATING SUPERPOLYAMIDE THREADS

Louis Antoine Billion, Lyon, France; Jacques Billion, executor of said
    Louis Antoine Billion, deceased
Application July 11, 1947, Serial No. 760,490
In France April 25, 1947
Six Claims (Cl. 57-157)

Claim 1. A method for producing superpolyamidic yarn having
permanent crimping and fluffing properties which consists in highly

Fig. 5. Patent 2,564,245.

twisting a superpolyamidic yarn, allowing the yarn to shrink freely, setting the yarn, back-twisting the yarn to a low twist, releasing the filaments of said yarn and plying the thread obtained with a similar thread which has been back twisted to a low twist after having initially been highly twisted in an opposite way.

Leesona Corporation, Providence, Rhode Island, U.S.A.

Patents licensed to manufacturers of torque-crimp thermoplastic yarns:

U.S. Patent 2,803,105 APPARATUS FOR PROCESSING TEXTILE YARNS

Nicholas J. Stoddard, Berwyn, and Warren A. Seem, Chester Springs, Pa., assignors, by mesne assignments, to Universal Winding Company, Cranston, R.I., a corporation of Massachusetts
Application January 4, 1954, Serial No. 401,952
Seven Claims (Cl. 57-34)

Claim 1. Apparatus for thermally processing thermoplastic yarn comprising a support for a supply of yarn, wind-up means for the processed yarn spaced from said support and operable to draw the yarn continuously at a selected linear speed from the supply to said wind-up means, an electrically energized heating device defining a restricted thermally isolated heated zone for passage of the yarn therethrough to heat the yarn to a prescribed temperature, means operable to twist the yarn before passage thereof through said heated zone, control means operable automatically to regulate the supply of heat energy to said zone compensatively according to the rate of transfer of heat to the yarn to maintain said zone uniformly at the temperature required to heat the yarn to said prescribed temperature, tension means operable to maintain the yarn at a uniform tension during passage thereof through said heating device and to the wind-up means, and means to regulate the tension means to control the tension of the yarn in correlation to the prescribed temperature and linear speed of travel of the yarn to maintain the latter at a selected uniform tension relative to the contractile force and thermal characteristics of the yarn.

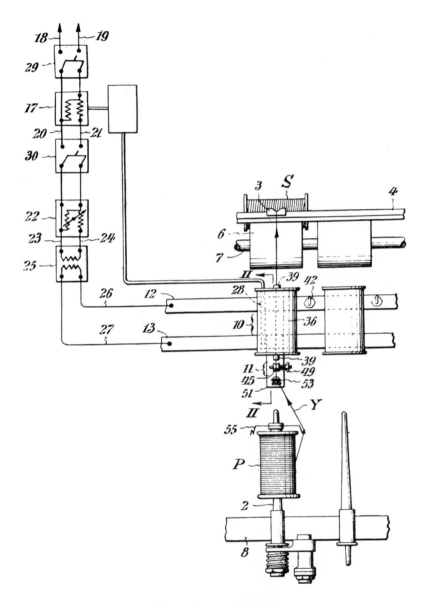

Fig. 1.   Patent 2,803,105.

U.S. Patent 2,803,108 METHODS OF PROCESSING TEXTILE YARNS

Nicholas J. Stoddard, Berwyn, and Warren A. Seem, Chester Springs,
   Pa., assignors, by mesne assignments, to Universal Winding Com-
   pany, Cranston, R.I., a corporation of Massachusetts
Application January 4, 1954, Serial No. 401,803
Eleven Claims (Cl. 57-157)

Claim 2. A method of thermally processing thermoplastic yarn
which comprises continually drawing the yarn from a source of supply, continually passing the yarn at a selected linear speed through
a restricted thermally isolated and uniformly heated zone to uniformly heat the yarn to a prescribed temperature to yarn-set the
same, controlling the supply of heat energy to said zone compensatively according to the ambient temperature and rate of transfer
of heat to the yarn to thereby maintain said heated zone uniformly
at the temperature required to uniformly heat said yarn to said prescribed temperature, continually cooling the yarn to stabilize the
same after passage under tension through said heated zone, winding
the processed yarn, maintaining the yarn under a uniform tension
during heating, cooling and winding thereof, and correlating the tension in said yarn to said prescribed temperature and linear speed of
travel of the yarn to maintain the yarn at a selected uniform tension
relative to the contractile force and thermal characteristics of the yarn
resulting from heating thereof.

U.S. Patent 2,803,109 METHOD OF PROCESSING THERMOPLASTIC YARNS

Nicholas J. Stoddard, Philadelphia, and Warren A. Seem, Gwynedd,
   Pa., assignors, by mesne assignments, to Universal Winding Com-
   pany, Cranston, R.I., a corporation of Massachusetts
Application January 4, 1954, Serial No. 401,951
Eleven Claims (Cl. 57-157)

Claim 1. A method of producing evenly and permanently crimped,
wavy or fluffed multi-filament thermoplastic yarn having improved
and uniform physical characteristics which comprises, continually
drawing the yarn from a source of supply, continually twisting the
yarn drawn from said supply, continually passing the yarn at a selected linear speed under uniform tension through a restricted thermally isolated and uniformly heated zone to uniformly heat the yarn
to a prescribed temperature to reorient the molecules of the yarn to
the twisted formation of the yarn and yarn-set the same, controlling
the supply of heat energy to said zone to thereby maintain said

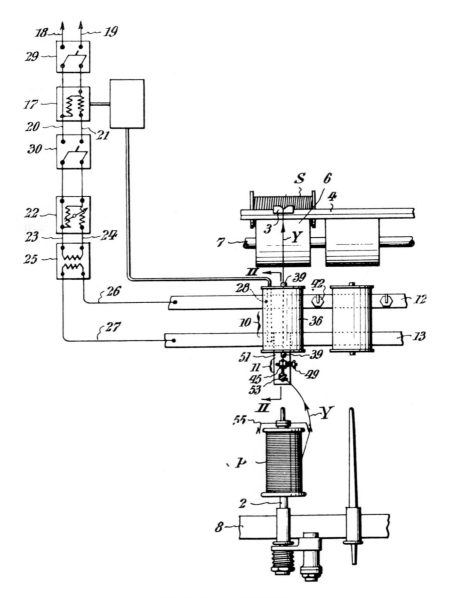

Fig. 1.   Patent 2,803,108.

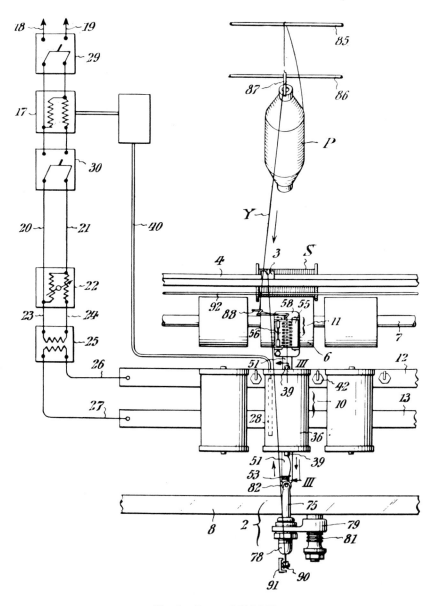

Fig. 1.   Patent 2,803,109.

heated zone uniformly at the temperature required to uniformly heat said yarn to said prescribed temperature, continually cooling the yarn to stabilize the same after passage under tension through said heated zone, continually untwisting the yarn after cooling the same, and finally continually collecting the processed yarn, the tension upon the heated yarn being correlated to said prescribed temperature of the heated yarn to maintain the yarn under tension adequate to preclude substantially any ductility in the cooled yarn.

Patents Not Currently (1963) Licensed Indicating Probable Trends in Yarns Produced for Textured Fabrics

It is suggested that workers in the fields of textured yarns and fabrics should benefit from reading the body as well as the claims of the five following patents.

U.S. Patent 3,025,659 METHOD OF THERMALLY PROCESSING NON-THERMOPLASTIC YARN

Nicholas J. Stoddard, Philadelphia, and Warren A. Seem, Gwynedd, Pa., assignors to Leesona Corporation, Providence, R.I., a corporation of Massachusetts
Filed February 21, 1955, Serial No. 489,693
Seven Claims (Cl. 57-156)

Claim 1. A method of imparting to non-thermoplastic yarns the capability of being thermally shrunk, stretched, stabilized and otherwise processed and yarn-set, which comprises, continually drawing the yarn from a source of supply, continually applying to the traveling yarn material selected from the group consisting of thermoplastic and thermal setting resins, continually twisting the yarn, continually passing the yarn at a selected linear speed under uniform tension through a restricted thermally isolated and uniformly heated zone to evaporate the excess liquid and uniformly heat the applied material and yarn to a prescribed temperature to heat the applied material and yarn-set the yarn, controlling the supply of heat energy to said yarn to thereby maintain said heated zone uniformly at the temperature required to uniformly heat said applied material and yarn to said prescribed temperature, continually cooling the yarn to stabilize the same after passage thereof under tension through said heated zone, continually untwisting the yarn after cooling the same, continually collecting the processed yarn, and controlling the tension upon the heated yarn relative to the thermal characteristics of the

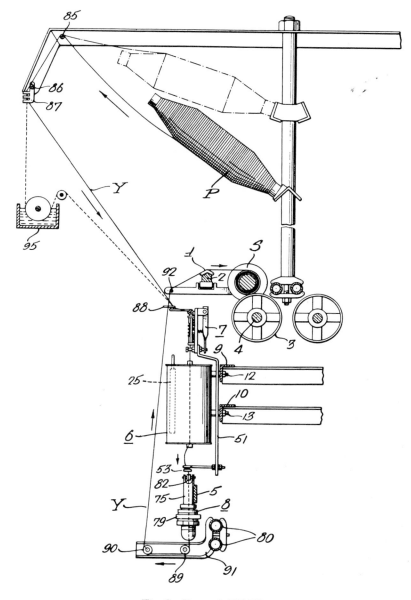

Fig. 2.   Patent 3,025,659.

treated yarn at said prescribed temperature to maintain the same under uniform tension adequate to preclude substantially any ductility in the cooled yarn.

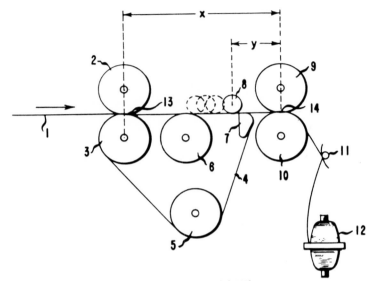

Fig. 1.   Patent 3,007,227.

U.S. Patent 3,007,227   STAPLE FIBER BLENDS

George Leslie Moler, Newark, Del., assignor to E. I. du Pont de Nemours and Company, Wilmington, Del., a corporation of Delaware

Filed April 30, 1957, Serial No. 656,128

Twenty-five Claims (Cl. 28-81)

Claim 1.   A blend of intermingled fibers of staple length comprising a major proportion by weight of a hard inelastic staple fiber, and a minor proportion by weight of essentially straight synthetic elastomeric staple fiber, said elastomeric fiber being present in an amount sufficient to impart cohesiveness to said blend characterized by resistance to separation of said intermingled fibers and recovery upon release of separating stress, said elastomeric fiber having a breaking elongation of at least 100% and an essentially complete and quick recovery from stretching to an elongation less than its breaking elongation, said synthetic elastomeric staple fiber having a denier of less than about 30.

Fig. 39.   Patent 3,009,309.

U.S. Patent 3,009,309   FLUID JET TWIST CRIMPING PROCESS

Alvin L. Breen, West Chester, Pa., and Martin V. Sussman, Wilmington, Del., assignors to E. I. du Pont de Nemours and Company, Wilmington, Del., a corporation of Delaware
Filed July 16, 1956, Serial No. 598,135
One Claim (Cl. 57-139)

The Claimed Invention. A sheaf-yarn characterized by random intervals along its length of substantially parallel fibers separated by areas in which ends of fibers are twisted tightly about the circumference of the yarn bundle, the yarn resembling sheaves of wheat attached end to end and tied at random intervals by yarn fibers.

Note. The only claim granted in this patent, listed above, is very limited. The patent should be read carefully from beginning to end particularly because it describes in detail the production of false-twisted yarn at a rate of in excess of one million turns per minute.

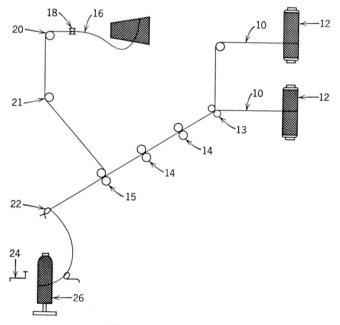

Fig.   Patent 3,017,740.

U.S. Patent 3,017,740 PROCESS FOR CORE SPINNING SMOOTH ELASTIC YARN

Charles R. Humphreys, Wilmington, Del., assignor to E. I. du Pont de Nemours and Company, Wilmington, Del., a corporation of Delaware
Filed December 24, 1958, Serial No. 782,742
Ten Claims (Cl. 57-163)

Claim 1. A process of spinning smooth elastic yarn comprising the steps of drafting at least one roving of staple fibers; stretching at least one continuous filament of a segmented elastomer to increase its length substantially; gathering the drafted roving and stretched filament; twisting the filament and roving, using a twist multiplier of more than about 4.4, to produce a composite yarn having the filament as a core and the roving as a sheath; permitting appreciable contraction of the composite yarn from its initially stretched condition; heating the composite yarn at a temperature less than the degradation temperature of the core; and cooling the composite yarn at a length substantially equal to the length at which it was heated.

Fig. 2. Patent 3,038,295.

U.S. Patent 3,038,295 ELASTIC HIGH BULK YARN

Charles R. Humphreys, Wilmington, Del., assignor to E. I. du Pont de Nemours and Company, Wilmington, Del., a corporation of Delaware
Filed December 24, 1958, Serial No. 782,744
Fourteen Claims (Cl. 57-152)

Claim 1. A high-bulk elastic yarn comprising, an initially stretched elastic core including at least one straight, uncrimped, elastic filament and a sheath consisting of at least one staple fiber roving surrounding the core in a series of helical turns, said yarn having a core content of less than 40% by weight and a twist multiplier of less than about 4, said sheath and the fibers thereof being adapted to bulge outwardly when the core is permitted to contract.

Index

355